# ETHNICITY, CLASS AND ASPIRATION

## Understanding London's new East End

Tim Butler and Chris Hamnett
with Sadiq Mir and Mark Ramsden

First published in Great Britain in 2011 by

The Policy Press
University of Bristol
Fourth Floor
Beacon House
Queen's Road
Bristol BS8 1QU
UK

Tel +44 (0)117 331 4054
Fax +44 (0)117 331 4093
e-mail tpp-info@bristol.ac.uk
www.policypress.co.uk

North American office:
The Policy Press
c/o International Specialized Books Services (ISBS)
920 NE 58th Avenue, Suite 300
Portland, OR 97213-3786, USA
Tel +1  503 287 3093
Fax +1 503 280 8832
e-mail info@isbs.com

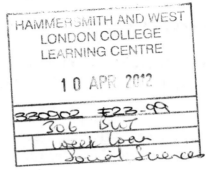
British Library Cataloguing in Publication Data
A catalogue record for this book is available from the British Library.

Library of Congress Cataloging-in-Publication Data
A catalog record for this book has been requested.

ISBN 978 1 84742 650 5 paperback
ISBN 978 1 84742 651 2 hardcover

Cover design by Qube Design Associates, Bristol
Front cover: image kindly supplied by www.alamy.com
Printed and bound in Great Britain by Hobbs, Southampton
The Policy Press uses environmentally responsible print partners.

FSC
www.fsc.org
MIX
Paper from
responsible sources
FSC® C020438

We dedicate this book to our daughters

# Contents

# List of tables, figures and illustrations

## Tables

## Figures

## Illustrations

# Acknowledgements

Like most academic projects, this one has been long in the making and we have accumulated a series of debts to those who have helped us out. First, we thank the Economic and Social Research Council (ESRC) who, in their wisdom, agreed back in 2004 to fund a research project by us on 'Gentrification, ethnicity and education in East London' (RES-000-23-0793), which enabled us to undertake the basic research of which this book is the outcome. In a sense, that project was itself the outcome of previous research projects we had both undertaken separately on the changes that have been taking place in London over the last 30 odd years. We therefore owe a considerable debt to all those who supported our separate research trajectories which came together in this project.

In regard to this project, however, our biggest debt must be to Dr Mark Ramsden and Dr Sadiq Mir, who worked as research fellows on the project. Mark undertook much of the secondary analysis of existing data sets and they both worked on the survey and carrying out the interviews which are at the heart of the book. They also contributed to the drafting of papers and presentations which we have drawn on here. They made a considerable contribution not only to gathering the data but also to making sense of it. They had very different interview styles but both succeeded in getting people to talk about their hopes for, and fears about, their children and the futures they wanted to build for them.

We also wish to thank Professor Richard Webber, who very generously shared with us his access to the Pupil Level Annual School Census (PLASC) to which he had added categories from the Mosaic geodemographic database. He talked us, and Mark in particular, through how to work with this for the East London schools which we draw on substantially in the later chapters of the book. Lidija Marva did an excellent job of transcribing some of the tapes while at the same time finishing off her own PhD. We would also like to thank the editors of the following journals for publishing papers from the research, most of which we have drawn on in writing this book: *Journal of Education Policy*, *Urban Studies*, *Environment and Planning A* and *Children's Geographies*.

We would also like to thank the professional services staff in the Department of Geography at King's College London and in particular the Departmental Manager, Rob Hydon, for all the little ways in which we were supported in getting the research done. Thanks also to Lester Jones, our cartographer, working on the other side of the Atlantic, who produced many of the diagrams and figures. Our biggest intellectual debt is to the Cities Group at King's College.

Finally, we would like to thank those 350-odd people in East London who agreed to talk to us, in some cases on more than one occasion. Without them, this book would not have happened. Emily Watt and her colleagues at The Policy Press and their three anonymous readers have been all that one should expect of a publisher: professional, supportive and persistent.

# About the authors

**Tim Butler** is Professor of Geography at King's College London. He is the author of several books on the gentrification of London and also on the regeneration of East London as well as a jointly authored book on *Understanding Social Inequality*. He is now embarking on a comparative study of the middle classes in London and Paris. He is currently the Vincent Wright visiting professor at Sciences Po in Paris.'

**Chris Hamnett** is Professor of Geography at King's College London. He is the author of *Winners and Losers: Home Ownership in Britain* (1999), *Unequal City: London in the Global Arena* (2003) and other books. He is currently looking at the geographical impact of the government welfare cuts in Britain.

# List of abbreviations

| | |
|---|---|
| BME | black and minority ethnic |
| CCS | county comprehensive school |
| COS | Charity Organisation Society |
| DCSF | Department for Children, Schools and Families |
| ESRC | Economic and Social Research Council |
| EU | European Union |
| GIS | geographic information system |
| GLA | Greater London Authority |
| GLC | Greater London Council |
| ICS | Institute of Community Studies |
| ILEA | Inner London Education Authority |
| IMD | Index of Multiple Deprivation |
| LCC | London County Council |
| LDDC | London Docklands Development Corporation |
| LEA | local education authority |
| NPD | National Pupil Database |
| Ofsted | Office for Statistics on Education |
| ONS | Office for National Statistics |
| PLASC | Pupil Level Annual Social Survey |
| SEC | socioeconomic class |
| SEG | socioeconomic group |
| SEN | special educational needs |
| UDC | Urban Development Corporation |

# ONE

# Introduction: the social transformation of East London

'This area of London has always been a place that people aspire to, the first stop for people who are immigrants, so they come in to the East End and they work very hard in not very pleasant jobs, then they save enough money and they want to move to here then a lot of them will move on again, they're not going to all stay here, a lot will want to move to more rural areas, that's my view.' (White British, female, Redbridge)[1]

## Introduction

London is now one of the world's leading global cities. One of the characteristics of this is the role of the City of London and its position in global financial flows; another is the role of London in global migration, both at the top and bottom ends of the labour market. On the one hand, there are the highly paid workers in the City who come from the US, France, Germany and other Western countries (including Japan and increasingly China) and on the other hand, there are the less skilled, the 'huddled masses' from Africa and Asia. The former are mainly white, the latter predominantly non-white (Wills et al, 2010). At the same time, 40 years of de-industrialisation have dramatically reshaped London's economy, its occupational class structure and its housing market. As a result of these changes, London today is a very different place, both socially and economically, from what it was in the 1970s.

This book examines the dramatic social changes that have taken place in East London over this period of time. Although the empirical focus of the book is on East London, the argument it develops is a wider one regarding the importance of the role of aspiration and education in understanding social change in contemporary Britain. The book examines the effects that class, ethnicity and aspiration have had on spatial and social mobility in a part of London that was, until relatively recently, a bastion of the white working class. We show how large-scale de-industrialisation and a subsequent growth of both upper and lower middle classes and an increase in international immigration have transformed its social structure. We focus on the way that this has played out in relation to education as minority ethnic groups have struggled to achieve their aspirations by putting distance between themselves and their places of origin in inner East London and by trying to achieve the best for their children in today's competitive and increasingly market-oriented education system. Although the importance of education figures centrally in the book, it is not just a book about education, but also one about ethnicity, housing and class change, aspiration and social reproduction more generally.

The notion of aspiration was adopted by New Labour in the run–up to the 1997 General Election and continued as a core theme under the successive leaderships of Tony Blair and Gordon Brown; it looks set to continue under David Cameron's Conservative–Liberal Democrat coalition government. Despite a widening of social inequality during New Labour's time in office, the notion of aspiration has been widely embraced not least by many minority ethnic groups who have seen an opening up of social and educational possibilities over the last 20 years in ways that were not open to their parents. As a result, higher proportions of some minority ethnic groups are going on to higher education and subsequently into intermediate and higher middle-class jobs and, even when this has not happened, they often have high educational aspirations for their children. Some are also 'suburbanising' from the inner London areas where they or their parents lived into outer London in the search for the contemporary equivalent of the 'good life'. At the same time, some white residents in both inner and outer London are moving further afield in a process that can sometimes only be described as 'white flight', while others who lost their jobs as a consequence of de–industrialisation are continuing to live in East London, struggling to keep their heads above water, often having become dependent on benefit payments.

One issue the book does not explicitly address is that of gender. This is not that gender is unimportant: quite the contrary. However, given our focus on class change, ethnicity, education, housing and location and their interactions, and the magnitude of the changes that have been experienced in recent decades in East London, to attempt to explicitly add gender to the analysis as a specific dimension would have been a step too far. In practice, gender issues pervade the book as, for example, when we discuss the impacts of industrial and occupational change, educational attainment and attitudes to education. What we have not done, however, is to treat gender as a distinct dimension of analysis – this would have been a different book. Equally, although we discuss the issue of faith-based education and school choice, we have not taken religion as a separate dimension of analysis. We have chosen to focus on the implications of the massive shift which has taken place in ethnic composition in East London which, along with the major change in industrial and class structure, comprise in our view, two of the most important social changes in the region in the last 30 years.

The second issue the book does not explicitly address is that of educational policy. Although issues of educational aspirations, attainment, the structure of educational opportunities and the key role of school choice, or more accurately, preferences, play a major role in the book, we have explicitly chosen to focus on how the structure of educational provision operates and the basis on which places are offered and on how parents deal with this structure in terms of their strategies and behaviour. There is an explicit criticism of the 'choice' agenda which has pervaded education in recent years which, given the shortage of places in popular schools, we view as being largely illusory in terms of offering real choice to parents. We are also very critical of the concept of 'failing' schools given that their performance is strongly related to the social composition of their intake. We also pay considerable attention to the role played by distance to school and catchment areas in the allocation of school places and thus of the reproduction of area social differences in terms of school composition, but we do not set out to provide a separate and distinct analysis of school policy in contemporary East London, let alone London or England as a whole.

While based on East London, the book seeks to locate the area as an example of the wider changes in ethnic and class structure that are taking place in many major British cities. At the broadest level, the book looks at the competition for urban space and social resources between different groups, and the various strategies they adopt for social reproduction. As such it engages debates in urban studies whose origins lie in the Chicago School of (Urban) Sociology and, more recently, W. Julius Wilson's eponymous account of what happens 'when work disappears' (Wilson, 1996; see also Park et al, 1925). In our study, work (or more specifically the jobs associated with the docks and related processing industries) disappeared nearly a generation ago, although not perhaps on the catastrophic scale of inner Chicago, and we address the consequences of that in what has, at least until recently, been the backyard of a resurgent urban economy. One of the themes that we address is the apparent 'contraflow' of gentrification, suburbanisation and re-urbanisation in a single-city region. Education in such circumstances becomes central to the language of aspiration and strategies of social and spatial mobility and it is clear that many respondents view education as the key to achieving upward social mobility for their children. Issues of social reproduction are therefore important for all groups.

Our focus is on East London, rather than some other part of London, for a number of reasons. It was here (in the 'East End', as it was termed) that many of the dirty trades took place from the 17th century onwards, and it was in London's rapidly expanding docks that much of the trade with the expanding Empire was conducted from the mid-19th century. It was here that the various dock processing and consumer goods industries developed (Hall, 1962; Coppock and Prince, 1964). The result was that the East End became not only London's gateway but also its backyard. It has long been London's poorest quarter and, until comparatively recently, the area most resistant to the gentrification that has affected the rest of the city over the last 30 or so years. One of the reasons that the UK won the right to stage the 2012 Olympic Games in East London was because of the putative regeneration benefits from its legacy in what remains one of the poorest areas in the UK in one of the European Union's (EU's) wealthiest regions. The closure of the docks, its de-industrialisation and subsequent redevelopment as a post-industrial economic space (predominantly around the Canary Wharf development) has transformed the economic base of the area. More recently, the area has undergone a dramatic ethnic transformation and a less marked shift in its class structure with the growth of a minority ethnic middle class. As such, it provides a fascinating lens through which to study the interaction of class, ethnicity and aspiration in an increasingly multi-ethnic city. Platt (2005) has shown that some minority ethnic groups have experienced upward social mobility in Britain in recent decades – this is in marked contrast to what has occurred in some other European countries.

The social division between the East End and the West End of London is longstanding. Whereas the West End was traditionally the locus of wealth and power, the East End was one of poverty and deprivation and, with the development of the docks in the 19th century, the working-class culture of East London became more firmly established. The work of Mayhew and Booth in the late 19th century documented the concentration of poverty in the area, and subsequent research by Stedman Jones (1974) and Green (1986, 1995, 2010) has highlighted the deprivation of the area. The East End became a bastion of London's working classes and this continued with the development of large areas of working-class housing in areas such as West and East Ham, Plaistow and Leytonstone in the late 19th century. For many readers these names will mean little or nothing. Unlike West London, East London is a *terra incognita*: the territory of films such as *Lock, Stock and Two Smoking Barrels* and *The Long Good Friday* as opposed to that of the middle-class *Notting Hill* or *Sliding Doors*. There were concentrations of middle-class housing in East London, for example, around Tredegar Square in Bow and Victoria Park in Hackney in the 19th century (Coppock and Prince, 1964), but much development was for the working class (Wohl, 1977).

Although there was suburban development in East London in the interwar period, with the exception of a few upmarket areas such as Barkingside and Chingford, East London retained its reputation as one of the poorer parts of London with an over-representation of the lower social classes and under-representation of the managerial and professional social classes (Willmott and Young, 1973). This was reinforced by the large-scale council redevelopment of much of Tower Hamlets and Newham after the Second World War, which replaced streets of bomb-damaged terraced houses with high-rise council estates. At the peak in 1981, before the redevelopment of Thames riverside for private housing, 82% of households in Tower Hamlets lived in council housing – one of the highest proportions in Britain.

In 1957, when Young and Willmott (1962) published the first edition of their classic study of Bethnal Green, *Family and kinship in East London*, the East End of London was still a largely white working-class residential area with tight social links based around kinship and class. Although the more affluent were beginning to suburbanise out to Woodford and elsewhere (Willmott and Young, 1961), East London retained many of its traditional characteristics. In the last 30 years however, East London has witnessed many dramatic economic, social and physical changes, starting with the closure of the Docks from the late 1960s onwards, the subsequent de-industrialisation of the area and finally, the redevelopment of Canary Wharf and associated riverside housing from the late 1980s onwards. This development has transformed the area, bringing large numbers of white-collar jobs in financial and business services and new groups of residents who have bought or rented luxury apartments along the river (Butler, 2007; Davidson and Lees, 2005).

In addition, much of the traditional white working class has now disappeared and has been replaced, in large measure, by a new multi-ethnic population: many are still poor, but they are no longer largely white. Instead, large parts of East London, initially the inner boroughs but more recently spreading to the outer ones, have witnessed one of the most dramatic ethnic transformations of any part of Britain in the last 30 years. Although the East End was subject to large-scale immigration in the 19th century, mostly by Eastern European Jews escaping persecution, the area retained its overwhelmingly white character. In the last half century, however, this has changed dramatically with the immigration of large numbers of Asian, Black Caribbean and Black African migrants. Since 2004, and the accession of the Eastern European countries to the EU (the 'A8'), the area has also seen a major influx of Eastern European workers.

One thing London shares with early 20th-century Chicago is the key role played by migration. In 1925 Park and Burgess published *The city* (Park et al, 1925). This book was the manifesto for what became known as the 'Chicago School' of Urban Sociology and Burgess's concentric ring model of Chicago went on to influence generations of urban geographers and urban sociologists until it was displaced by the new Marxist approaches in the 1970s that consigned it, possibly temporarily, to the dustbin of history. What made Chicago the 'shock city' of the 1920s, parallelling Manchester in the 1840s and New York in the late 19th century, was the massive wave of immigration that poured into the central city. To a very large extent, the social character of the city was based on mass immigration. It would be an exaggeration to say that this has been the same in London, but in the last 20 years the city has certainly seen a rapid growth of overseas immigration (Gordon et al, 2007), allied to a large increase in the size of the minority ethnic population of London which grew no less than 57% from 1991 to 2001.

We argue that East London is still functioning today as an immigrant reception area much as it did in the 19th century and before. What has changed is the nature of the recent immigrants, first Indian, Pakistani and Black Caribbean, and from the 1970s large numbers of Bangladeshi and then Black African migrants, the more successful of whom are gradually pushing out into the suburbs, following the East End Jews of the earlier generations who moved out to the suburbs in the interwar period. Many of the more traditional white working class have disappeared, partly by upward social mobility and/or out-migration and partly by retirement, economic inactivity and death. The most recent groups making their presence felt in East London have been the Eastern European recent entrants to the EU and also refugees, many of whom seem to be disproportionately represented in private rented housing. The area (particularly in Newham) is thus functioning as a classic 'zone in transition', as a sort of migrant reception and sorting area for London, from which the more successful move outwards, which they take to be a signifier of their success in consolidating and improving their social and economic position.

## New flows of population

East London forms the expanding 'wedge' running out north and east from the City of London to an outer periphery now marked by the M25 motorway which today circles the whole metropolitan area (see Figure 1.1). The area defined as East London has, over the past 150 years, with London's expansion in the 19th and early 20th centuries, steadily radiated out from a relatively narrow belt of deprivation surrounding the City of London to incorporate an increasingly wider and more suburban hinterland. It followed the railway lines out of London Liverpool Street Station in the 19th century, and was partially facilitated by cheap 'workmen's tickets' (Kellett, 1969). In the mid–20th century this radial development was continued with the building of the Central underground line eastwards and the construction of a road network (A10 to Cambridge, A12 to Colchester and A13 to Southend) linked by the North Circular 'arterial' road around what was then suburban London. These transport systems were conceived and built specifically to move people in and out of the City of London to and around the new suburbs – from Walthamstow in the 19th century to places like Gants Hill and Redbridge in the 1930s. The M25 orbital motorway now provides the *de facto* outer marker for London. Nowhere

**Figure 1.1: The study area showing London and the surrounding region**

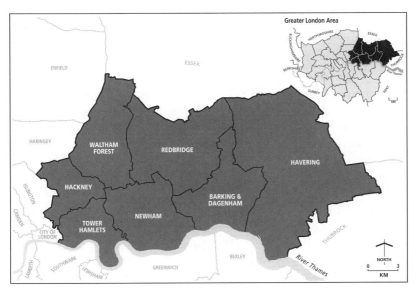

is this more apparent than in East London between the outer London boroughs and the shire county of Essex.

If the marker between the outer London boroughs and Essex used to be one of social class, it is increasingly one of ethnicity. The non-white (specifically Asian) populations of inner East London (particularly Newham) have been moving steadily outwards; until recently, however, the M25 borderlands were overwhelmingly white (Havering and, to a lesser extent, Barking & Dagenham). Paul Watt's (2009) ethnography of two estates on these white borderlands both sides of the M25 focused on the interweaving of aspiration, class and ethnicity. For example, he demonstrates that many of these moves were driven by the desire to maintain a sense of whiteness and what he terms, in a well-turned pun on Savage et al's (2005) eponymous concept, a sense of '*se*lective belonging'. Beyond the boundaries of Greater London, the minority ethnic population is far smaller and concentrated into a handful of small industrial centres such as Slough or High Wycombe. Watt (2008) also noted the presence of black middle-class Nigerians and Chinese in one of his case study areas just across the M25 in Thurrock. The former populations of many of these places have either been slowly dying out or considering a move across the M25, even as far as the coastal towns of Essex, in a gradual process of white out-migration and replacement (Hobbs, 1989; Cohen and Rustin, 2007; Stillwell, 2010).

The place of those white residents who have moved on has increasingly been taken by an aspiring black and minority ethnic (BME[2]) middle class, many of whose members are themselves in flight from what they see as the long-term decline of the inner London boroughs in which they were – for the most part – born and raised. The 'push' may be scenarios of decline, under-achieving schools, new migrant groups and the spread of 'buy-to-let' housing; the 'pull' is one of high-achieving and, for the most part, non-selective schools, single-family housing with a front garden (even if it is paved over to provide off-street parking) and what can only be termed a 'group effect' as they emulate members of their peer group who have moved out. Redbridge is now a very multicultural place yet, even in the remaining predominantly white boroughs of Havering and Barking & Dagenham, our analysis shows that the proportion of *middle-class* BME residents (and particularly Black Africans) is rising fast – faster than that for the middle class as a whole (Butler et al, 2006). There is some further support for this trend in the finding that the number of non-white secondary school children is currently approximately 50% higher in 2009 than 1999, indicating that ethnic change is occurring here as well (see Chapter Five, this volume). This is an important finding because, contrary to the experience of some other European countries, where minority ethnic groups have remained firmly at the bottom of the economic and social pyramid, Britain has seen significant upward social mobility among some minority ethnic groups, particularly among Indian and Chinese groups, many of whom have moved into middle-class professional, managerial and entrepreneurial positions. In this respect, the major ethnic divide in Britain today is not, perhaps, between whites and minority ethnic groups, but between different minority groups who have experienced very different educational, employment and housing trajectories (Modood, 1997). Working-class whites and Black Caribbean groups are, to some extent, conjoined by their more limited mobility (Fieldhouse, 1999).

Class has long played a distinctive role in defining East London's social economy, as we argue below and in subsequent chapters, but the hegemony of the white working class and its culture has been subject to radical transformation in recent decades in particular; as the lines of class demarcation between those in employment have become increasingly fuzzy so those between the economically active and inactive have sharpened and become reflected in an increasingly divided housing market which we discuss in subsequent chapters. What lies across all these divisions, however, is ethnic difference: if East London was a largely working-class place with its lower middle-class suburbs spreading out to the North Circular Road and then to the M25, it was also largely socially and ethnically homogeneous – white and predominantly working or lower middle class. This is no longer the case: Newham was the first borough in which no ethnic group formed a majority and today its population of young people under 15 is overwhelmingly non-white. It is this group and their parents and grandparents who are leaving – some might say 'fleeing' – Newham for the rest of outer East London in search of better schools and more attractive neighbourhoods of people like themselves. Thus both the social structure but more importantly the flows of people have changed dramatically in the last few decades.

## It's the economy ...

Despite its relatively well-defined physical boundaries (the River Thames to the south, the City to the west and the M25 orbital motorway marking its outer limits), East London has long been demarcated by its social and cultural geography. From the end of the 19th, and for much of the 20th, century East London came to symbolise a form of working-class culture and resistance that set it apart from the working class elsewhere in the country. The reasons for this are complex, but in essence are a function of the East London labour market and the peculiarly insecure nature of the forms of employment engendered by its dominant industries (docks, food markets and the small sweatshops of consumer goods industries needing to be near their customers). While located close to the heart of the world's most advanced imperial economy, these industries were largely pre-industrial and low skilled in their labour processes. London was an exception in Victorian Britain and nowhere was this more so than in the East End, whose social and political (dis-)organisation was a continual source of fascination and fear to the late Victorian establishment. If the division elsewhere was between skilled and unskilled labour, East London's labour market was characterised by the insecurity of its workforce, a phenomenon first systematically documented by Charles Booth (1889) and subsequently by Gareth Stedman Jones (1974) in his pioneering book *Outcast London*.

## Beginnings of organised capitalism

The emergence of a London – and specifically an East London – organised working class may have occurred later than elsewhere in Britain but it did so around a different demographic. In place of the pre-existing model of unions of skilled workers, the model in the capital was different, with politically ambitious leaders forming trades unions from the semi-skilled general workers who worked in the capital's leading industries. From the start and throughout the first half of the 20th century, this involved a three-way relationship between capital, labour and the state, often referred to as 'Fordism' (Amin, 1994). This was highlighted by the decision of the Ford Motor Company to set up its UK operations on marshland at Dagenham in East London in 1929 for which the London County Council (LCC) built a whole new dormitory settlement for its workers on what is known as the Becontree Estate (Willmott, 1963; Olechnowicz, 1997). Car production finally ceased at Dagenham in 2002 and it is now solely focused on manufacturing diesel engines.

The East London working class and its closely knit occupational communities continued therefore to play a key role in both challenging and transforming the relationship between the state and its working-class citizens. This manifested itself in the aftermath of the First World War with the emergence of what came to be known as 'Poplarism' (Branson, 1979). This hinged on the refusal of some working-class councils in East London to means test its ratepayers during the economic crisis of the early 1920s when world trade began to shrink, which would have further penalised some of London's poorest areas.

Ultimately, following the experience of the Great Depression in the following decade, the rise of extremism and the experience of the Second World War (in which the state effectively nationalised large parts of the economy 'for the duration' [of the war]) led to an overwhelming popular acceptance that citizens had social as well as economic and political rights in which it was the duty of the state at a national level to balance the burden of poverty across society. The first formal articulation of this came in the 1942 Beveridge Report (Beveridge, 1942), written in some of the darkest years of the Second World War, with the clear objective of banishing the five 'giant evils' (of Want, Disease, Ignorance, Squalor and Idleness) through 'cooperation of the state and the individual'. It offered a better future for all once the war was won. A significant number of the many steps that were trod on the path to setting up the welfare state were made in East London, which became a social laboratory for the charting of social policy in Britain. In one sense this was unsurprising as it provided an area of extreme deprivation within a few miles of the centre of power, unlike the northern cities that occupied a different world from the golden triangle of Oxford, Cambridge and London, in which policy was decided in Britain. More than that, however, the cause (although not necessarily the effect) of poverty was different in London where the *structure* of large parts of the labour market was built around permanent insecurity and demanded the kind of structural change that only a welfare state and nationalisation of the key parts of its economic infrastructure could offer. The experience of the Second World War itself formed therefore the third element in the changing relationship between the working class and the wider society, and once again much of this was forged in the East End of London.

For much of the 20th century then, East London can be seen as the laboratory for creating what Rex (1961) referred to as a 'truce situation' between labour and capital (Dahrendorf, 1959). This involved a tripartite agreement by labour to legitimate a market economy and by capital to agree to the state funding of what Castells (1977) termed the 'means of collective consumption', which involved not simply the provision of a welfare safety net but also the 'reproduction of labour' which previously had been borne either directly by the working class or had had to be subsidised by capital. The coming together in the postwar years of Keynesian demand management with the welfare reforms inspired by the wartime Beveridge Report has been referred to as the 'Keynes-Beveridge settlement', and gave rise to a broadly bipartisan form of national government in pursuit of these objectives and a long postwar boom which lasted until the 1970s (similar to the period in France referred to as the '*trentes glorieuses*').

## Remaking East London under the aegis of neoliberalism

The end of the long boom and the subsequent economic crisis of the late 1970s, coupled with the election of a Conservative government under the leadership of Margaret Thatcher, with its commitment to monetarist policies, led to a rapid de-industrialisation of the UK economy and the irretrievable breakdown of this postwar settlement. This hit London and particularly East London hard as it lost much of its industrial base and working-class employment leading, as we shall show in Chapter Two, to a massive shrinking of the city's working-class population and an increase in the economically inactive population. At the same time, London has become an increasingly middle-class city on the basis of what one of us has argued to be a process of 'professionalisation not proletarianisation' (Hamnett, 2003). This is not to argue that there has not been an increasing inequality; many of those who lost their jobs as London de-industrialised have never effectively re-entered the formal labour market. Indeed, earnings and income inequality have increased dramatically in London since 1979 and this continued under New Labour, largely as a result of the massive increases in earnings and incomes of the top decile, particularly by those working in financial services, and a concomitant driving down of real wages at the bottom – the minimum wage notwithstanding. These impacts have been particularly keenly felt in East London, which has perhaps changed more dramatically than any other area of London. We summarise the sociodemographic changes here and discuss the greater nuances in subsequent chapters. The crude characterisation is of a change from a predominantly white working-class inner east London and lower middle-class outer suburban belt to an increasingly multi-ethnic and multi-class sub-region, segregated in new and complex ways. This process of class change and ethnic diversification has resulted in a very different kind of distribution of class places and conceptualisations of ethnicity, aspiration, mobility, culture and community from those that characterised East London for much of the 20th century.

It has also given rise to new debates not only about how to characterise and theorise this (Devine et al, 2005), but also about how to research it – with some arguing that the old language of social class and the social survey need to be updated in the light of new cultures of consumption and the development of a new 'commercial sociology' (Savage and Burrows, 2007, 2009). It is also taking place within a much changed economic context (which we detail in Chapter Two); when London began to de-industrialise in the mid-1960s, it was East London (the part of the city with the most extensive industrial infrastructure) which was most severely affected, resulting in high levels of job loss and subsequently high rates of long-term unemployment and economic inactivity (Buck et al, 1986). The resulting economic devastation was compounded by the recessions of the 1980s and early 1990s which left large parts of inner East London resembling an economic ghost town from which it has only slowly recovered. When the recovery came, it was on the basis of a completely different kind of economy (Butler and Hamnett, 2009; Imrie et al, 2009). The Docklands were left almost entirely derelict and the once busy riverside areas were largely deserted. This was the economic nadir of East London and the tragedy was that its population, which had some of the worst levels of education in the country, was ill-placed to benefit from the recovery as it required a new kind of educated, customer-facing worker who was unlikely to tell a banker flying out to Frankfurt from London City Airport (LCY) to 'have a nice day' (Kennedy et al, 2000).

The turnaround, if it can be called that, came with the redevelopment of the Isle of Dogs (the Canary Wharf area of Docklands) into one of Europe's leading financial centres. The office blocks and towers which were built there from the late 1980s onwards now form a joint financial centre with the City of London and, along with the proliferation of luxury residential apartment buildings which line the river, has revitalised this area of London. How far the economic effects have spilled over into neighbouring deprived areas is open to question. Despite this juxtaposition of great wealth and deprivation there has nonetheless been a huge transformation, and not just in Docklands. The redevelopment of Stratford's 'rail lands' for the 2012 Olympics is just one further example of how the area will continue to be transformed, but it seems unlikely that it will do other than further increase inequality in the poorest area of London.

## The 'new' East London

The exploration of the relationships between neoliberal forms of economic governance and the sociopolitical settlement being reached in new places and old cities alike (Hackworth, 2007) is not an explicit focus for this book; nevertheless it can be argued that, as an area created and subsequently transformed by a previous mode of accumulation, East

London will continue to act as a laboratory for a future urban form. Our main goal in this book is more modest, which is to chart what happens when one type of work and one resident group disappears and is replaced by another. Unlike the Chicago of W. Julius Wilson's (1996) study, work has not disappeared from East London, but those who did that work previously have gradually been replaced in a process by which a new workforce has emerged – drawn in part from minority ethnic groups who migrated to London during the long boom and settled into its eastern quarter (Wacquant, 2008). Perhaps because of the manner in which the white working class was incorporated into the 'labourism' of the postwar consensus, many minority groups were excluded from the state-sponsored jobs and services that dominated East London. As a result, they were often forced to rely on their own initiative and entrepreneurial skills. Dench et al (2006) have focused on the sense of white working-class resentment at their loss of entitlement (see also Cohen's 'All white on the night', 1996). This book therefore focuses in part on the ways in which minority ethnic groups have pursued their aspirations for upward social mobility for themselves and particularly for their children through the education system in this new socioeconomic environment. For many, this has meant thinking about moving away from the areas in which they were born and brought up, which were the areas of first settlement for their parents and even grandparents. These moves have not taken place in a geographic or social policy vacuum and we draw on data we derived from a research project funded by the Economic and Social Research Council (ESRC)[3] to interweave these personal accounts into the structural mesh of occupational, class and ethnic change and the changing provision of education across East London.

Given the legacy of the area's postwar history of class and ethnic homogeneity and its inhabitants' expectations for state provision and collective consumption which resulted in some of the lowest educational outcomes in the country, we might expect the transitions to a more aspirational and individualist form of mobility to be dramatic if not traumatic, but in fact the slow decline of the white working class has often been marked more by 'exit' than by 'voice', while some of their minority ethnic replacements seem to have adjusted relatively easily to the recent culture of aspiration. This book takes up some of these themes by looking at what happens when an area whose institutions were nurtured on a previous set of sociopolitical assumptions finds not only that they have disappeared but that so too have some of the population who made use of them, to be replaced by a new population with a different set of expectations and assumptions. It is for this reason that we have devoted part of our focus to the concepts of aspiration and social mobility – which have changed so dramatically over the last 30 years – and to their achievement. Crudely, we argue that many of the ethnic groups who now make up a sizeable part of East London's middle-class population, having struggled against the 'institutional racism' of the previous modes of collective mobility, are likely to be receptive to the more individualised and 'open' modes offered by successive Conservative, New Labour and now coalition governments, and nowhere more so than in the new 'market' in education with its widely published attainment statistics and its stress on school choice. These groups have, to an extent, taken what is on offer at face value but have not necessarily been best pleased when they discover that every choice has its structural constraint. These constraints are, in part, the outcome of an education system developed for a working class in a different era – raising questions about its fitness for purpose in an area that is gradually becoming more middle class. Securing an appropriate schooling for your child has become one of the most stressful aspects of being a parent in East London. What might once have been a private concern is now part of the everyday discourse among peer groups over what it means to be a 'good parent' and how 'to do the best' for one's child. The account we offer in this book is about what happens when a predominantly single-class mono-ethnic group, nurtured on collective rather than individual mobilisation, is replaced – over time – by a different group of people with a different set of expectations about what the education system should be doing to meet their aspirations for their children. The fact that the schools are improving and, in some cases, are doing so quite dramatically, cuts little ice when parents come up against the very real structural limits of educational choice and opportunity.

## The book

The book therefore deals with a set of contemporary issues about the transformation of social structure in an area undergoing rapid social and economic change – in which social and structural factors interact across time and space. Much of East London once seemed immune to the gentrification and change happening elsewhere in the city but it is now changing in ways not previously seen. This change reflects not only endogenous factors – notably the aspirations of previous postwar generations of immigrants to move up the social ladder and their fears about what would happen if they didn't take actions to achieve this – but also the consequences of some of the external factors that have impinged on London, notably economic globalisation and large-scale immigration. The book, which is being published either as the UK belatedly emerges from the longest recession in 60 years or just as it enters its 'double dip', charts the consequences of past problems (de-industrialisation and high economic inactivity rates particularly among white and black working-class groups) against those of more recent successes (post-industrial growth) and the emergence of new social groups (such as recent migrations from Eastern Europe).

Our account is of how these various groups have attempted to manoeuvre around each other to gain advantage and minimise the risk of failure according to their particular sets of values, aspirations and fears. It should be borne in mind that this strategising has occurred during one of the biggest periods of investment in the public sector since 1945; how it will play out in a period of large-scale spending cuts still remains to be seen. The resentments and frustrations that we recount, however, are likely to become more entrenched and more acute in this process of jockeying for position, as individuals 'play the game'. Education becomes a crucial terrain on which these manoeuvres take place and is one in which state policy has been more active than any other area of policy in recent years. Our research has focused on the effects that class and ethnicity have had on spatial and social mobility in a part of London that had, until the 1990s, changed least in the context of London becoming a 'global city' but has, over the last decade, witnessed a huge turnover in its population, 'pushed' in large part by international migration and 'pulled' by an individual sense of aspiration. The book locates these changes that are occurring in East London as an example of wider changes in ethnic and class structure that are taking place in major cities across the world and have been discussed at length in the 'global cities' literature.

At the broadest level, the book looks at the competition for urban space and social resources between different groups and the strategies they adopt to achieve this. As such, it engages with an urban studies literature whose origins lie in the Chicago School of Urban Sociology. In contrast to much of this literature, including such modern classics as Wilson's (1996) *When work disappears* and Bourdieu and Wacquant's (1999) *The weight of the world* and Wacquant's more recent writing *Punishing the poor* (2009) and *Urban outcasts* (2008), our focus is on the relatively advantaged who have survived the impact of de-industrialisation and, at least until recently, prospered from the growth of the service and business sector as opposed to the absolutely deprived whose fate has dominated much social science writing.

In our study, of an area where manufacturing work disappeared nearly a generation ago, we argue that we need to understand how class, ethnicity and, to a lesser extent, gender[4] have been reconfigured in the context of de-industrialisation, the development of a post-industrial economy and international migration within a single-city region. We need to consider the links between these dimensions of stratification and how they relate to narratives of *individual* accounts of aspiration and social mobility within a fast-changing urban landscape in which the desire to escape 'the other' and to achieve some degree of upward social and spatial mobility is important. For many of our respondents, the 'fear of falling back' is never far distant (Ehrenreich, 1989). In these circumstances, education takes on a central meaning – whether people are on the way up or hanging on to their relative privilege. While housing, and success in the housing market, is an indicator of mobility and aspiration, it does not have the same salience in the respondents' minds as educational achievement, which is the key marker for the kind of lives they hope their children will be able to live. The 'right to buy' and 'buy to let' phenomena within the housing market over the last 30 years have often been the means by which they have been able to measure their own progress, but it is the ability to get their child into a 'decent' school and – crucially – away from a 'failing' one, that is a key measure of their success as parents and their sense of self.

## Structure of the book

Following this introduction, the book is organised into chapters dealing with the historical background of East London's development in the 19th and 20th century, and then moves on to a discussion of the four crucial dimensions of change: social class, ethnicity, housing and education. In a sense these are all in dialogue with each other and 'come together' in the dilemmas that parents across East London face when addressing the issues of social reproduction and their aspirations to move on in a society which has increasingly become one based on competition rather than cooperation.

Chapter Two outlines the changes that have taken place in London's economic role over the last 40 years as its manufacturing industry has largely disappeared and as it has become one of the major global financial centres. East London has been one of the poorest parts of the capital for several hundred years, and during London's period of massive urban expansion in the 19th century this was reinforced by the growth of the docks and the casual labour system. By the late 19th century acute poverty was widespread in London as a whole and in East

London in particular; growing labour unrest and social concern led to the state playing a wider role in welfare, leading to the setting up of the welfare state post-Second World War. Against this background, the last 40 years have witnessed the closure of the docks, de-industrialisation and the associated changes in occupational class structure as London's traditional working class has shrunk to be replaced by a growing managerial and professional class and, more recently, the rapid growth of a routine intermediate and lower middle class. East London remains one of the poorest areas of London but it, too, is seeing a gradual change in its class composition.

Chapter Three highlights the dramatic changes in the ethnic composition of London and East London over the last 40 years. This period has seen London change from a largely white mono-ethnic city to a multi-ethnic one, with a substantial minority ethnic population that was 29% in 2001, and is likely to be near 40% by the next Census in 2011. The 10 years from 1991 to 2001 saw the minority ethnic population increase in size by over 50% while the white population decreased. These changes have been particularly dramatic in East London in which two boroughs – Newham and Tower Hamlets – have the highest proportions of minority ethnic populations in London after Brent. The chapter argues that what has happened over the last 30–40 years is that as the number of people from minority ethnic groups has grown in size, they have also moved outwards into suburban outer East London, often replacing older white residents in the process, many of whom have either died or moved further out. Consequently, we have seen the increasing suburbanisation of minority ethnic populations, and a significant growth of minority home ownership, although this has been offset by the growth of private renting and social housing. This is part and parcel of a wider process of social and spatial change of which the ethnic changes in residential tenure are some of the clearest 'markers' available to us.

Chapter Four goes on to consider the importance of aspiration. It argues that the concept of aspiration underwent something of a rediscovery in the New Labour renaissance, when Tony Blair, Peter Mandelson and Gordon Brown found common ground in asserting that individual aspiration was not a dirty word but a key part of the New Labour project. This notion resonates strongly with many of the minority ethnic respondents who see aspiration and educational achievement, if not for themselves then for their children, as a key part of the process of upward social mobility which, if successful, they believed would take them into the middle class and give them the educational credentials, occupational skills and professional incomes and status they aspired to. Going to university has become particularly important in an era where a much larger proportion of the age group now go on to university. A university degree is now an essential requirement for many kinds of middle-class jobs.

Chapter Five moves on from the general discussion of educational aspiration to examine how education attainment is differentiated by geography, social class and ethnicity. It shows that London overall has a history of low educational attainment, which poses problems for many parents who wish to see their children in high-attaining schools. There is a wide variation in GCSE attainment levels across London by borough and by school. East London has major variations in attainment, with some of the lowest scores in London in Hackney, Tower Hamlets and Barking, and also some of the very highest scores in Redbridge and Havering. At school level the variations are even more marked, with some of the highest performing schools seeing 100% of pupils gaining 5+ GCSE grades A*–C while some schools gain little more than 20%. There is thus a distinctive geography of attainment in London. There are also major variations in attainment by both ethnic origin and residential area and the chapter analyses the respective contributions of these factors to attainment, showing that while both play an important role in influencing attainment, class is slightly more important than ethnic origin.

In Chapter Six we consider the limits to choice and the highly constrained nature of parental decision making. We focus initially on the policy context and the way in which both main political parties have played up choice but neither has found how to reconcile this with a dearth, particularly in some urban areas like East London, of 'good schools'. In this context, we argue that choice becomes little more than a rationing device and that, as it has been embraced by increasing numbers of parents, it has had the unintended consequence of limiting choice on the basis of where you live. We examine in detail both the attainment and recruitment patterns not only of the seven boroughs in our study area but also, more importantly, of the individual schools. In terms of attainment, most boroughs (the main exception being Redbridge) have one or two high-performing schools and a long 'tail' of average and below-average schools. In the context of the cross-London allocation process, which was instituted in 2006, there is less and less opportunity for middle-class parents to 'play the system', and where you live has become increasingly critical in getting into a popular school. We present the data on the numbers of applicants and places in different schools across East London to show that some popular schools are only able to offer places to pupils living very near to the school whereas the less popular schools are allocated pupils from a much wider area. As such, the 'best' schools tend to be heavily oversubscribed although we question whether highly popular necessarily equates with the best in schooling. Nevertheless, the reality for many parents is that, whether they exercise choice or not, they often find themselves allocated to their nearest school. We draw on our in-depth interviews to examine parental reactions to this and how they deal with the situation they find themselves in. This might include 'going private', dusting off a long-dormant faith or moving house into the catchment of a popular school. We examine what parents look for in a 'good school' — the extent to which it is attainment-driven, the extent to which it reflects an 'evasion of unpopular groups' and the extent to which it embraces a wider view of education.

In Chapter Seven we continue this theme about school reputation and working the system by drawing extensively on our interviews with parents across the sub-region. We try to pin down what is meant by a good school and what differentiates it from the least popular. While most parents articulate a desire to get their child into a high-achieving, non-selective school, they are generally accepting of the fact that most of the time they will fail unless they live nearby, get out their chequebook (and this doesn't always work) or devote a lot of time to their local church. What they are adamant about, however, is that they will not send their children to what are clearly often demonised as 'failing' schools — the words 'over my dead body' were used by more than one parent. We examine how parents deal with the failure to get into their chosen schools and how, to some extent at least, the policy of choice is creating a sense of failure among schools that perform perfectly well given the social background of their intake. We look at the extent to which issues around discipline and values are important and suggest that this is particularly so among groups who are concerned about their children being 'brought down' by disruptive pupils — usually seen to be white and Black Caribbean working-class boys. It is often in these circumstances that 'faith assets' are relied on in order to get their children into religious schools, without the family having to move from where they live.

In the concluding chapter, we attempt a synthesis of these themes in the wider context of East London as a classic 'zone in transition', in which there has been a process of upward and outward mobility by some groups as new groups come in. We rather more tentatively suggest that East London represents, in exaggerated form, the future of the social composition of a number of British cities and those elsewhere. The broad outcomes of the book are to interweave our four dimensions of change (social class, ethnicity, housing and education) into an account of urban change as neoliberalism faces its first serious social and economic crisis.

## The bigger picture

We make the argument over the course of this book that the interaction of class and ethnicity, in the context of a resurgence in international migration over the last decade, has spurred a new dynamic of urban change which, while specific to East London, has wider implications for an understanding of contemporary urban change. Specifically, we argue that these interactions between class and ethnicity require a reworking of the previously separate narratives of gentrification and suburbanisation into a wider theoretical understanding of the contemporary urban fabric. The analysis of the 'warp' of structural change (de-industrialisation, service sector growth, changes in ethnic structure, class mobility and change, economic globalisation and international migration) is combined with narratives drawn across the 'woof' of individual aspirations, household mobility strategies and a sense of culture – all of which are highly contextualised within their respective class and ethnic cultures. Our drawing of London's changing social landscape thus interweaves an analysis of structural change with accounts of individual social action.

In East London, as in many other parts of the western world, the late 1960s marked the high water mark of manufacturing employment. The 1970s saw the 'perfect storm' of massive oil price rises, rapid inflation and rising international competition allied to a growing trend to shift production to cheaper locations overseas. The result was a round of plant closures, job losses and increasing unemployment, which peaked in the early 1980s. In many areas employment in the once traditional industries of iron and steel, manufacturing, textiles and other key industries never recovered, marking the end of 'Fordism' and large-scale mass production. This restructuring of industrial production was accompanied in Britain by the emergence of 'Thatcherism', a Conservative political programme which was an early iteration on neoliberalism and led, among other things, to large-scale privatisation, a weakening of trades union power and a shift in the relative balance of power between capital and labour, allied to the growth of banking and finance, the service sector and a marked increase in earnings inequality. The consequences of this for East London have been dire for some while opening up new opportunities for others (Mason, 2009; Callinicos, 2010).

The Chicago School of Urban Sociology focused around a model of outward process of 'invasion and succession' in the expanding, industrial city of the early 20th century in the context of massive inward migration; we argue that there are significant similarities and differences in contemporary East London. These revolve around the interactions between class and ethnicity in the context of high inward migration. East London, long a mono-cultural working-class 'quarter' of London, has simultaneously – and not always painlessly – become an increasingly multicultural and post-industrial area in a complex process of class and ethnic interchange. It is this interaction of class and ethnicity which is central to the account we develop in the rest of the book and return to in the conclusion. Some of the white working class 'upped sticks' for the outer reaches of London and Essex, while others slipped into economic inactivity. Some members of the professional middle classes headed for the terraced housing of its inner areas in a now familiar process of gentrification. Some of the long-settled immigrants of the 1960s and 1970s, many of whom had bought their houses in those inner areas which have now become gentrified, moved out to the suburbs, seeking semi-detached owner-occupation and a system, as they saw it, of guaranteed good schooling. Many others were desperate to follow them. Many were fleeing what they saw as the deterioration of these areas as their schools became publicly labelled as failing and houses fell into private letting – in some cases by the very neighbours who had made the suburban transition. This occurred during the boom years of the last decade at precisely the same time as new groups of migrants (mainly from the Balkans, sub-Saharan Africa and more recently the eight EU accession countries, the so-called 'A8') began to move into these areas (particularly in Newham). We thus have a four-way class/ethnic split in East London that, we argue, has patterned its changing social structure during the last decades of the 20th century and opening years of the 21st:

- First, the resident traditional white working class has contracted or moved further out of the East London area, towards the M25 and beyond.
- Second, the immigrants of the 1960s and 1970s (mainly of New Commonwealth and Pakistani origin) have grown rapidly in numbers, as a result of family reunification and high rates of natural growth, and have been moving into the areas and housing vacated by the white working class.
- Third, some white professionals (what David Lockwood has termed the 'urban-seeking' middle classes), unable to afford those areas

gentrified during the 1980s and 1990s, have been moving into the inner-city areas (notably in Newham) vacated by outward-moving, and largely Asian, groups referred to above.

• Fourth, the new (largely economic) migrants from Africa and, more recently, the A8 countries, have been coming to London, and particularly Newham, in both cases replacing a largely Asian indigenous working and lower middle class referred to above who have, in turn, been replacing similar white groups from outer areas, such as Redbridge.

The new poor of economic 'inactives' – often black and white, and more rarely Asian, who now occupy positions of what Wacquant terms 'advanced marginality' (2008) – are the absent actors in this research. Their voices have only occurred off-stage but their importance should not be under-estimated, not only in terms of their increasing precariousness but also for the way in which the relatively advantaged have created a new imaginary of the 'urban other' out of them. The fear that this group engenders among many of our respondents cannot be exaggerated, in particular the fear of infecting the carefully nurtured hopes of aspiration for their children.

We end this introduction, where we started, by emphasising the importance of international migration at both ends of the labour market. Two recent studies embrace this: Adrian Favell's *Eurostars and eurocities* (2008), which is an articulate ethnography of young European professionals working in London's leading sectors and, on the other side, the less-skilled, the huddled masses who have come from Africa and Asia, discussed by Jane Wills and her colleagues in *Global cities at work: New migrant divisions of labour* (Wills et al, 2010). Both are outstanding pieces of scholarship about the two sides of the new urban realm; this book fits somewhere between them, with its focus on those who represent at least part of the new 'middle' middle class of London.

## A note on the research areas

The findings in this book are the result of detailed survey and interview work that we undertook in East London. We focused on five areas across East London (see Figure 1.2). We chose these areas with a number of points in mind: first, to try and capture a number of inner and outer East London places that had been undergoing social class and ethnic change; second, to ensure that we got a good mixture of ethnic and class backgrounds; and third, to capture the differences in educational provision. We made our selection on the basis of an analysis of census

**Figure 1.2: Map of the East London study area showing individual research areas**

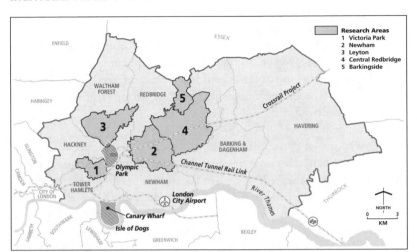

and other data, and detailed on the ground explorations of a number of areas. We finally chose the following five areas:

1. Victoria Park (falling in the London Boroughs of Hackney and Tower Hamlets)
2. East Ham (London Borough of Newham)
3. Leyton (London Borough of Waltham Forest)
4. Central Redbridge (London Borough of Redbridge)
5. Barkingside (London Borough of Redbridge).

Our first research area was centred on Victoria Park, straddling the London Boroughs of Hackney and Tower Hamlets. It was chosen because our initial research indicated that it contained a large cluster of higher managerial and professional workers. Victoria Park has long been a middle-class enclave in East London, and it was originally built as such in the late 19th century. It is an estate agent's delight, often described as an 'architectural gem', with an elegant curve of terraced housing opposite the Park, the highest performing primary school in Hackney literally over the fence from the back garden and an appropriate infrastructure of shops, pubs and restaurants. To the south of the Park, the area around Tredegar Square, with its Georgian houses, provides equally elegant gentrified living with prices to match. Both areas have become increasingly desirable given the increasing importance of the City of London and the need to minimise journeys

**1.1: Victoria Park North, the elegant terrace of housing at its centre**

**1.2: Victoria Park North, the upmarket pubs and shops**

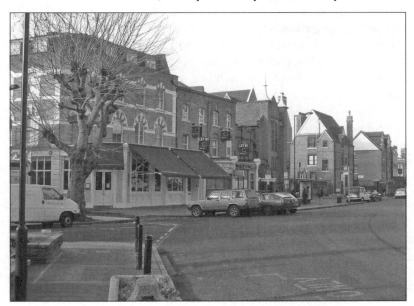

### 1.3: Victoria Park South, Tredegar Square

to work with the lengthening of the working day. We also included a number of new-build and ex-council high-rise flats towards Hackney Wick at the eastern end of the Park, which provided a rather different environment and from which people often tried to move when they had children but found that they could ill afford to move to the more elegant and larger housing at the western end of the Park.

Our second area was based in Newham around Central Park in East Ham and also in the Forest Gate area. Both of these are characterised by terraced housing, much of which had been owner-occupied by Asian families but was now increasingly a destination for incoming white middle-class professionals. These people, for the most part, worked in the public sector as lower managers and professionals, and approximated to an earlier generation of gentrifiers, such as those studied by one of us 20 years earlier in Stoke Newington (see Butler, 1997), but were no longer able to afford Hackney prices. They were classic examples of what Lockwood (1995) has termed the 'urban-seeking' middle classes. There were, however, many Asian and some Black African and Black Caribbean professionals among our respondents in this group. Most of the white professionals valued the socially and ethnically mixed nature of the area and were prepared to educate their children in its schools despite the relatively low standards of attainment – although these were improving rapidly at the time at which we undertook our research.

## 1.4: Plashet Park and its surrounding housing in Newham

## 1.5: Green Street, one of the prime Asian shopping streets in London

### 1.6: Leytonstone, near to Wanstead Flats

The third area was in Leytonstone and Leyton in the London Borough of Waltham Forest. In many respects, this was a destination of necessity rather than affection compared to the other areas. People tended to choose it precisely because they got more housing for their money and it had good transport links to the centre – via the Central line. Many of the white respondents had left areas like Hackney, including Victoria Park, because they could not afford a house there that they needed for a growing family, but they did not want to become suburbanites. It also had the advantage of being on the borders of Redbridge, which gave access to its selective schools without its prices or its suburban feeling. Prior to the tightening up on application procedures in 2006, Leyton offered a reasonable chance of gaining access to other schools in Redbridge or in Havering. As such, it was a favoured destination for black respondents from Newham and to a lesser extent Hackney. While most respondents did not like its built environment, its position between the city and suburbs was often highly valued.

Our last two areas were both located in the London Borough of Redbridge. We have called them Central Redbridge and Barkingside, respectively, and both comprised relatively large areas. Central Redbridge was located centrally in the borough and took in some of the catchment areas of its most popular non-selective schools, notably Seven Kings School. A previously largely Jewish area, it is now heavily populated by Asians, many of whom had moved from Newham or elsewhere because of its high-quality schooling and its suburban

## 1.7: Redbridge, streets around our Central Redbridge area

## 1.8: Redbridge, larger housing in Barkingside

ambience. Many had left Newham because of what they perceived as its poor education and also the arrival of new migrant groups, many of whom were moving into buy-to-let private rented flats and houses which they regarded as putting a blight on the area. Ironically, the attractiveness of the schools in Redbridge was causing the same to happen there. Barkingside was located further to the east and abutted the M25 motorway and the shire county of Essex. It is an area that includes large semi-detached and detached houses as well as some of the larger peripheral council housing estates and, until relatively recently, was largely white. Many of the white residents have begun to move out and have been replaced by Asians who have been unable to afford housing nearer the centre and south of the borough around the high-performing schools. Issues of ethnic change and 'white flight' were often addressed most explicitly by our respondents in this area.

The questionnaire-based survey in each of these areas was undertaken face to face. We collected 300 responses to this, more or less evenly spread across the five areas. We aimed to interview middle-class respondents with school-age (or pre-school) children. We defined 'middle class' quite broadly and did not restrict ourselves to owner-occupiers although we excluded council estates and focused on areas of owner-occupation. We also aimed to make the respondents broadly representative of the area's four major ethnic groupings – White, Black African, Black Caribbean and Asian. We largely succeeded in this aim. Rather more respondents were female than male.[5] The interviews lasted approximately an hour and apart from questions about the respondent and their education, occupational and housing history, we explored their hopes and aspirations for their children's education, how they chose schools for them and what their feelings were about their children's schooling. We subsequently undertook in-depth semi-structured interviews with 100 of these respondents, some of which took over two hours. These focused particularly on the issue of schooling. We draw on both sources of data in the book but particularly on the in-depth interviews which were transcribed and coded using Nvivo software.

The survey areas were selected in part on the analysis of census data on social class and tenure and in part from ethnographic evidence. We also used the census extensively in the analysis of housing tenure and ethnic change. As we discuss later in the book, we also analysed data from the Department of Education's Pupil Level Annual School Census (PLASC) in terms of attainment, area social composition (through the Mosaic classification derived from pupil postcodes) and ethnicity. Finally, we undertook extensive analysis of published borough education data on school catchment areas, applications, offers and appeals for all the seven boroughs of East London. This work provides the context for the questionnaire surveys and in-depth interviews.

## Notes

[1] Where necessary we have omitted information that might identify individuals.

[2] BME stands for black and minority ethnic; sometimes it is referred to as BAME – black, Asian and minority ethnic. How to refer to non-white groups is a political minefield and many such terms rapidly become politically unacceptable. In Europe such longstanding minorities are often referred to as 'immigrants'; this would be unacceptable in the UK.

[3] RES-000-23-0793 'Gentrification, ethnicity and education in East London'.

[4] We have not given gender the same emphasis and this is something that we have been taken to task for by at least one of the anonymous readers who read the original outline and the final draft. It is probably significant that more of our respondents were female than male, reflecting the concerns about education that still remain predominantly the responsibility of women within the household. Indeed, given the importance of education to this book, the salience of gender as an issue should not be under-estimated and our relative silence on this is an issue. It remains a hidden theme in the book compared to the more overt ones of ethnicity and class. A cynic might argue ''twas ever thus' against which we have little defence, except to argue that we have had to focus on what appear as the key issues of change in recent decades – in a sense we are writing about change, and issues of class and ethnicity have been subject to massive change in East London, gender less so.

[5] For those interested, further details are to be found at www.esrcsocietytoday.ac.uk/ESRCInfoCentre/, entering RES 000 23 0793 in the search box.

# TWO

# Changing economy and social structure of East London

'... in my parents' area [...] in Ilford there was a bit more of a ... all of the households were there for a long time so there was a sense of neighbourhood. But here it's constantly changing. I mean, you know, because it's constantly changing you don't know how long somebody's going to be there. If you know someone's long term I think you make an effort. Like next door is rented and although I'm nice and friendly to them I don't go out of my way because I don't know who's going to move in next door. Whereas, like in my childhood home where my parents were, the neighbours were the same for so many years and they kind of watched me grow up and in that sense we kind of look out for each other so there was this semi–community spirit.' (Indian, female, Redbridge)

## Introduction

In this chapter and Chapter Three we point to the changes that have taken place in class and ethnic structure and how these changes and the interactions between them have been particularly marked in East London. These changes could be regarded as a marker for the future, particularly in large metropolitan areas. They have also not occurred within a political and economic vacuum and we locate them in the context of London's recent re-making as a major financial services economy under conditions of neoliberal governance (Hackworth, 2007). This chapter is focused mainly on class change; Chapter Three looks at changes in ethnicity and how this has interacted with the changing class and housing tenure structure. We explore this interaction through an analysis of changes in the housing market in East London. We use this analysis of changes in social class and ethnicity in East London as the jumping-off point for our discussion in subsequent chapters of how our respondents have put their aspirations into practice. More often than not, 'moving up' has involved 'moving out' and this has been particularly governed by a wish to access 'good' (or perhaps more accurately, 'popular') schools.

In the mid-1960s, London's physical and human geography was neatly summarised by Peter Willmott and Michael Young (1973), as a 'cross' following its river basins (the Thames flowing west to east and the rivers Fleet and Wandle to the north and south respectively) and the railway lines which hugged the low-lying ground of the river valleys (see Figure 2.1). Working-class housing and factories tended to cluster around the railway lines while middle- and upper-class housing tended to be on the higher ground in the surrounding quarters of the cross, to escape what William Petty in 1772 called 'the fumes, steams and stinks of the *whole easterly pyle*'. The central area was an exception to this rule, forming an oasis of upper-class housing. This model of the 'cross' provided a clear integration of human and physical geography in accounting for the distribution of London's population. As London has de-industrialised, many of these areas of working-class housing, transportation and industrial production have become the focus of regeneration and, all too often, gentrification. By the 1990s, East London remained the only largely un-gentrified and working-class quarter of London.

**Figure 2.1: The 'cross'**

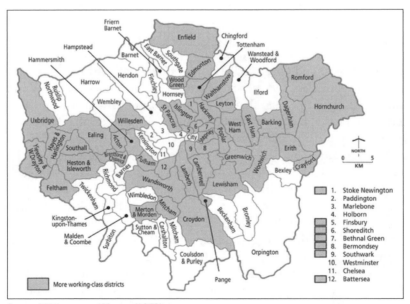

*Source:* Willmott and Young (1973)

East London has, as we claimed in Chapter One, long been the bastion of the London working class, and with good reason. After the 'Great Fire of London' in 1666, more and more high-quality development took place in Westminster to the west of the City of London, much of which was (and still is) owned by large landed estates who tightly controlled the nature of development. To the east, however, ownership was small-scale, and the development which took place was much less controlled. It was here that the growing working class expanded in the 19th century (Stedman Jones, 1974). Our focus is on the changes at the end of the 19th and 20th centuries and the processes of persistence and change in between and their legacy in terms of contemporary class structure. Both periods were ones of rapid social and economic change and, in the case of the 19th century, of social crisis. Out of this social crisis emerged the working-class culture that dominated East London for much of the 20th century.

However, even while it was being researched, this close-knit 'occupational community' based around the proximity of work and home was breaking down, and many of the younger East Enders were making the move out of London to some of the new towns in Essex, with their relatively well-paid and secure jobs in new manufacturing industries and newly built homes with all the 'mod cons'. These changes speeded up with the de-industrialisation of London that began in the 1960s, and particularly affected inner East London with its dependency on the docks, food markets and other riverside industries. By the 1970s most of the docks and with them their associated industries were closed or in the process of closing, resulting in the loss of an estimated 200,000 manual working-class jobs (Buck et al, 1986). During the last quarter of the 20th century, East London began to restructure around a financial services economy that has come to dominate London's economy (and for that matter, the economy of the UK as a whole). This new economy has required a workforce with an entirely different 'skill set' – not just for those working in it at various levels but also those servicing it. East London has moved from being a production and distribution economy based around a workforce that was largely male and working full-time in semi-skilled manual occupations to one that services the consumption and work-related needs of the financial services economy and is more female and part-time. This new economy is largely based in the City of London, the new financial districts of Docklands (notably Canary Wharf) and outlying centres such as Stratford and Thurrock. The requirements for this labour force vary but often include a need for either customer-facing or sophisticated data analysis skills. None of these were part of the skill set of the traditional white, male East End working class.

## From East End to East London: marking out East London

The social division between the East End and the West End of London is long-standing. The work of Mayhew (1850) and Booth (cited in Fried and Elman, 1971) in the second half of the 19th century confirmed the existence of concentrated poverty in East London. The working-class nature of the East End spread east across the River Lea to West Ham, East Ham and Plaistow in the late 19th century. Working-class housing also expanded out to the north east to Waltham Forest, with the building of the railways out of Liverpool Street from the mid-19th century (Kellett, 1969). It was in the 'East End' from the 17th century onwards that many of the dirty trades took place and it was through London's rapidly expanding docks that much of the trade with the Empire was conducted. The development of the docks also led to a growth in related dock-processing and consumer goods industries (Hall, 1962; Coppock, 1964). The East End and its subsequent 19th-century eastward extensions along the Thames became not only London's gateway but also its backyard, which status it retains today. In 1998 Hackney, Newham and Tower Hamlets ranked first, second and fourth nationally on the Department for Communities and Local Government's ranking of social deprivation by local authority in Britain. This has been, and continues to be, a very poor area.

From the end of the 19th, and for much of the 20th century, East London came to symbolise a form of working-class culture and resistance that set it apart from the working class elsewhere in the country. The reasons for this are complex and were outlined in the previous chapter but, in essence, are a function of the East London labour market and the peculiarly insecure nature of the forms of employment engendered by its dominant industries. While located close to the heart of the world's most advanced imperial economy, these industries were, in a classic illustration of uneven development, largely pre-industrial and low skilled in their labour processes. British manufacturing industries, with their dependence on skilled artisanal labour, were – with a few exceptions (Crossick, 1978) – located well to the north, in the Midlands, the North West, the North East and in Scotland (Gray, 1974, 1976). These areas were often well unionised. London was an exception in the economic geography of Victorian Britain and nowhere was this more so than in the East End, whose social and political disorganisation was a continual source of fascination which increasingly turned to fear among the middle classes of late 19th-century London (Stedman Jones, 1974). To the contemporary middle class, the East End was the embodiment of a deprived, disorganised and socially threatening but little known 'other'.

## London's governance

In 1889 London was organised into 28 metropolitan boroughs that made up the London County Council (LCC), which, together with the City of London, accounted for the 29 named boroughs in Figure 2.2. These included the metropolitan boroughs of Hackney, Shoreditch, Poplar, Stepney and Bow, all located to the east of the City. The River Lea marked the eastern boundary of the County of London from the County of Essex that incorporated such places as the County Boroughs of East Ham and West Ham.

London was, however, always more extensive than its administrative boundaries; the *de facto* boundary of (East) London moved outwards with the building of the North Circular road in the 1930s surrounded by new suburban housing in such places as Gants Hill (Jackson, 1974). The construction of the largest housing estate in the world in Dagenham in the late 1920s to service the new manufacturing plants being built by companies such as Ford and May & Baker (in chemicals) marked a further expansion into Essex (Olechnowicz, 1997). The post-Second World War Green Belt that was meant to put a stop to its

**Figure 2.2: The old LCC boroughs**

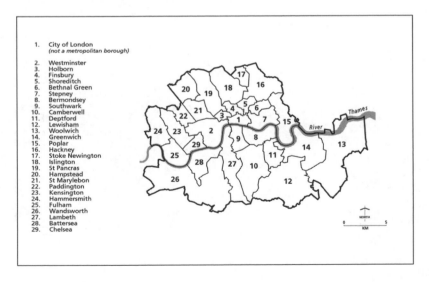

1.  City of London
    *(not a metropolitan borough)*

2.  Westminster
3.  Holborn
4.  Finsbury
5.  Shoreditch
6.  Bethnal Green
7.  Stepney
8.  Bermondsey
9.  Southwark
10. Camberwell
11. Deptford
12. Lewisham
13. Woolwich
14. Greenwich
15. Poplar
16. Hackney
17. Stoke Newington
18. Islington
19. St Pancras
20. Hampstead
21. St Marylebon
22. Paddington
23. Kensington
24. Hammersmith
25. Fulham
26. Wandsworth
27. Lambeth
28. Battersea
29. Chelsea

further outward sprawl did little to frustrate the continued expansion. The building of the M25 orbital motorway in the 1970s–1980s marked yet another *de facto* boundary between London and its surrounding exurbia. In effect, as Buck et al (2002) argue, London functionally now reaches out to include a huge travel-to-work area extending into most of south-eastern England.

The LCC was replaced by the larger Greater London Council (GLC) in 1965, incorporating (on its eastern flank) parts of the surrounding county of Essex into the new London Boroughs of Barking & Dagenham, Havering, Newham, Redbridge and Waltham Forest; Hackney brought together the metropolitan boroughs of Hackney, Shoreditch and Stoke Newington while Tower Hamlets included those of Bethnal Green, Poplar and Stepney (see Figure 2.3). These seven boroughs make up our East London study area (see Figure 1.2 on page 24). The GLC was itself abolished by Margaret Thatcher in 1986 having become under Ken Livingstone's leadership the *de facto* opposition to her government (Carvel, 1984). Following its abolition, London was left with no strategic government until New Labour set up the Greater London Assembly (GLA) in 2000.[1] The GLA comprised all 32 London boroughs and the City of London.

The remainder of the chapter is divided into four parts. First, it considers the 'social crisis' of London in the late 19th century and the consequences for its working class are traced through the first half of the 20th century. In particular we develop the idea that East London

**Figure 2.3: The GLC boroughs**

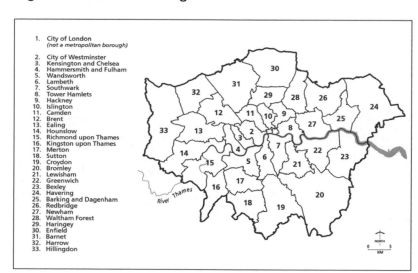

1. City of London
   *(not a metropolitan borough)*
2. City of Westminster
3. Kensington and Chelsea
4. Hammersmith and Fulham
5. Wandsworth
6. Lambeth
7. Southwark
8. Tower Hamlets
9. Hackney
10. Islington
11. Camden
12. Brent
13. Ealing
14. Hounslow
15. Richmond upon Thames
16. Kingston upon Thames
17. Merton
18. Sutton
19. Croydon
20. Bromley
21. Lewisham
22. Greenwich
23. Bexley
24. Havering
25. Barking and Dagenham
26. Redbridge
27. Newham
28. Waltham Forest
29. Haringey
30. Enfield
31. Barnet
32. Harrow
33. Hillingdon

became a 'social laboratory' for the development of state-led welfare as part of a wider 'partnership' between the state, capital and labour. The high point of this era, sometimes characterised as 'Fordism', was reached in the aftermath of the Second World War with the so-called Keynes-Beveridge settlement. The next two sections provide brief overviews of the decline of the East End and its subsequent regeneration; these are associated with the closure of the docks and allied riverside industries and their subsequent redevelopment by the London Docklands Development Corporation (LDDC) following the Conservative Party's election victory under Margaret Thatcher's leadership in 1979. This renaissance heralded the beginnings of a different kind of East London economy, the emergence of new social groups and a much-changed relationship with the state. In the fourth and final section, we discuss the changing class structure of London in the closing decades of the 20th century, with particular reference to the East London study area. Like the rest of London, there has been a decline in working-class employment but the increase in the middle class has been less dramatic and more focused on lower middle class and intermediate occupational positions than elsewhere in London – with relatively low degrees of gentrification except in Hackney and Tower Hamlets, where riverside housing development has partially transformed the area.

## Social crisis of 'outcast London' and the growth of welfare

By the end of the 19th century, the British economy was slowly emerging from the 'long depression' that began in 1873. However, at the same time as the broader economic situation began to improve, what can be termed London's 'social crisis' sharpened and was increasingly perceived as a threat to London's social and political stability. Gareth Stedman Jones, in his eponymous study of 'outcast London' (Stedman Jones, 1974), argues that the underlying causes of London's social crisis lay in the structure of its labour market which was characterised by insecurity of employment – particularly in East London, where the seasonal nature of much employment was reinforced by the widespread extent of 'sweating' in which workers were paid 'by the piece', usually for labour carried out in the home. It was this, together with the necessity for the workers to live near to potential employment, that contributed to the overcrowding and poverty in the East End – in 1881, 18.7% of the population lived more than two per room, with an infant mortality rate of 152 per 1,000 live births. Paul Thompson (1967, p 13) quotes a government survey of 28,000 London working men undertaken in 1887, which showed that over 70% of the dock labourers, building craftsmen, tailors and boot makers had been unemployed for over two months the previous winter. Thompson and Stedman Jones both stress the lack of social stability in most working-class areas of London, and Charles Booth's surveys indicated a continuously shifting working-class population, where it was common for a third of the population to move during the course of a year. In 1850 Mayhew observed that:

> I believe that we may safely conclude that out of the 4½ million people who have to depend on their industry for the livelihood of themselves and their families, there is barely sufficient work for the regular employment of half our labourers, so that only 1½ million are fully and constantly employed, while 1½ million are employed only half their time and the remaining 1½ million wholly unemployed, obtaining a day's work occasionally by the displacement of some others. (Mayhew, 1850, vol 2, pp 322-3)

Most middle-class people were unaware of, and uninterested in, the poverty in working-class areas. Andrew Mearns' pamphlet 'The bitter cry of outcast London' (1883) was largely responsible for opening up the public discussion on poverty. Mearns claimed that most work in East London was casual and often in sweated trades, for which the wages were commonly a shilling or less a day. The description of poverty and living conditions of the poor was one of criminality, immorality and general depravity, where marriage was rare and incest common. He did little to challenge the predominant view of poverty as pauperism that was seen as 'individual failing'; his prescription was to build more mission halls! It was the publicity that the crusading *Pall Mall Gazette* gave to Mearns' pamphlet and the ensuing debate that made it so influential.

Charles Booth, a bourgeois ship owner from Liverpool recently settled in London, was dissatisfied with both mainstream 'solutions' to poverty – that of socialism ('a pernicious invasion of human rights') and philanthropy ('hopelessly ineffective'). The appearance of another series of articles in the *Pall Mall Gazette* in 1885 based on a survey carried out in working-class areas by the Social Democratic Federation (SDF),[2] which claimed that 25% of Londoners lived in abject poverty, moved Booth to carry out his own investigation to disprove what he considered to be a mere propaganda exercise by the SDF. The findings of his work (which involved surveying every house in London) are well known – that approximately 30% of Londoners were living in abject poverty and that the major cause was want of regular employment (in 85% of cases) and not 'habit' (that is, drink or mendacity, which only accounted for 15% of cases). The initial findings were published in 1889 as *Life and labour of the people in London, Volume 1* and concentrated on the work he had undertaken in what is now Tower Hamlets. He later produced data on the rest of the capital that confirmed his finding that just under a third of the total population were living in poverty.

Stedman Jones argues that during the 1880s a transformation occurred in middle-class perceptions away from this focus on pauperism (caused by individual failings) to one of chronic poverty (caused by structural forces). Despite the slowly improving economic situation, unemployment remained high, as did the fear of continued social unrest. The intermittent disorder and riots of 1886, when the dispossessed from the East End had camped out in the squares and parks of the West End, had continued into 1887. This culminated in the events of Bloody Sunday on 13 November 1887 when troops were used to clear the mob forcibly from Trafalgar Square. The riots were therefore symptomatic of a widespread, endemic and chronic poverty in which hundreds of thousands lacked work or hope; in other words, the problems were structural and, as such, they were beyond both the selective long-term casework approach favoured by the Charity Organisation Society (COS)[3] and 'ad hoc' funds such as those administered by the Mansion House Appeal.

The dock strike of 1889 was a key moment in the social crisis of London. The strike had gained wide support – politically and financially – not just from within the UK but also from overseas. Its partially successful outcome, which mitigated some of the worst aspects of casual labour, offered evidence in support of those who claimed that the problem was primarily one of irregular work. Indeed Charles Booth (1892) argued that the effect of the dock strike on labour practices, especially with decasualisation, showed beyond doubt that regular work makes better labourers; drunkenness had declined, he claimed, which showed that decasualisation was the way to break the cycle of poverty. According to Stedman Jones, the dock strike convinced the ruling class that there were essentially two groups in London among the working class – the 'respectable' and the 'rough' (known as the residuum). Effectively the strategy they adopted was to separate the two and, as Thompson (1967) shows, the closing decade was one of frenzied activity by all political parties to recalibrate their organisations and policies to this newly perceived environment that ultimately led to the Liberal electoral landslide of 1906.

The decasualisation achieved as a result of the strike – despite the dramatic social benefits demonstrated by Booth – was relatively limited and short-lived. For the majority of households in East London, work – such as there was – remained casual, sweated or both. Despite the relative optimism achieved after the dock strike and the hyper-activity by sections of the establishment that 'something must be done', the realisation at the beginning of the new century that up to 60% of potential Army recruits in the Boer War had been rejected due to physical weaknesses caused near panic in Whitehall. The result was the setting up of the Inter-Departmental Committee on Physical Deterioration that reported in 1905. The findings of the Committee were a key influence on the incoming Liberal government that came to power in 1906. They legislated to provide free school meals and low-cost land for housing for low-income workers and in 1917 Lloyd George put forward his policy of 'Homes fit for heroes', which introduced direct subsidies for council house construction (Swennarton, 1981). Once the principle of state involvement had been won, what followed was a long struggle to widen the range of provision until the comprehensive reforms setting up the so-called welfare state in the late 1940s. Local authorities in East London were among the first to provide free school meals and continued to press for further extensions in the involvement of the state for the next four decades. In a period of less than 50 years, between the first tentative pieces of legislation following the election of the Liberal government in 1906 and the 'roll out' of the welfare state in the late 1940s, the national and local state became increasingly important in the lives of East London's working-class population. The Liberal Party's election victory also led to the setting up of labour exchanges (under the direction of William Beveridge), rudimentary forms of unemployment insurance, the provision of old age pensions and the introduction of subsidised council house building. During the Second World War, the government commissioned a series of reports into how the postwar world would be run, designed to stiffen the resolve of the population. The first articulation of this came in the 1942 Beveridge Report written in some of the darkest years of the Second World War with the clear, if unstated, goal of offering a better future once the war was won. For the people of East London, this form of social protection, together with the nationalisation of key parts of the transport network (including the docks), finally provided a measure of regular and secure employment for its working class.

## Economic change and the decline of working-class community in East London

The years following the Second World War marked the high point for East London as a working-class community, not withstanding the massive bomb damage to the East End, but they were relatively short-lived. There was a huge postwar interest in what seemed the lost world of the working class and particularly of its occupational communities, not only in the burgeoning social science literature (Zweig, 1952; Dennis et al, 1956; Hoggart, 1958; Williams, 1958) but also in popular novels (*This sporting life*, *Saturday night and Sunday morning*, *The loneliness of the long distance runner*, for example). However, it was the publication in 1957 of Young and Willmott's (1962), study of Bethnal Green, *Family and kinship in East London*, from the Bethnal Green-based Institute of Community Studies (ICS),[4] that did more to popularise the sociological study of working-class culture than probably any other book published in the postwar period. The study, undertaken between 1953 and 1955, compares a group of working-class respondents remaining in the tightly knit communities of Bethnal Green with a mainly younger generation attracted by seemingly secure jobs in manufacturing industry out of London.[5] 'Greenleigh' is a thinly disguised synonym for Basildon, one of the New Towns developed beyond the Green Belt in Essex after the war as part of the Greater London Plan (another example of war-time planning). The picture of working-class life painted by the Young and Willmott study was reinforced by Peter Townsend's (1963) study of old people (*The family life of old people*), which was undertaken at ICS at approximately the same time. This study pointed to the growing isolation of elderly people in a world where kinship obligations were declining yet in which the state was either unable or unwilling to fill the gap. The characterisation of the East End working class in these studies became, not for the first time, popularised as part of a fascination with the nature of working-class culture more generally.

Michael Young and Peter Willmott built on this earlier work by looking at how the East End working class was changing, particularly focusing on the process of suburbanisation. *Family and class in a London suburb* is a study of the middle-class suburb of Woodford and the ways in which postwar notions of aspiration and social mobility were beginning to take shape, and the authors investigate how these were affecting long-standing assumptions about social class (Willmott and Young, 1961). Another study (*Evolution of a community*), led by Willmott (1963), investigated how the Becontree Estate had evolved 30 years after it was built in the market gardens of Essex to provide employment for the newly built Ford factory at Dagenham. Many of these people moved out of East London to find work and better housing in the interwar years and then, a generation later, the lack of housing opportunities for their children was identified as a major social problem for the sustainability of the community, with many young people forced to move further away to find housing. Thus, while there were 'modern' jobs in the car plants and chemical works in Dagenham, workers often had to travel long distances to such work.[6] The housing issue was an important one in the heart of the old East End in Tower Hamlets and Hackney as a great deal of the housing stock was destroyed during the war, and it was subsequently cleared and rebuilt in the form of large, high-density and often high-rise, local authority housing estates. As a result, at its peak in 1981, before the impact of the Conservative right-to-buy legislation took effect, council housing accounted for 82% of all households in Tower Hamlets and 57% in Hackney. As a result, the East End became increasingly synonymous with the high-rise council housing that subsequently spread rapidly across Britain's inner cities (Dunleavy, 1981).

## Decline of manufacturing and the rise of financial and other services

The importance of the manufacturing industry in London's economy reached its peak in the early 1960s when almost a third (32.4%) of the labour force worked in manufacturing and just 10% in financial and business services. As a result of an emerging international division of labour, greater competition, factory closures and de-industrialisation, the share of the manufacturing industry fell to 19% in 1981 and under 8% in 2001. The number of manufacturing jobs in London fell by over half, from 1.45 million in 1961 to 684,000 in 1981, and it halved again to 360,000 in 1991. East London fared particularly badly in the decline and it was hard hit by the closure of the docks that took place between 1967 and 1981 (Hamnett, 2003). The effect on Dockside employment was particularly harsh, falling from around 30,000 in the 1950s to 2,000 in 1981 (Porter, 1994). Since manufacturing and heavy port-related industries were the major employers of the working class, it is not surprising that East London boroughs in particular felt the cost of this decline. Largely as a result of rises in productivity and falling demand, those boroughs with the highest proportion of employees working in manufacturing generally experienced the largest falls. For example, manufacturing employment in Barking & Dagenham dropped from around 30% in 1981 to 15% in 1991 and 10% in 2001 (Rix, 1997). Similar changes took place in all the East London boroughs that in 2001 had less than 10% of their employment in manufacturing. Despite the general trend of decline, however, East London retained a higher proportion of residents employed in manufacturing industries than London as whole, thus contributing to East London retaining a more working-class population than elsewhere in London (see Figure 2.4).

Since the late 1970s, the major sector of job growth in Britain has occurred within service-related industries (Hamnett, 2003). In London, employment within the business and financial sector, as well as within producer and communication services sectors, has increased. Despite the damaging economic recession of the early 1990s, in which approximately 100,000 jobs were lost within the service sector, business and financial services have become the largest sectors of employment in London (Butler and Rix, 2000; Hamnett, 2003). Since the 1980s, the shift from a predominantly industrial to a post-industrial economy has continued within the city. London now occupies a key role in the global financial and legal services sectors; the consequences of these changes for the population of East London have been profound as those sectors that had previously underpinned employment in the area rapidly declined or disappeared, to be replaced by sectors with different skill requirements.

**Figure 2.4: Decline of manufacturing employment, East London boroughs, 1981–2001**

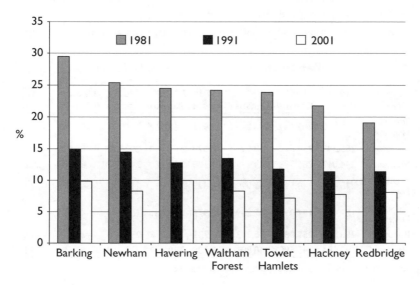

## Redevelopment of Docklands: the emergence of a new East London?

The population of East London, like inner London as a whole, increased dramatically during the 19th century as a result of rapid urban development, high birth rates and immigration. Large tracts of new housing were rapidly built, and overcrowding was widespread. The population of the inner London boroughs reached a peak around 1901, but during the interwar years, the growth moved outwards to the newly built suburbs that doubled in physical area between the wars. Inner London's population went into steep decline in the postwar period from 1951 to 1981, largely as a result of the clearance of high density privately rented housing areas and its redevelopment as lower density local authority estates (Hamnett and Randolph, 1983) and outmigration to the new and expanded towns around London. East London displays a classic pattern (see Table 2.1). Tower Hamlets saw its population fall by 39%, Hackney by 32% and Newham by 29%. The suburban borough decreases were much lower (12% in Redbridge), and Havering even saw its population grow by 25%. The changes parallel those in inner London as a whole, where population declined for 30 years post war, largely as a result of housing clearance and redevelopment and conversion of multi-occupied rented housing to owner-occupied single-family dwellings.

Population loss that was at its height in the 1970s continued through the 1980s, until it stabilised, and eventually began to grow again, in the late 1990s. The turnaround has been driven by a number of factors: high fertility rates, particularly in Newham and Tower Hamlets, new housing developments across most of inner East London and, more recently,

**Table 2.1: Population change, East London, 1951–81**

| Borough/ city | 1951 Census | 1961 Census | 1971 Census | 1981 Census | 1991 Census | 2001 Census | Change 1951–81 | % change |
|---|---|---|---|---|---|---|---|---|
| Tower Hamlets | 230,790 | 205,682 | 164,349 | 139,996 | 161,064 | 196,121 | −90,794 | −39.34 |
| Hackney | 265,349 | 257,522 | 218,594 | 179,529 | 181,248 | 202,819 | −85,820 | −32.34 |
| Newham | 294,017 | 265,388 | 233,699 | 209,128 | 212,170 | 243,737 | −84,889 | −28.87 |
| Waltham Forest | 275,468 | 248,591 | 235,929 | 214,595 | 212,033 | 218,277 | −60,873 | −22.10 |
| Barking & Dagenham | 189,430 | 177,092 | 161,849 | 148,979 | 143,681 | 163,944 | −40,451 | −21.35 |
| Redbridge | 256,902 | 250,080 | 238,383 | 224,731 | 226,218 | 238,628 | −32,171 | −12.52 |
| Havering | 192,094 | 245,598 | 248,801 | 239,788 | 229,492 | 224,248 | 47,694 | 24.83 |

*Source:* Population census, various years, compiled by authors

international migration. The resurgence of the London economy, after the recession of the late 1980s and early 1990s, has now created new employment opportunities particularly in the City and Docklands, providing jobs for those living in East London and beyond.

Since the 1980s, East London has been characterised by the presence of very high proportions of young people, particularly in boroughs with large minority ethnic populations. The proportions of elderly people have declined although some of the riverside wards in Newham and, to a lesser extent, Barking & Dagenham and Tower Hamlets, have high numbers of elderly and economically inactive white working class, many of whom lost their jobs in the restructuring and recessions of the 1980s and have not re-entered the labour market since. What is particularly striking are the changing household forms, with a high number of single-parent households with dependent children, particularly among the white and Black Caribbean groups. In the past 30 years East London has therefore witnessed many of the dramatic economic, social and physical changes experienced by the UK as a whole but sometimes in a particularly exaggerated form – the most notable being its transformation from a largely mono-ethnic area to one with some of the highest ethnic mix in the country, which we discuss in the next chapter.

The changes in East London's built environment have been dramatic: starting with the closure of the Docks, a process which began in the late 1960s, leading to wide-scale de-industrialisation and finally, from the 1980s onwards, to the redevelopment of Canary Wharf and its associated riverside housing. Some of the largest infrastructure projects in Europe have been based in East London (Docklands, Stratford City, the Olympic Park) coupled with some major transport developments such as the Jubilee line extension, the building and expansion of the Docklands Light Railway, the Channel Tunnel Rail Link and London City Airport (see Figure 1.2 on page 24). These developments have transformed the area, bringing large numbers of white-collar jobs in financial and business services and new groups of residents who have bought or rented luxury apartments along the river. What is much less certain is the extent to which the existing residents of East London have benefited from this regeneration.

The acute unemployment in East London at the end of the 1970s hastened the incoming Conservative government in 1979 to try a bold experiment in hands-off regeneration, where the state 'facilitated' development rather than actually taking responsibility for doing it. The legislation enabled Urban Development Corporations (UDCs) to take charge of the regeneration process in selected urban areas. By far the most important UDC set up by this legislation was the LDDC. The LDDC was charged with developing the riversides of the three dockland boroughs of Newham, Tower Hamlets and Southwark. It was given a limited life of 18 years, at the end of which the planning powers would be handed back to the respective boroughs. It was this control of planning and the ability to trade the land owned by nationalised industries (Port of London Authority, British Rail and the Gas Board primarily) that were the corporation's main assets – it had no formal budget other than its ability to trade its assets. The LDDC used these powers to the full to get the area rebuilt: social cohesion was very much a secondary consideration compared to persuading investors to invest in what seemed financially attractive projects, which invariably meant commercial and high-end residential developments. Mark Goodwin (1991) even suggests that the focus of new housing development on market housing functioned to 'replace a surplus population'. The planning powers given to the LDDC enabled them to create an Enterprise Zone, which meant that investors paid no taxes for the first decade, and there were few of the usual restrictions on land use or building style.

The most spectacular of these developments was Canary Wharf, the huge complex of high-rise office buildings located across the narrow neck of the Isle of Dogs, which was designed to provide major new office space for London's financial complex. Initially, there were well-founded doubts about the viability of such a development just three miles from the City of London but, by the mid-1990s, these had been dispelled as the success of the development became steadily clearer. It was a slow process persuading private investors to put their money into an area that was previously associated with communist shop stewards and to which there was no public transport or much prospect of any. By 1987 a new phase of development began; sufficient progress had been made on the construction front to enable some attention to be paid to issues of social inclusion and to the neglected issue of transport to connect the Isle of Dogs to the rest of London, the lack of which was beginning to threaten the success of the project (Foster, 1999). This more inclusive approach was, however, all but killed off by the major recession beginning in 1988 that plunged the project back into crisis. The developers of Canary Wharf, Olympia & York, owned by the Toronto-based Reichmann brothers, went bankrupt, and a coalition of the government and the banks had to provide the finance for the Jubilee line extension (which linked Docklands to the West End) and finish off the building of 1 Canada Square (the building often known as 'Canary Wharf'). By the time the LDDC was wound up in 1997, it was widely felt to have been a success in developing what was once the most run-down and degenerated part of London, albeit at the cost of continued social exclusion and displacement (Hamnett, 2003). In the end, it has been calculated that the public sector contributed something like £3 billion to building Docklands, a far cry from the original intention that it should be a private sector project (Rhodes and Tyler, 1998). At the time of writing (spring 2010), the massive reconstruction and regeneration in the area around Stratford is well advanced in preparation for the 2012 Olympics.

## Changing class structure of East London: persistence and change?[7]

East London was once the most solidly white working-class area of London, and remained so as other areas of the city gentrified and suburbanised; it can, however, no longer be described in such stark terms. In the final section to this chapter, we consider the ways in which East London changed in the last decades of the 20th century by focusing on the changing occupational structure. In the next chapter we consider the changes that have taken place in its ethnic mix in the light of these changes in occupational class. We suggest that a new matrix of class and ethnic positions is emerging into sharper focus in East London. This is partly in contrast to its previously white and largely working-class history. In 1981 inner London had a lower proportion of people working in higher managerial and professional occupations (socioeconomic groups [SEGs] 1–4) compared with outer London, South East England and the country as a whole. However, by 2001 the proportion in this category was higher in inner London than elsewhere (see Table 2.2), while the rate of growth in outer London was roughly at the national average of five percentage points.

In the 2001 Census only one of the seven boroughs making up the East London study area (Redbridge) had a proportion of higher professional and managerial workers (defined as those in SEGs 1–4)[8]

**Table 2.2: SEGs 1–4 as a proportion of SEGs 1–15 (%)**

| Year | East and West | South East | Greater London | Inner London | Outer London |
|---|---|---|---|---|---|
| 1981 | 15.9 | 20.5 | 17.6 | 15.0 | 19.1 |
| 1991 | 20.1 | 24.6 | 24.1 | 24.2 | 24.0 |
| 2001 | 20.9 | 24.0 | 26.0 | 28.7 | 24.3 |
| Percentage point change 1981–2001 | 5 | 3.5 | 8 | 13.7 | 5.2 |

higher than the respective inner or outer London averages. The remaining six boroughs are near the bottom of the distribution. What is most striking is the degree of persistence – only Tower Hamlets demonstrated a dramatic increase in the proportion of senior professionals and managers. The rapid growth in Tower Hamlets was a result of the huge regeneration programme in the Docklands areas in the south of the borough, which has led to widespread gentrification by mainly professional and managerial households without children and/or single-person professional and managerial households (Hall and Ogden, 1992). Across East London, the change is from a very low base, generally lower than elsewhere in London. Therefore a combination of below-average rates of change and the very low base from which it has started indicates that the occupational class structure has changed less in East London than elsewhere. It might be expected that rising house prices across London would be pushing gentrification into East London but, with the exception of Tower Hamlets and to a lesser extent Hackney and now perhaps Newham, this does not seem to be happening, and East London's relative deprivation is perhaps more uniform than elsewhere in the city. This is not to say that it has not been witnessing large increases in property prices (Hamnett, 2009). On the contrary, the percentage increase in property prices from 1995 to 2007 has been more marked in Newham and Barking than any other boroughs, as discussed next in Chapter Three.

What we appear to be seeing is an increase in the proportion of lower professional and managerial workers and administrative workers. The classification used by the ONS, until the 1991 Census, of SEGs, classified this group as SEG 5. We have recoded the data from the 2001 Census to make it compatible with the 1991 classifications.[9] The growth in SEG 5 across outer London has been dramatic – Preteceille (2004) points to a similar pattern in Paris. The increasing proportion of higher managers and professionals (SEGs 1-4) in inner London has continued to fuel its gentrification; this has gone hand in hand with an associated decline in working-class occupations and an increase in SEG 5 (Hamnett, 2003). The geography of this change in inner London is significant in that the growth in the lower middle classes (SEG 5) has been concentrated in the east in Hackney, Tower Hamlets and Newham. In outer London, the growth of this group (SEG 5) has been dramatic as it has more than doubled in size compared with an increase of approximately a third for SEGs 1–4 (see Figure 2.5).

Most of the growth in SEG 5 occurred between 1991 and 2001. Outer East London has shown below-average growth for both upper and 'middle' middle-class groups and has retained more of a

**Figure 2.5: Growth in SEG 5.1 during 1999–2001 for seven East London boroughs**

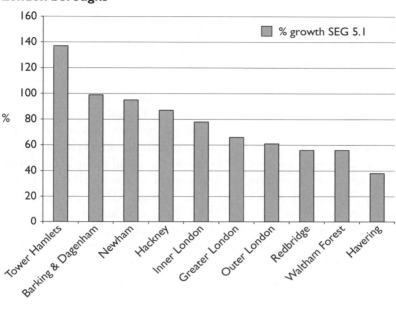

working-class and intermediate-class profile than elsewhere in London in the overall context of a loss of working-class occupations. This finding should not, however, be read to imply that East London has avoided the processes of class change and 'social upgrading' that have swept across London over the past 25 years. East London is currently experiencing a demographic transition that is rather different from the rest of London. While the 'horseshoe' formed by five of the seven boroughs – the exception being the relatively affluent boroughs of Redbridge and Havering – remains the most deprived area in London and retains something of a working-class heritage, in other respects the area has been in the vanguard of the ethnic reshaping that has been accelerating across London over the past 15 years. Social mobility and processes of class change have heavily influenced the contours of this ethnic reshaping. In other words, although the class change profile may be less dramatic than elsewhere in London, when taken with the changing ethnic composition, these changes take on a considerable social and sociological significance, as we show in the next chapter.

East London is therefore experiencing a complex pattern of social mobility in which the interactions of class and ethnic change give greater significance to the experience of social change than the data might suggest. It remains London's largest working-class sub-region and includes a high proportion of economically inactive (ex-)working-class residents. Its three inner boroughs (Tower Hamlets, Newham and Hackney) remain at the top of the Index of Multiple Deprivation (IMD) while – in the case of Hackney and particularly Tower Hamlets – being subject to gentrification by the higher professional and managerial groups, thus indicating high levels of social inequality. Following the Olympic-led developments in Newham, a similar process is under way there. Each of these boroughs have large minority ethnic populations, some of whom have been upwardly socially mobile; when this has occurred our data indicate that these groups have shown a tendency to move out of inner London. The reasons behind this reflect a long-standing desire by those who have been successful to put some (social and spatial) distance between their present situation and that of their place of origin. This is reinforced by the operation of markets in housing and increasingly in education. The inner London private housing market is now all but closed to those on middle incomes, and this has acted as a driver for those wanting to buy into the owner-occupied sector, particularly in relation to Redbridge, Havering and, to a lesser extent, Waltham Forest, where housing is seen as affordable and there is the perception of decent schooling. We suggest in the next chapter that perceptions about schooling, which are now firmly etched in the public consciousness through the publication of 'league tables' and individual school assessments by the Office for Standards in Education (Ofsted), are becoming critical in this process of residential choice.

## Conclusions

In this chapter we have painted a broad historical picture of East London as the focal point of the 'social crisis' of London in the last decades of the 19th century. This was caused, as Stedman Jones made crystal clear, by the casual nature of much working-class employment in the East End. This period also provided the cradle for sociological thinking about the nature of the social crisis in which the persistence and extent of the poverty could no longer be denied but nor could it be explained (or more accurately rationalised) as the consequence of individual failing or fecklessness ('pauperism'). The middle class of London began to fear the mobs of destitute East Enders. The more far-sighted 'social bookkeepers' – such as Charles Booth – found that poverty was pervasive and widespread. In so doing, they also had to look for a cause and a solution. In identifying the cause as lying in London's casualised and sweated labour market, they were forced to confront the ideology of laissez faire. Repression and charity having failed, it seemed to many that in order to satisfy the greater good, the state needed to become involved in at least mitigating the causes of poverty and malnutrition. This growing consensus laid the grounds for the election of the reforming Liberal government in 1906, which passed a raft of measures enabling the state to become involved in the welfare of the nation. The impetus for much of this legislation flowed directly from the 'social crisis' in East London and the perception that if 'something' was not done then the greatest imperial power in the world could find itself unfit to defend itself and liable to the kind of instability at its centre for which the riots of 1886/87 had provided a preview.

The story of the long 20th century in East London was one of increasing state involvement, both in the management of the economy in order to at least mitigate the effects of the slumps to which capitalism was clearly subject and in the provision of a safety net of social support. As we have seen, the postwar decades were the high water mark of this three-way collaboration between capital, labour and the state. However, just as this was occurring, so were the seeds of its destruction, which largely eliminated the economic base of the white working class of East London, many of whom were already moving out from the East End to the suburbs and out of London altogether. In a sense, the last quarter of the 20th century marked a social and economic transformation no less dramatic than that of the end of the 19th, and was one in which East London was once more at the forefront of the kinds of more general economic changes occurring across the country. Over a period of 25 years a white working-class population in inner East London was declared redundant and replaced by a working and lower middle class, one drawn from a mosaic of ethnic groups, many of whom had a more ambivalent view towards the state than those they had replaced. It is to these groups that we turn next.

## Notes

[1] The Government Office for London took on some of the strategic planning roles but this was a central government body and thus lacked any sense of local accountability.

[2] The SDF was a group of radical and influential socialists that was a forerunner to the Labour Party and in which Karl Marx's daughter played an active role (Kapp, 1976). Eventually the SDF became one of the groups that formed the Labour Representative Council, the forerunner to the modern Labour Party.

[3] COS was the forerunner for the Family Welfare Association and laid the groundwork for what is now seen as casework-based social work. It firmly rejected any but the most targeted aid as being likely to lead to 'mendacity'; indeed, its original full title was the 'Society for the Organisation of Charity and the Repression of Mendacity' (Loch, 1977).

[4] Now The Young Foundation (www.youngfoundation.org/).

[5] The problem was that the book was published just as the East End working-class culture that it set out to study entered its period of terminal decline; it is not the authors' fault that the message that people remember is about the extended matrilocal working-class family living in Bethnal Green rather than the nucleated families who settled in Basildon.

[6] There is perhaps an interesting contrast here to the so-called Luton studies by Goldthorpe and Lockwood (Goldthorpe, et al, 1969) which looked at similar industries (Vauxhall, Laporte chemicals and Skefco ball bearings), but in the context of one of the towns that expanded post war and was able to offer housing and work to the ambitious young working class wanting to escape the pre-modern industries of East London; that is the point made by Gavin Mackenzie (1974).

[7] We are particularly grateful to Mark Ramsden for undertaking the data analysis that underpins this section.

[8] The Office for National Statistics (ONS) moved to a new form of social classification for the 2001 Census based around socioeconomic classification (SEC) which replaced the previous classification known as the Registrar General's measurement of social class and the occupation-based SEG (see Rose et al, 2005). Broadly the new social class 1 of the SEC corresponds to the old SEGs 1–4, and in both cases incorporates what is termed in the narrative 'higher professional and managerial' occupations. The overlap between these two groups is high, according to Rose et al, 2005. We have converted the 2001 figures to the old SEG using a matrix supplied to us by Professor Rose. For details of the transformation and a justification of its use, see Butler et al (2008). Somewhat more problematic is the conversion of what might be termed the 'middle' middle class of intermediate workers such as teachers, nurses and other routine non-manual workers which used to be found in SEG 5, and particularly SEG 5.1, and is now largely, but not exclusively, classified by SEC as social class 2, 'lower professional and managerial occupations', although some fall into social class 3, 'intermediate occupations'. In London the largest social class group in the 2001 Census by a considerable margin (assuming that those

who are not classified are omitted) was social class 2, at 22%, which is approximately 10 percentage points greater than either social class 1 (12.1%) or social class 3 (10.2%).

[9] For details of how this transformation was undertaken, see Butler et al (2008).

# THREE

# Changing ethnic and housing market structure of East London

'Well, if I was a white working-class person I would notice that there are more and more Asians coming into the area. I mean, this street is a classic example. Ten years ago when I bought this house there were a few Asian families. Now, on this road, let's say there are 50 families, I would say that about 42 are Asian families. Non-Asian families, white families mostly, have moved out – moving out towards Essex, Southend, further and further away. You know, they haven't moved to Ilford or Gants Hill, they have moved further out to Southend, Canvey, a lot of them have sold their house [here] and got a smaller house out there. But, yeah, a lot of the white working-class families have moved and shifted out towards Dagenham and other areas.' (Pakistani, male, Newham)

## Introduction

Over the last 30–40 years the ethnic composition of London has undergone a dramatic transformation from that of a predominantly white, mono-ethnic city to an increasingly multi-ethnic city with large minority ethnic populations. In 2001, 29% of the population of Greater London were drawn from minority ethnic groups and in inner London the proportion reached a third. In terms of ethnic population, London is becoming more like some major North American cities such as New York and Los Angeles (Storkey and Lewis, 1996; Peach, 1999; Johnston et al, 2002a). Although London's minority ethnic groups are still minorities, they have grown very rapidly during the 1980s and 1990s, and in 2001 in two boroughs (Newham, 61% and Brent, 55%) minority ethnic groups comprised the majority of the population and a near majority in Tower Hamlets (49%). The bulk of the changes have been within the last 20 years. By the 2011 Census the figure is likely to be higher, with over 40% of inner London's population classified as non-white. In this respect, London is a laboratory for the future of ethnic change in some other British cities.

Nowhere has this process been more marked than in East London which, because of its proximity to the docks, was traditionally the first destination for many of London's waves of immigrants. The first group to arrive were the Huguenots in the late 17th century following the persecution of the Protestants in France. From 1670 to 1710, some 40,000–50,000 Huguenots sought refuge in England, about half of whom settled in London, many in Spitalfields, on the northern edge of the City of London, where they developed the silk weaving industry. The second big group to arrive were the Jews in the late 19th century and early 20th century, as a result of persecution and pogroms in Eastern Europe. In 1880 there were 46,000 Jews in London, but by 1900 the figure had trebled to 135,000, and most were living within in a small area of Whitechapel.

By the early 20th century, with growing prosperity, the Jews began to move out of their cramped, overcrowded accommodation in Whitechapel into the adjacent areas of Hackney, and further afield, and today there are relatively few Jews left in the old East End. They were replaced by new minority ethnic groups, notably the Bangladeshis, who first arrived in the early 1960s, but the vast majority arrived from the 1970s and were concentrated in Tower Hamlets. By 2001, there were some 65,000 Bangladeshis in the borough, mainly living in the areas of Whitechapel around Brick Lane, previously occupied by the Jews. The impact of the successive waves of immigration into East London is highlighted by the successive transformation of the Huguenot church in Fournier Street, first into a Synagogue, and subsequently into a Mosque. This is perhaps the single most emblematic symbol of the ethnic transformation of East London.

Of the successive waves of immigrants into London, by far the largest has been the wave of immigrants from what was termed the New Commonwealth (India, Bangladesh and the British ex-colonies in the Caribbean and Africa) and Pakistan, who have come in the years since the arrival of the *Empire Windrush* in Tilbury in 1948, which first brought labour migrants from Jamaica. There was a more recent flow of immigrants in the 1990s, many of whom were refugees fleeing war in the Horn of Africa, the Balkans and elsewhere. Most recently, the accession of the so-called 'A8' Eastern European countries to the EU from 2004 has led to another major wave of immigrants to London and the rest of Britain (Gordon et al, 2007). In addition, the growth of London as a major global financial and business centre has led to many other migrants from developed countries such as France, the US and Germany (White and Hurdley, 2003; Favell, 2008).

We analyse the growth of East London's minority ethnic populations below and argue that in many respects East London continues to function in the same way that Burgess noted of early 20th-century Chicago – as an immigrant reception area and 'zone in transition' from which some migrant groups make moves both upwards and outwards. These changes have not been without their associated social, cultural and political conflicts, as different ethnic groups have competed for space, housing and political representation. The anti-Semitism of the interwar period was replaced by the white East End dockers marching in support of Enoch Powell in 1968, and by the continuing white support for the British National Party (BNP) in East London (Husbands, 1988). More recently competition for social housing has led Dench et al (2006) to argue that the allocation of council housing to minority ethnic groups and refugees is a major source of social resentment for some of the old East End white working class who feel they have been marginalised and left at the back of the queue. This is currently a 'hot issue' in Barking & Dagenham, where the BNP had 12 seats on the local council; in the General Election in May 2010 they failed to take control and replace local Labour MP, Margaret Hodge, who argued that Labour had neglected social housing issues for long-term white residents (Mattinson, 2010).

The structure of the chapter is as follows. First, we examine the rapid growth of London's minority ethnic population and the associated but smaller decline in the white population. Second, we outline the geography of ethnic change in London from 1991 to 2001, focusing specifically on East London, and discuss whether the process is one of replacement and differential growth and the extent to which there are elements of 'white flight'. Third, we look at the growth of the minority ethnic middle class in London, and fourth, we examine how the changes in ethnic structure have linked to changes in the housing market of East London. There have been major changes in housing tenure across East London in the last 20 years, with the rapid growth of private renting and social housing, combined with the slower growth of home ownership and a sharp decline in the council housing sector. The changes in the ethnic structure of housing tenures show that almost all the net growth in home ownership has been among minority ethnic groups and the decline of whites in council and social housing has been parallelled by a major increase in the minority ethnic groups' share in these tenures. Finally, we examine perceptions of minority ethnic suburbanisation and ethnic change and white flight and their links to education, drawing on the voices of some of our respondents. Many minority ethnic groups want to move to the suburbs to escape the inner city and to get better housing and education but, at the same time, some whites are moving out because they are unhappy with the social and ethnic changes in their areas. There is thus a game of what the sociologist John Rex once described as 'suburban leapfrog' going on.

## Recent growth of London's minority ethnic population

Forty years ago, the proportion of London's residents born in what was termed the 'New Commonwealth and Pakistan' was tiny: less than 250,000 or about 3% of London's population in 1961 (Deakin, 1974). The proportion increased relatively slowly: 6.4% in 1971, 9% by 1981 and 11% in 1991. While these figures on the New Commonwealth and Pakistani residents who were born abroad are a useful measure of the size of the minority ethnic populations in the early decades of settlement when most minority ethnic residents were immigrants, they excluded the rapidly growing minority ethnic population who were born in Britain. This situation was rectified with the 1991 Census, which asked a question about the ethnic background of respondents. It revealed that non-white minority ethnic groups totalled 1.35 million, or 20%, of London's population (Peach, 1996). The 2001 Census (which also included various categories for mixed ethnicity for the first time) showed the minority ethnic population of London had grown by just over half (53%) from 1991 to 2001, and it is likely to show a further substantial increase by the time of the 2011 Census.

The population of Greater London grew by about half a million between 1991 and 2001, but this was made up of an increase of 723,000 (53%) in the non-white population and a decrease of 230,000 or 4% in the size of the white population. The most rapidly growing group was Black African (152%), followed by Bangladeshi (79%), Pakistani (63%) and those of Black Caribbean origin (42%). The number of people of Indian origin grew by a relatively modest 26%. Of the total increase in the minority ethnic and mixed ethnicity groups, half (49%) were born abroad, and half (51%) were born in the UK (see Figures 3.1 and 3.2). The growth of the minority ethnic population is thus not just a result of immigration but of a large and growing number of UK-born children. This is important when it comes to looking at housing and education, as growth of the proportion of minority ethnic school population far exceeds that of minority ethnic groups as a whole, as we show in Chapter Five.

**Figure 3.1: Persons born in the New Commonwealth and Pakistan and minority ethnic groups as a percentage of the population of Greater London, 1961–2001**

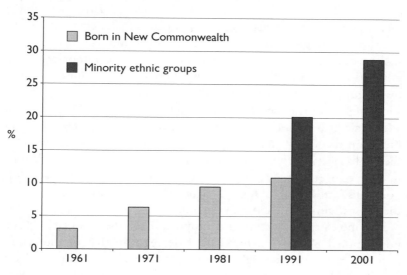

**Figure 3.2: Components of change in London's population by ethnic origin and birthplace, 1991–2001**

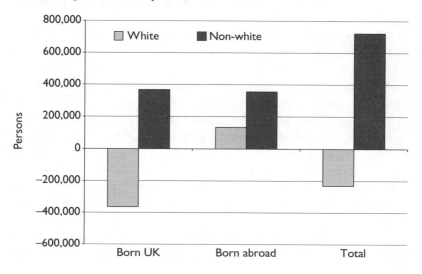

It is important to note that the growth of the minority ethnic population was not confined to the areas of initial settlement in inner London boroughs such as Lambeth, Hackney and Newham. On the contrary, all London boroughs have experienced large percentage increases in their minority ethnic populations in recent years. All but three boroughs had increases of over 30% and half of over 65%. In five boroughs, the increase was over 80%. The minority ethnic population grew more rapidly in outer London than in inner London (see Figure 3.3). In East London, the percentage change ranged from a low of 43% in Waltham Forest to a high in Barking & Dagenham of 148% (albeit from a low base), with Redbridge, Tower Hamlets and Newham recording increases of 80%, 66% and 64% respectively. Of the 15 districts in Britain with non-white minority ethnic populations in 2001 of over 30%, all but two (Leicester and Slough) were London boroughs (Stillwell and Duke-Williams, 2005). London is thus one of the most multi-ethnic cities in Britain.

The increase in the size and proportion of the minority ethnic population has been mirrored by a decrease in that of the white population in most boroughs. The largest decreases were in Newham (−21%) and Harrow (−18%), but five other boroughs including Waltham Forest (−11%) and Redbridge (−15%) had decreases in their white population of over 10% (see Figure 3.4). In East London, there is thus a broad gradient in terms of ethnic composition from the inner boroughs to suburban Havering. Newham saw its minority ethnic population grow from roughly 40% to 60% of the total while the share of the white population fell correspondingly. All the other East London boroughs, with the exception of Havering, saw the share of the minority ethnic populations grow rapidly (see Figure 3.5).

What this suggests is a process of outward minority ethnic expansion and succession in London, with previous white residents either dying or moving outside London and being replaced by non-whites. The figures for East London show a rapid replacement of whites by minority ethnic groups in most boroughs (see Table 3.1). A clear indication of the scale of the change in minority ethnic composition of East London is shown in Figure 3.6, which compares the percentage of residents with both parents born in the New Commonwealth in 1971 to the percentage of minority ethnic groups in 1991 and 2001. The increases are dramatic.

It is unclear whether we are seeing the sort of process documented in many US cities of 'white flight' to the suburbs and ethnic expansion (Frey, 1995; Deskins, 1996) or a process of replacement or even displacement of the white population. This question is impossible to answer from these kinds of data although analysis of migration trends

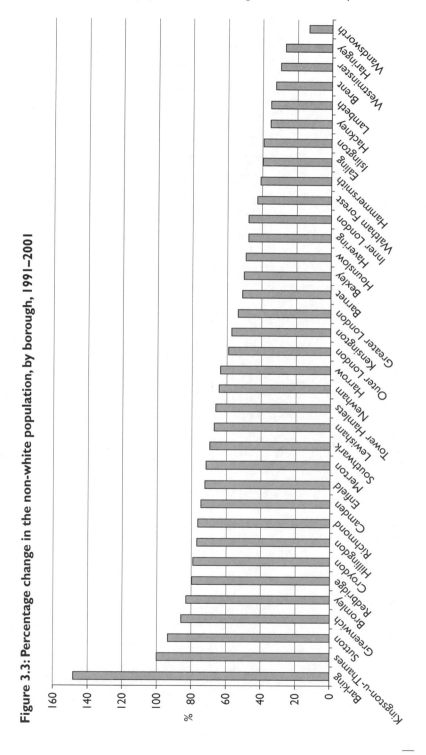

**Figure 3.3: Percentage change in the non-white population, by borough, 1991–2001**

**Figure 3.4: Percentage change in the white population, by borough, 1991–2001**

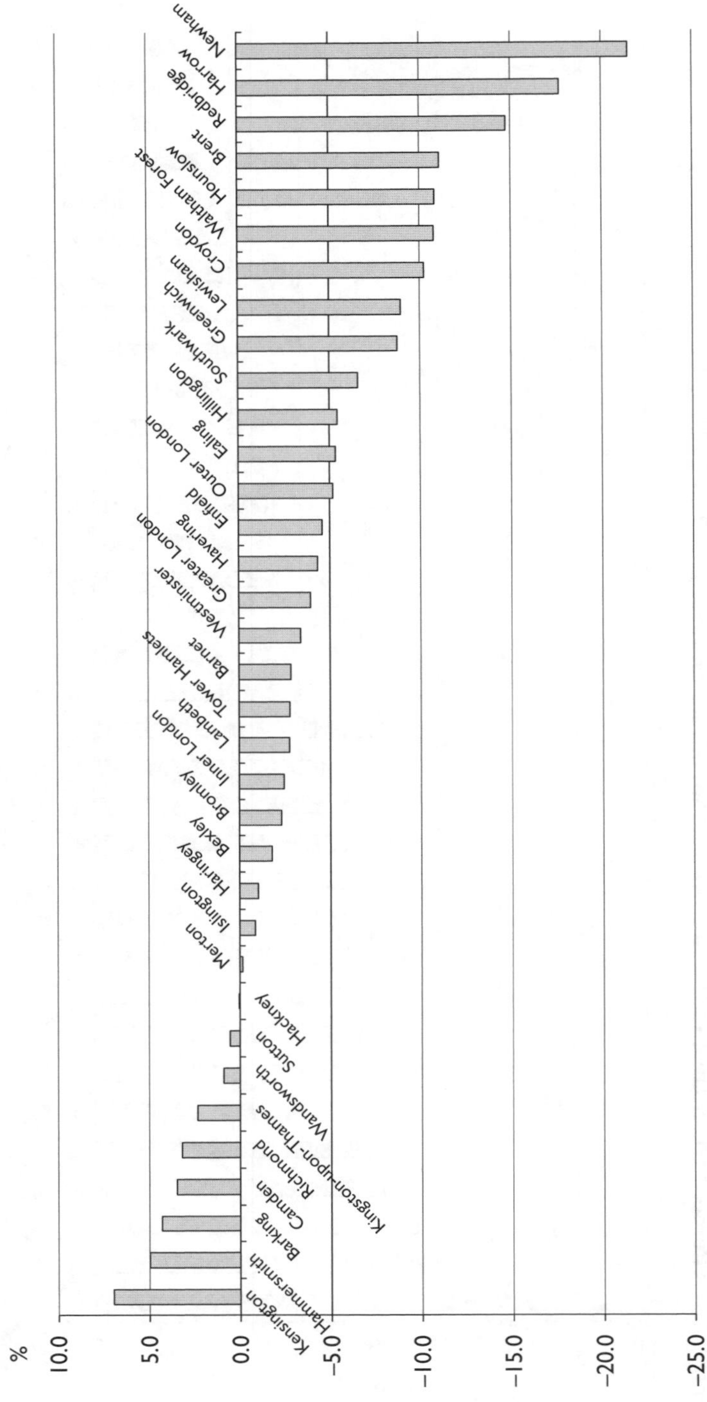

**Figure 3.5: Percentage change in white and non-white populations, East London boroughs, 1991–2001**

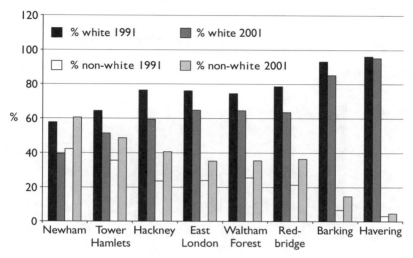

**Table 3.1: Absolute changes in the white and non-white populations, East London boroughs, 1991–2001**

| | Change | | | Change | | |
|---|---|---|---|---|---|---|
| | 1991 non-white | 2001 non-white | Non-white | 1991 White | 2001 White | White |
| Newham | 89,767 | 147,607 | 57,840 | 122,403 | 96,130 | −26,273 |
| Tower Hamlets | 57,307 | 95,322 | 38,015 | 103,757 | 100,799 | −2,958 |
| Redbridge | 48,421 | 87,041 | 38,620 | 177,797 | 151,587 | −26,210 |
| Waltham Forest | 54,209 | 77,474 | 23,265 | 157,824 | 140,803 | −17,021 |
| Havering | 7,324 | 10,827 | 3,503 | 222,168 | 213,421 | −8,747 |
| Barking | 9,778 | 24,277 | 14,499 | 133,903 | 139,667 | 5,764 |
| Hackney | 60,839 | 82,351 | 21,512 | 120,409 | 120,468 | 59 |
| East London | 327,645 | 524,899 | 197,254 | 1,038,261 | 962,875 | −75,386 |

*Source:* Population census, borough statistics, 1991 and 2001

by ethnicity in 2000–01 show that there is a general trend for borough-level minority ethnic in-migration to be accompanied by white out-migration (Stillwell, 2010). What is clearly happening is that the minority ethnic population of East London is now expanding rapidly both in the East End boroughs of Tower Hamlets and Newham and in a ring of outer suburban boroughs; this is being accompanied by a decline in the white population.

**Figure 3.6: Percentage non-white population, East London, 1971, 1991, 2001**

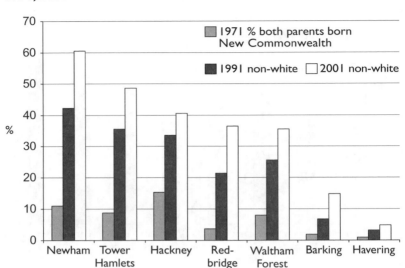

We argue that East London is still functioning today as an immigrant reception area much as it did in the 19th century and earlier. The more successful of the earlier groups of immigrants from the New Commonwealth and Pakistan are gradually moving out into the suburbs, following the East End Jews of the earlier generations who moved out in the interwar period. The traditional white working class is shrinking and being replaced and, in some cases, moving out to 'escape' what are seen as unwelcome ethnic changes. A new group is now making its presence felt in East London, namely the Eastern Europeans, many of whom appear to be living in the burgeoning private rented sector of 'buy-to-let' homes. The area is thus functioning as a classic 'zone in transition', a migrant reception and sorting area for London, from which, over time, the more successful move outwards in a bid to improve their housing and living conditions and to escape the perceived social problems of the inner city.

## The variety of ethnic groups in East London

In terms of the individual minority ethnic groups found in East London, there is a huge variety. In 2001 the largest groups were Bangladeshi (100,000 or 8% of the total population of East London) followed by Black African (7.2%), Indian (6.7%), Black Caribbean (6%) and Pakistani (4.7%). The importance of individual minority ethnic groups varies considerably from borough to borough. Bangladeshis are by far the largest minority group in Tower Hamlets (33% of the borough population) but just 9% in Newham and a minimal percentage in the other boroughs. Newham is the most ethnically mixed borough with 13% Black African, 12% Indian, 9% Bangladeshi, 8% Pakistani and 7% Black Caribbean. In Hackney, by contrast, the largest groups are Black African (12%) and Black Caribbean (10%) with Asian groups of limited numbers. In Waltham Forest, the largest groups are Black Caribbean and Pakistani (both 8%), while in Redbridge by far the largest group is Indian (14%). Havering and Barking & Dagenham remain predominantly white (see Figure 3.7).

**Figure 3.7: Ethnic composition (%), East London boroughs, 2001**

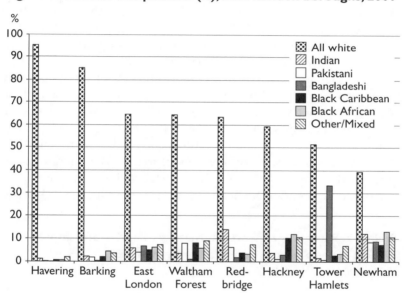

## The changing minority ethnic class structure of London

Over the last two decades, a dramatic social upgrading has accompanied London's de-industrialisation and emergence as a major post-industrial city, partly associated with gentrification. Whereas in 1981, as we saw in Chapter Two, the proportion of professional and managerial middle classes was higher in outer London than inner London, this pattern had reversed by 1991, by which time inner London had seen a disproportionate increase in the size of its professional and managerial group; this trend continued during the 1990s. By 2001, the proportion in this group in inner London was significantly higher than the rest of England and Wales, the South East (excluding London) and outer London, a major reversal of the position 20 years earlier. While there has been a general 'upgrading' of the social class composition of England and Wales, this has been particularly noticeable in London, and the biggest growth in both inner and outer London has been in the lower managerial and professional occupations (the old SEG 5, which correlates predominantly with the new NS-SEC 2) (Butler et al, 2008). Whites showed the greatest proportional middle-class (SEGs 1–4) growth during the period 1991–2001, followed in order by Asian Other, Indian, Black Caribbean, Black African and Pakistani, with Bangladeshi at the bottom (see Table 3.2). However, when we examine percentage point changes in SEGs 1–5 we see that the largest increases were among the Black Caribbean (13) and Indian (12.9) groups, followed by White (10.9) and Black African (9.5). Read together, these data show that several major minority ethnic groups are moving up into the middle class, particularly in outer London (see Table 3.3).

We are therefore faced with a complex process of social class and ethnic change in outer London. The region is witnessing the highest rate of growth of lower managerial and professional workers – most of whom are inevitably white given the large size of this group – of any region in the country, while it is also becoming home to increasing numbers and proportions of members of minority ethnic groups. It appears that many of the white working class and intermediate social classes in outer London are being replaced by both higher social class

**Table 3.2: Percentage growth in managers and professionals (SEGs 1–4) as a proportion of all growth in SEGs 1–15, 1991–2001**

|  | England and Wales | South East | Greater London | Outer London | Inner London |
|---|---|---|---|---|---|
| Asian Other | 23 | 26.2 | 23 | 17.4 | 51.9 |
| White | 14.3 | 12.7 | 32.4 | 14 | 45.4 |
| Indian | 23.3 | 29.5 | 26.7 | 25.1 | 34.3 |
| All | 15.4 | 13.8 | 27.6 | 19.3 | 35.5 |
| Other | 37 | 34.8 | 32.3 | 35.6 | 26.3 |
| Caribbean | 25.5 | 24.9 | 28.6 | 29.3 | 28.7 |
| Chinese | 20.7 | 22.6 | 23 | 23.1 | 22.8 |
| African | 22.2 | 25.2 | 21.7 | 23.5 | 20.4 |
| Pakistani | 15.8 | 18 | 22.8 | 22.6 | 23.5 |
| Bangladeshi | 7.9 | –0.1 | 11 | 11.8 | 11 |

**Table 3.3: Percentage point change in SEG classifications, Greater London, 1991–2001**

| SEG | All ethnicities | White | Indian | Black African | Black Caribbean | Pakistani | Asian other | Black other | Bangladeshi | Chinese |
|------|------|------|------|------|------|------|------|------|------|------|
| 1–5 | 10.0 | 10.9 | 12.9 | 9.5 | 13.0 | 9.6 | 7.0 | 5.7 | 0.6 | −1.9 |
| 6, 8, 9, 12 | −6.4 | −7.6 | −8.4 | 4.3 | −3.3 | −5.7 | 1.1 | −5.1 | 21.8 | 8.3 |
| 7, 10, 11 | −4.7 | −4.4 | −5.8 | −14.7 | −10.7 | −5.5 | −9.3 | −1.6 | −23.9 | −7.7 |
| 13, 14, 15 | 1.1 | 1.1 | 1.3 | 1.0 | 1.0 | 1.5 | 1.2 | 0.9 | 1.4 | 1.3 |

whites and upwardly mobile socially aspirant members of minority ethnic groups whose proportionate increase far exceeds their absolute numbers. As a result, outer London is becoming more middle class and increasingly non-white. There are both parallels and differences from the situation in other European and North American cities where many, but not all, minorities are often stuck at the bottom of the occupation and income pile (Mollenkopf and Castells, 1991; Waldinger, 1996). As in the US and Canada, the Indian and Chinese and some Black groups are making significant headway both occupationally and in terms of the housing market. As Modood (1997, p 84) has pointed out: 'insofar as there is a fundamental divide in employment by ethnicity, it is not a black–white divide, but a divide between Whites, Chinese, African-Asians on the one hand, and Bangladeshis and Pakistanis on the other, with Indians and Caribbeans in perhaps an intermediate position'.

## Minority ethnic groups in the London housing market

We have summarised the changes that have taken place in the ethnic composition of East London over the last 30–40 years. It is now important to examine how these changes have been linked to the changes in the housing market. As discussed in Chapter Two, East London in the 1950s was still overwhelmingly white and working class and most households lived either in private rented housing or the rapidly growing high-density and often high-rise council sector which replaced postwar bomb-damaged housing. While some of the white working class were already beginning to move out to home ownership in outer London and Essex, the newly arrived immigrant minorities faced a struggle to secure housing. Research on the social segregation and housing market position of minority ethnic groups in Western European cities has shown that minorities have typically been confined either to poor-quality inner-city rented housing or to the least desirable social rented housing (see Hamnett and Butler, 2010, for a summary). The issue we want to examine here is the housing experience of minority ethnic groups in London – have they become more concentrated in private rented or social housing, or have more of them achieved home ownership?

Given the recent debates over whether Britain is 'sleepwalking to segregation' (Phillips, 2005), this raises the important issue of whether minority ethnic groups have become more concentrated in a few areas and sectors of the housing market, as some have argued, or whether they have dispersed across a wider area (see Peach, 1996, 1998; Simpson, 2004; Johnston et al, 2005a). As we will show, the evidence of the 1990s in London suggests a *dual* process of both increasing minority ethnic home ownership, largely concentrated in suburban outer London, and a much larger minority 'ethnicisation' of social housing by particular groups. There is little research evidence to support the idea that there is increasing residential segregation.

Given the labour market position of most minority ethnic groups on arrival, they have traditionally occupied the lower rungs of the housing market. Thus, when the first New Commonwealth migrants arrived in Britain in the 1960s, they generally lacked the money to buy and were also ineligible for council housing because they lacked the necessary residence requirements then in force (Rex and Moore, 1967). Even if they managed to get onto council waiting lists they would generally have a long wait as points were allocated for length of time on the waiting list. As a result, New Commonwealth and Pakistani immigrants in London and other cities generally found themselves in poor quality, overcrowded, private rented accommodation (Milner Holland Committee, 1965; Sarre et al, 1989). After 1970, the housing careers of New Commonwealth immigrants began to diverge. While some West Indian migrants managed to buy houses in the cheaper parts of London, the majority began to make headway getting into the council rented sector, particularly after 1974 when discriminatory barriers to entry began to be removed as a result of the Cullingworth Report (Cullingworth, 1970). Many Indian and Pakistani migrants who had managed to accumulate some capital, often borrowing from families, began to buy owner-occupied housing. These differences intensified during the 1980s and, by 1991, the housing market position of the various groups of migrants, and their children, were very different. Whereas those of West Indian, African and Bangladeshi origin had become strongly concentrated in the council sector, those of Indian and Pakistani origin had become increasingly concentrated in home ownership (Peach and Shah, 1980; Peach, 1997).

To some extent, the concentration of Bangladeshis and Black Africans in the social rented sector was a result of their more recent arrival and the fact that they had not yet become well established in the labour market (Dench et al, 2006). In the case of Bangladeshis it was also a result of their extreme concentration in one borough – Tower Hamlets – and because they were from lower social class rural backgrounds than many Indian migrants. Many of these groups were found to be concentrated in the worst parts of the local authority sector, either in high-rise, high-density unpopular estates or in older, poor quality property (Parker and Dugmore, 1978), and Phillips (1988) found that minority ethnic groups tended to be allocated poorer quality housing on worse estates than the indigenous population in Tower Hamlets. The reasons for this were complex, sometimes involving direct discrimination or a decision to concentrate minorities in specific areas and parts of the stock, and sometimes the interaction of urgent housing needs with the quality of the available stock. From the 1960s a process of socio-tenurial polarisation began to emerge in Britain in which the council sector lost its higher SEGs to ownership and saw a growing concentration of lower SEGs, the unemployed and economically inactive (Hamnett, 1984). In London, this was accompanied by a growth of some minority ethnic groups in council housing (Hamnett and Randolph, 1987). The result has been that council housing became increasingly socially residualised at the same time as the proportion of minority ethnic groups increased in the sector. This process was intensified by the rapid increase in house prices in London from the early 1970s onwards, which made access to home ownership more difficult for low-income groups (Hamnett, 2009).

Much of the international literature sees minority ethnic groups as being concentrated in inner-city areas. While this is not true of all cities (in Paris, immigrants are concentrated in peripheral social housing; see Rhein, 1998a, 1998b), the distribution of minority ethnic groups in London is different, with Asians increasingly living in owner-occupied suburbia in outer London, and Black Caribbeans and Bangladeshis in inner London (Peach, 1998). As we have argued, the period 1991–2001 witnessed increasing minority ethnic suburban growth in London which is linked in part to upward social mobility (Platt, 2005; Butler and Hamnett, 2007) and gradual outward geographical diffusion in addition to in situ population growth. Thus, as we noted in the previous section of this chapter, minority ethnic groups are no longer confined to inner-city areas in London but are dispersing into suburban boroughs, partly for reasons of aspiration and a desire to escape some of the social problems in inner London, and partly as a response to rising house prices in inner London. Before looking at ethnic change in the housing market, however, it is important to summarise briefly overall changes in the structure of the housing market in East London in the 1990s and how it differs from previous decades.

## Changing housing market of East London

East London forms a classic wedge, running outwards from the city centre to the outer suburbs, and it contains a wide range of housing situations, ranging from the inner boroughs dominated by council housing to the suburban boroughs such as Redbridge and Havering dominated by home ownership. The area has seen dramatic changes in the structure of its housing market over the last 40 years, particularly in the inner boroughs of Tower Hamlets, Newham and Hackney. The key to understanding the structure of the housing market in the different boroughs is that the three inner-city boroughs, and the southern part of Waltham Forest, were all initially built in the late 19th century as private rented terraced housing. Redbridge and Havering were built up in the interwar period as classic detached and semi-detached single-family housing, much of it built for home ownership. Barking & Dagenham is different again in that it was largely developed in the interwar period and after in the form of large-scale council estates, notably the Becontree Estate (Willmott, 1963; Olechnowicz, 1997). All the inner London boroughs saw a dramatic increase in the size of the council rented sector from 1961 to 1981 and an even more rapid decline in the private rented sector, but by 2001 the size of the council sector was back to its size in 1961 while home ownership had grown rapidly and private renting grew in the 1990s as a result of the growth of buy-to-let housing.

There are marked differences in housing tenure between the East London boroughs. At one extreme is Tower Hamlets, which was severely damaged in war-time bombing and then redeveloped for local authority housing which reached a peak of 82% in 1981, the highest share of any borough in London. Conversely, home ownership was less than 5% until 1981 – by far the lowest of any borough in London. Big changes took place from the late 1980s with the construction of large numbers of riverside luxury apartments linked to the redevelopment of Canary Wharf, which increased the percentage of home ownership and private renting. Even today, however, Tower Hamlets has the lowest level of home ownership of all London boroughs.

Like Tower Hamlets, large areas of poor housing were cleared in Hackney in the 1960s and 1970s and replaced with council housing estates and tower blocks. This has declined since 1981 and gentrification has led to the growth of home ownership. Newham also saw a rapid decline in private renting but less council redevelopment. All three boroughs have seen the rapid growth of housing associations in recent decades, largely as a result of changes in government housing policy that favoured other forms of social housing over council housing. In all the East London boroughs, private rented housing has staged a major comeback from the 1990s in the form of buy to let (see Figure 3.8).

Looking at the outer boroughs of East London, Barking & Dagenham is an anomaly in that a large part of the borough was built for council housing and 70% of its households were council tenants in 1971, although this has now fallen to about a third. Redbridge and Havering are classic suburban boroughs, built in the interwar period and after, primarily for home ownership in the form of detached and semi-detached houses. Both boroughs had almost 80% ownership by 1991. In many ways they represent an aspirational target for households living in the inner parts of East London. When people seek to move out east, these are the places where they tend to go.

Taken as a whole, East London saw a growth in the number of households from 1991 to 2001 of almost 600,000, or 12%. As in the rest of London, this overall growth contained a number of very

**Figure 3.8: Housing tenure (%), East London boroughs, 2001**

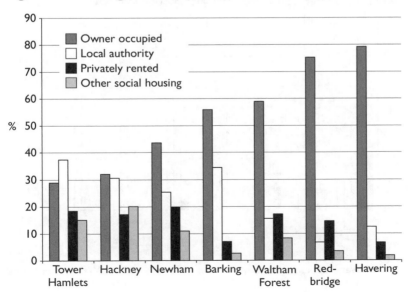

different components. Private renting and the social rented sector approximately doubled (growing by 85% and 106% respectively), while council renting fell by 18%. Home ownership grew by just under 9%. However, the overall changes concealed very different changes both between boroughs and between different ethnic groups. The boroughs can be ranked in terms of housing market change from rapid change to stability (see Figure 3.9). At one end of the spectrum, Tower Hamlets saw a growth of 28% in the total number of households, followed by Barking & Dagenham and Hackney. All three boroughs saw a marked growth in their levels of home ownership (55%, 25% and 36% respectively) but the most dramatic growth was in private renting and social rented housing. At the other end of the spectrum, the more suburban boroughs of Waltham Forest, Redbridge and Havering had low growth in household numbers (4–6%) and virtually no growth in home ownership, although there was a high degree of change in the social composition of those owner-occupiers, as discussed earlier.

**Figure 3.9: Percentage change in tenure, East London boroughs, 1981–2001**

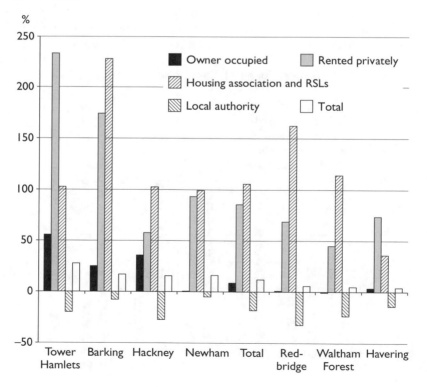

All the boroughs experienced growth of private renting, which was particularly marked in Tower Hamlets and Barking as a result of high levels of new building, much of which was for rent. All boroughs also saw declines in council renting, ranging from 32% in Redbridge to 8% in Barking, and all saw big increases in the social rented sector, partly the result of new building and partly of stock transfers to social landlords. Next we look briefly at the changes in the structure of house prices before turning to the interaction of these changes with the changing ethnic composition of the East London boroughs.

## House prices in East London

East London has long been the cheapest area in London in terms of house prices. In 1995, the three cheapest boroughs in London were Newham, Barking & Dagenham and Waltham Forest closely followed by Hackney, Redbridge, Havering and Tower Hamlets. Average house prices rose dramatically in London over the next 12 years and by 2007 average prices were some 230% higher than they were in 1995. In 2007, Newham and Barking & Dagenham were still the cheapest boroughs in London (although prices had risen by 340% in Newham, from £48,300 to £236,600), but the rate of house price inflation in the cheapest boroughs was much higher than in the expensive areas. Although the cheapest three boroughs in 1995 were still the cheapest in 2007, these boroughs had among the highest rates of house price inflation in London in 1995–2007, which has intensified problems of affordability for those attempting to buy, many of whom are effectively priced out of ownership and into private renting or social housing which have both grown dramatically. Prices in the cheaper East London boroughs have fallen back more markedly than elsewhere in London since the start of the financial crisis, which began in 2007 (Hamnett, 2009).

## Tenure and ethnic change in East London, 1991–2001

The question we address here is, how have the changes in tenure structure interrelated with change in ethnic composition? First and foremost, the number of minority ethnic households in East London grew by a remarkable 75% over the period while the number of white households fell by 1.3% – the population growth for the same period was 53%. In some boroughs overall, such as Newham and Redbridge, the number of white households has fallen by much more but this has been offset by the growth of white gentrification in Tower Hamlets and Hackney. Absolute tenure changes by ethnicity are shown in Figure 3.10, the percentage changes in Figure 3.11 and the percentage share changes in Figure 3.12.

The growth of minority ethnic households and the decline of white households has been very uneven by tenures. Both whites and non-whites have seen significant growth in the private renting and other social landlord categories. But the growth of owner-occupation among whites was minimal, less than 1% compared to 53% growth among non-whites.[1] Thus, almost all the overall growth of home ownership over the period has been in non-white households, although minority ethnic groups' share of the sector only grew from 15% to 21%. Conversely, while the council sector declined by 18% overall, this was made up of a decline of 31% in the white population and an increase of 32% in the non-white groups. This is indicative of the rapid minority ethnicisation of council housing and confirmed by the fact that minority ethnic groups comprised 20% of council households in 1991 but a third in 2001. A similar process has taken place in other social housing where minority ethnic groups have risen from 26% to 43% of total households (see Figure 3.12).

To summarise, minority ethnic groups have seen major growth across all housing tenures and a substantial rise in their percentage share of each tenure. Although their percentage growth and their share of the

**Figure 3.10: Absolute change in household tenure by ethnicity, East London, 1991–2001**

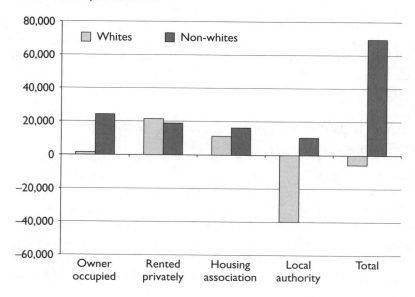

**Figure 3.11: Percentage change in whites and non-whites by household tenure, East London, 1991–2001**

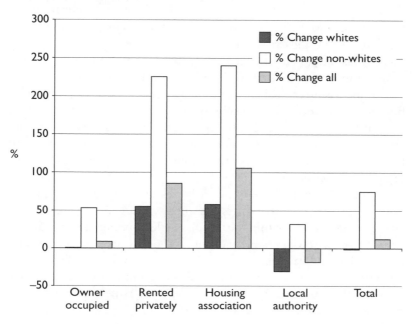

**Figure 3.12: Percentage shares of tenures: whites and non-whites, East London, 1991–2001**

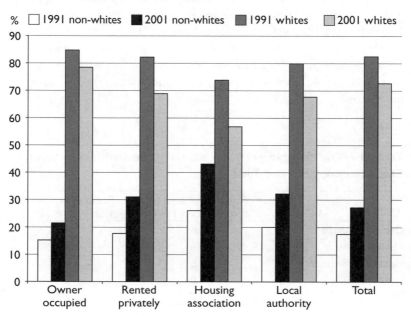

total was most marked in the private rented and other social rented tenures, the absolute growth was largest in home ownership. In 1991 there were 5.6 whites for every non-white in owner-occupation but this had fallen to 3.7 by 2001 (see Table 3.4). The corresponding ratios for council housing are 4.0 in 1991 and 2.1 in 2001, and for other social housing 2.8 and 1.3. It is clear that non-whites are becoming more strongly represented in the private and social rented sector as well as increasing their share of home ownership. This is an important finding which underpins our subsequent analysis of the out-migration to suburban home ownership by some of the more successful minority ethnic groups. This is a very significant process, but it is outweighed by the far greater numbers in the rapidly growing private and social rented housing sectors.

To discuss overall tenure trends it has been necessary to divide the population simply into whites and non-whites. This obscures the changes taking place within the minority ethnic population. We do not have the space to discuss these changes in detail here, but in absolute terms Indian and Pakistani groups have expanded most rapidly in home ownership and private renting, Black African groups have grown equally across all the tenures in absolute terms and the Bangladeshi groups in the council sector. The Black Caribbean group grew most strongly in the owner-occupied sector and scarcely increased at all in council renting. We are thus seeing a pattern of growing tenure differentiation between different ethnic groups, with Black African and Bangladeshi groups increasing most rapidly in the social renting sector and the Indian and Pakistani groups in home ownership. What is likely, although we cannot show this empirically, is that the growth in minority ethnic home ownership in East London has been concentrated among the middle classes with the occupations and incomes to support entry to the sector.

**Table 3.4: The changing ratio of whites to non-whites by tenure, East London, 1991 and 2001**

|  | Ratio of whites to non-whites, 1991 | Ratio of whites to non-whites, 2001 |
|---|---|---|
| Owner occupied | 5.6 | 3.7 |
| Rented privately | 4.6 | 2.2 |
| Housing association | 2.8 | 1.3 |
| Local authority | 4.0 | 2.1 |
| Total | 4.7 | 2.7 |

## Minority ethnic suburbanisation, education and 'white flight'

There has long been a process of out-migration within East London, dating back to the late 19th-century working-class suburbanisation associated with the growth of Victorian terraced housing in areas west of the river Lea such as East Ham. During the 1920s and 1930s there was another wave of suburbanisation associated with the growth of suburban owner-occupation in Redbridge and Havering. All this suburbanisation was white and it is likely to have intensified in the 1970s and 1980s, with the growth of the minority ethnic population in Tower Hamlets and Newham. More recently, however, the picture has become much more complex as there is now a process of substantial minority ethnic suburbanisation combined with continuing white out-migration which is pushing out of London and into Essex. The reasons for this are complex and are discussed in detail in the next chapter, but essentially involve a desire to escape inner urban areas which are seen as increasingly dirty, dangerous and congested; this is coupled with a desire to move to areas which are seen to offer greater opportunities in terms of housing, education, environment and general quality of life. In this respect, the process is associated with a complex mixture of both 'push' and 'pull' factors, with the suburbs being seen as part of a wider set of social aspirations for mobility, housing and educational improvement. In the following section we draw on our in-depth interviews to highlight some of the key issues. First we look at the issues of affordability and education and then at ethnic change.

### Role of affordability and education

One Asian respondent highlighted the key role of upward and outward mobility for his family:

> 'We've been living in Ilford for the past 30 years. We originally lived in East London and so when my parents decided to move out – we were originally in council accommodation within Lime House area, Tower Hamlets. But before that, prior to that, we lived in Stepney so you know it's just been a steady progression upwards.' (Asian male, Redbridge)

House prices were seen to be cheaper and education and social mix better in the suburbs.

In response to the question about whether there was much movement out to Essex, another respondent said:

> 'Certainly from my anecdotal evidence from my children's primary school which is very local to here is that, yeah, there is movement out to the eastern suburbs – Dagenham, Grays, anywhere out along Romford – all of that, out, out, out! A lot of it is as a destination for secondary schooling, but I think a lot of it is property-driven in that people can get a foothold on the property market here – they can get a flat – but they can't get up the mortgage ladder enough to buy a house. You know, if they have kids they want a house with a garden. I was just out with another mum this morning at the gym and that's her plan. They have a two-bedroom flat but they cannot up their mortgage enough to get a three-bedroom house around here, but they can get a three-bedroom house in Grays.' (White British, female, Victoria Park, Hackney)

Property prices in the suburbs are clearly a key factor in out-migration as respondents felt that they could get more space for the same money as in the inner-city areas; one respondent outlined the reasons they moved from Stoke Newington to Leytonstone as follows:

> 'Well, in Stoke Newington we had an upstairs flat and we had two young children, and we didn't have a garden, so we wanted a house with more space, but the prices in Stoke Newington at that time just skyrocketed and were just unaffordable. So it was a matter of finding somewhere that was ... a pleasant place to live that wasn't so expensive, basically. And also my husband was working in Walthamstow, so it was convenient for him to be able to get to work easily.' (White British, female, Leyton)

Another respondent in Barkingside highlighted the importance of affordability in the choice of an area to live:

> 'My wife wanted to live together – we weren't married at the time but we wanted to live together before we got married. We had just got, not financially independent, but just got promoted at work so we had a fixed income of about £70,000 that we had to spend on a house. The most

important thing was we had to get into work as well, so we looked at the tube map, picked an area that we possibly liked and then just worked our way to a place where we could afford to live. Barkingside fell into that category, and so we looked around here. We sort of had a wide search area to start with, then we sort of pinned it down to the Barkingside area.' (White British, male, Barkingside)

When the next respondent was asked why they moved from Hainault to Barkingside, she replied:

'We were aiming to get a bigger house in a slightly better area.'

['What was more attractive about Barkingside?']

'Um ... the social mix of people [laughs]. Should we call it a class issue? Hainault was becoming an area which, given my job at school, which was getting a lot of people from the East End moved out, and bringing a lot of problems with them. So there was a lot of families who had social issues, and that was reflected in the kids' behaviour, both in school and out of school, mainly out of school. Mainly it was the house was too small.' (White British, female, Barkingside)

The issue of educational aspirations is specifically discussed in the next chapter but it is clear that from what many respondents said, the quest for better schooling was a key driver of the minority ethnic suburbanisation process in East London as parents sought out the catchment areas of their preferred schools. The provision of schools is believed to be better in the outer boroughs, with the Redbridge grammar schools being a trump card in the eyes of many educationally minded minority ethnic families. Schooling issues seemed most potent for those parents whose children were about to make the transition to secondary schools as opposed to nursery or primary education, and it was at this point that desires to move elsewhere often crystallised:

'I think a lot of people are coming in from the neighbouring boroughs of Newham, Walthamstow – and my impression is, speaking to people who go to my daughter's school, a lot of people move in for the schools in Redbridge. So speaking to most of the people, most people moved in to the area (because I've kind of grown up here) none of the other mums have been here, in this borough, and they all said that they moved because they heard that Redbridge schools are very good.'

['So the schools are definitely something that attracts people?']

'Oh a hundred per cent. I think when … I mean if you look at all our family friends were in Newham, once their kids get to the 11 plus exam they definitely move beforehand. If not moving, they rent and because the prices in Newham have shot up they sell, you know, they bought houses for £50,000 and now they're worth at least two hundred and they have moved, and they may not have moved into nicer parts of Redbridge but they've moved into that borough.' (Asian, female, Barkingside)

The demand is especially high in the best schooling districts and an Indian interviewee from Seven Kings, a self-employed builder, saw this in operation in his own locality:

'[Most] of the people come here because they think the Redbridge schools are good and if they can't buy the property they rent. This morning I went to see somebody and they converted a house smaller than this one into four different flats!' (Indian, male, Central Redbridge)

The desperation of parents, often from outside the borough, wishing to secure a good school in Redbridge was seen by another as fuelling the buy-to-let market:

'That's definitely why people are renting [in Redbridge], they can't afford to buy a house so they rent. And the estate agents don't help by slamming "Seven Kings School catchment" across everything.' (White British, female, Barkingside)

Nor was this process restricted to Redbridge. This Indian respondent commented that many of his friends and family had moved out from Newham to Hornchurch in Essex, primarily for educational reasons:

'They moved to Hornchurch for the same reason. For studies. Some very good families are there who are mainly worried about studies. Most of the good educated families from other ethnic groups also are worried about studies. Other ethnic groups, they are not worried. They just think that they come here and are better off. They are getting government money, dole, DSS money and everything, they think that this money is there, so we can survive, we are ok. But we don't want ok. We want the top. I don't want my kids getting 40%, I want 99.9%.'

['I have noticed this movement of people out to Redbridge...']

'Massive, massive. Even my family, not my wife's family, my family, we have three daughters, everybody has gone, from the start everybody is going, now nobody is here...'

Talking of the movement of people out to Redbridge, he continued:

'The best schools are in Redbridge, we will have to move from here to there. You can't take your children from here to there, but they can take their children from there to here. They are looking for their own catchment area, but schools in Redbridge are not.' (Indian, male, Newham)

## Ethnic change

Many of the respondents, irrespective of ethnicity, were clear about the nature of the major changes in ethnic composition which had taken place in recent years in East London, as whites died or moved out and minority ethnic groups moved in to replace them.

A Tamil woman living in Barkingside perceptively commented on not wanting to move too far out from her original area because of the ethnic and cultural differences:

'... this is just our first step, and we didn't want to start too far because in Barkingside there is – it's not as diverse as East Ham – but there are Asians here. Whereas we noticed when we went out further from Barkingside – Chigwell, Loughton – it was completely English people, which I wasn't too keen on at the time to tell you the truth. And the other thing is, we would have been hypocrites as well, because we have to go back to East Ham for all our shopping, Asian food and things like that. So it wasn't so much that we wanted to completely cut off from East Ham, you know, because our parents still lived there. But, in Barkingside there was a difference from East Ham. It wasn't as congested.' (Tamil, female, Barkingside)

Numerous respondents noted this process of white out-migration and minority ethnic succession, for example:

'… white kids that have left different schools that I've been in contact with, they usually seem to end up emigrating to "Australia". They go miles, right out into the country. Many move out to Essex, that happens a lot. I've worked in schools in Barking & Dagenham, 10 years ago, they were very white schools, which I didn't like, because I like the mix of kids in the classroom, but now if I go there, I've been to a few lately, you've got many more black or Asian kids in the school, it might be 20 or 30% in the class, so that suggests that a lot of those type of families are moving out, unless there is some sort of housing policy going on which means they are putting, I don't know if they are putting in refugees or asylum seekers….' (White British, female, Leyton)

Another respondent of mixed African Caribbean and white heritage commented that:

'They are moving out … on this street there are less and less English people on this street. They are all Asian. And the white people you find here are tenants of other boroughs. There are no householders here who are actually English people. Everybody has sold out … the reason why they move out, because they didn't want to bring up kids in this community … because of the dominance of Asians.' (Mixed Race, female, Central Redbridge)

'… this area used to be quite a Jewish area and well, Gants Hill was more famous because they've got a Jewish synagogue there. But the Jewish people have moved further out to Chigwell and further out into Essex and so much so that we have a Jewish high school, King Solomon's, they've actually reduced by a whole year entry due to lack of Jewish people in the area and also apparently a new Jewish senior school has opened in Barnet. So this is an area, you know, an area of population which is definitely moving out. Now we seem to have a huge number of Tamils in the area – the largest ethnic group seem to be the Tamils.' (White British, female, Barkingside)

Regarding white out-migration, this respondent also observed that:

'Quite a few people are moving for racist reasons. They said the area is becoming too black and two people, one person who I know moved out a year ago and somebody who has got their house on the market at the moment, have actually said that. I mean actually come up and said it.'

A few respondents were very blunt in their description of the ethnic changes taking place and where they would rather live:

'Well I think there's more, as I said, the whites are moving out, the blacks are moving in, but Asians are already here. When you go to the train station you do see more of the blacks, and when you go shopping I am aware that we are getting an influx of black people moving into the area ... the whites are moving out, well, now they've even passed Romford. As far as I'm concerned all the blacks are coming into Romford now, so the whites move a little bit further out.... When I moved from Stepney I thought, I'm not going to Forest Gate because it's predominantly blacks. I moved into East Ham which is predominantly Asian. But, then, I wouldn't move too far out considering I had children at school. I didn't want to move too far away from my family because they were still in the Mile End area ... I didn't know much about Newbury Park so actually, I was probably a bit shocked when I saw the number of Asians that actually live here. If I was to move again I wouldn't consider Romford, I don't want to be stuck in a street where there are lots of blacks, or lots of Asians.... I think everyone is looking for a quiet life but they don't want to be stuck with a large amount of any one particular race.' (White British, female, Barkingside)

Interestingly, another respondent, living in Little Ilford, commented that when they bought, the vendor was happier to sell to West Indians than if they had been Asians:

> 'In five plus years I've seen the faces change. When we came here when we were looking for houses we came here and it was a white woman, an English woman who was living here, and [laughing] she was very cagey.... She didn't really want to show us the property *until* we said to her that we were from the Caribbean. I made a comment about the garden, I told my husband that you'll have garden space just like back home and she said, where is back home? I said we're from the Caribbean ... the lady literally ... everything changed and she agreed to sell us the property. She did not want to sell the house to an Asian person.' (British Asian of Caribbean descent, female, Central Redbridge)

There is a belief that the East London social fabric has become splintered with some groups, notably elements within the former white, working-class majority, feeling isolated. The following interviewee, a white grandmother, had lived in the same house in the Cranbrook area of Ilford all her life. She had plans to move out to a village near Chelmsford in the Essex countryside as soon as possible ("I can't wait to move") to be closer to her children:

> 'I don't like the feel of the place any more. It [was] bound to happen but I haven't noticed it as much as I have in the past five years ... we are getting far too many different cultures moving in ... I don't object to people coming in and living in this country but what I do object to is them not respecting our standards.' (White British, female, Central Redbridge)

Other white respondents made similar comments, in which the essence of their views was clear, for example:

> '... if you don't feel comfortable somewhere, and you don't feel right you shouldn't be there which is how I feel now to be honest. I feel like I shouldn't be here. I feel like a sort of spare part. It's a shame really we're doing the same as a lot of other people have done in this road, in this area. So we're moving somewhere else ... it's just going to get

more and more but that's just the way it will go. And that's the way it will go everywhere in the UK I reckon.' (White British, female, Central Redbridge)

This argument – of 'too many cultures' – underpins the motives of the many whites who have themselves drifted eastwards away from these former, white working-class localities. They are also sentiments shared by members of other ethnic-defined groups, a number of the non-white interviewees sympathetic with this particular perspective and saddened as mature and elderly East London 'originals' move away. As residents – and homeowners – they, too, are affected by the same insecurities relating to the spread of rental properties, and there is a tendency to romanticise about a time when social relations were more reassuringly predictable and formed around a dominant white, working-class ethic of social obligation to one's neighbours, moral commitment to the idea of the neighbourhood and reciprocal help between neighbours.

One white, long-term resident of Newbury Park had the following to say on the influx of Asian families to her neighbourhood:

> 'Well my theory is ... it's not a nice theory ... [but] I think a lot of them [come] from the East End, Manor Park and Forest Gate, and I think as they better themselves they want to move here. I mean, we've got a Muslim family moved in next door but one – they're no bother apart from smells being a bit overpowering when you're in the garden. Next door but two are a Sikh family. Now the poor lady who lives next door, who is the original person, she's 95 and bought her house brand new, she said [this is] the worst time in her whole life because [her neighbours] have built a massive extension on the side – the son's moved in – their culture's different, isn't it? They're family orientated.' (White British, female, Barkingside)

Another woman, of Caribbean descent, seemed sympathetic to the whites who had moved out as a result of ethnic and social change in the area. Her account illustrates again how class-based tensions can be as evident within the non-white population as they are between whites and non-whites:

> 'That's one of the negative changes, the white people [who] are moving out. The white people are moving out

because the council usually place people down on that
side [of East Ham]. Most of the houses there are council
accommodation.'

['Were those council houses there when you moved here?']

'Yes they were, but the people who were living there were
white ... we [had] no problem living in that setting because,
coming from the Caribbean, our customs are English. It
was no problem for us, but a lot of asylum seekers are
being placed in the area.... I mean, [at] two o'clock in
the morning you can hear people swearing in the road,
something that never happened in the past four-and-a-half
years [is] happening now. It is coming from African asylum
seekers.' (Black Caribbean, female, Newham)

The quotes from respondents discussed above clearly show the ethnic
change which has taken place in East London in the last 20 years. The
gradual suburbanisation of minority ethnic populations outwards from
the inner boroughs has been driven by a desire to escape the various
problems of inner-city living such as the densification and crowding
associated with the conversion of owner-occupied or rented houses
to buy-to-let flats, the influx of new minorities, either from Eastern
Europe or refugees and asylum seekers from Africa and elsewhere,
the increasingly transient nature of what were once long-established
residential areas, the increase in dirt, congestion and crime and the
perceived decline in collective community values and standards.
Suburbanisation offers a potential solution to these problems allied to a
move to areas seen to be more stable and affordable, which also offered
higher educational standards. The prospect of an owner-occupied
house, a car on the drive, better neighbours and good schools represent
a powerful attractive combination to aspirant minority ethnic groups
keen to achieve upward social and spatial mobility. But at the same
time, the influx of minority ethnic groups clearly represents a problem
to some of the longer-established white residents, some of whom have
made or are deciding to move further out, towards Havering or Essex.
To them, the very success of the minority ethnic groups in moving
out represents a threat to the traditional ethnic composition of their
areas and they, in turn, are moving out or being replaced when they
die. In this respect, East London is undergoing a rapid process of social
and spatial change that is changing its very nature.

## Conclusions

As we have seen, London in general, and East London in particular, has seen dramatic changes in its ethnic composition over the last 30 years, and particularly over the 10 years from 1991 to 2001. On the basis of current births data and school attendance data by ethnicity, the 2011 Census is likely to show a further continuation of these trends. London is now a major multi-ethnic city and more boroughs will move towards a situation where there is no majority ethnic population. As the minority ethnic populations increase, we expect to see the white population continue to shrink, in relative, if not in absolute, terms. The key point to make here is that this growth has been accompanied by a gradual outward expansion. All the boroughs of London have seen their minority ethnic populations increase, and this is likely to continue. At the same time, we have seen a significant rise in the size of the minority ethnic middle class. This has important implications for the housing market. As we have shown, there have been two, slightly contradictory, trends. First, minority ethnic home ownership has increased very substantially but second, because of the overall growth of the minority ethnic population, the growth in the private rented and social rented sectors has been even larger and we are seeing the gradual minority ethnicisation of social rented housing in East London.

The suburban growth of minority ethnic groups has been driven by two main goals: first, to escape what are seen as the social and environmental problems of the inner city, and second, to move towards the promised land of suburban home ownership. This has both a housing dimension – in that the suburbs offer the promise of a house, drive and garden, and for considerably less than in gentrified inner London – and an educational one, in terms of what is commonly seen to be better schooling. Ironically, just as some minority ethnic groups move out to escape the inner city so some white residents are moving out to escape minority ethnic groups, although it is perhaps more accurate to say that there is a process of white replacement as well as white flight. However we label the process, the outcome is essentially the same: London's outer boroughs are now seeing a rapid increase in their minority ethnic populations that is being reflected in the composition of the schools. This is a theme we take up in the next two chapters.

## Note

[1] This may, of course, disguise the 'churn' described earlier where some white groups have left and been replaced by others of a different class. This seems a likely scenario.

# FOUR

# Moving on, moving out, moving up: aspiration and the minority ethnic suburbanisation of East London

'This area of London has always been a place that people aspire to, the first stop for people who are immigrants, so they come in to the East End and they work very hard in not very pleasant jobs, then they save enough money and they want to move to here then a lot of them will move on again, they're not going to all stay here, a lot will want to move to more rural areas.' (White British, female, Central Redbridge)

## Introduction: aspiration, education and mobility

'Aspiration' (safely escorted by scare quotes) and its offspring, upward social mobility, were at the heart of New Labour's project. Not for nothing did former Prime Minister Tony Blair state in 1997 that his priorities for New Labour were 'education, education, education'. Aspiration thus offered some hope of 'getting on' (rather than simply 'getting by') to groups who were not previously on the radar of the major political parties as well as enabling New Labour to connect with a wider electoral community that had largely been neglected by the political establishment. In effect, Blair built on Nye Bevan's concept of 'poverty of aspiration' and successfully incorporated the idea of aspiration as New Labour territory. Gordon Brown consolidated this; for example, in his first speech to the Labour conference as Prime Minister he claimed that:

> 'I want a Britain where there is no longer any ceiling on where your talents and hard work can take you ... where what counts is not what where you come from and who you know, but what you aspire to and have it in yourself to become ... a Britain of aspiration and also a Britain of

mutual obligation where all play our part and recognise the duties we owe to each other.'

Brown reiterated this in a newspaper article in 2010: 'This is a country of aspirational individuals who, given half a chance, want to get on and not simply get by' (Brown, 2010). Brown thus continued the Blair focus on the translation of aspiration into achievement through education (Limb, 1999).

These ideas did not easily fit into the sociological truisms that underlay the politics of the postwar era – of collective advancement for the working class through the trades unions or the individual hopes of the more or less established middle classes. In this period Labour was seen as the party of redistribution rather than aspiration – somewhat unfairly given its emphasis on 'equality of opportunity' in the setting up of the post-Second World War welfare state. In the age of neoliberalism, aspiration, like the lottery, serves a useful function because it offers the opportunity (or illusion) – despite the odds – of 'making it', and the prospect of greater social mobility, notwithstanding recent research (Hills et al, 2010) which has shown that the postwar trend towards greater equality has been reversed under both Conservative and New Labour administrations since the 1980s. Raco (2009) makes a convincing argument that there has been a move from a culture of *expectation* to one of *aspiration* that has been engineered to win consent for the framing of what might be termed neoliberal welfare policy. The juxtaposition Brown posed between 'getting on' and 'getting by' was central to the largely successful attempt by New Labour to steal the Conservative Party's traditional clothes and distance itself from its own past. Labour's core appeal was traditionally to a sense of *collective social progress* in contrast to the Conservatives' emphasis on *individual* mobility and achievement – although there was some convergence between the two in the postwar years of 'one nation politics' (Judt, 2010). What Brown stressed as distinctively New Labour was the link between 'a Britain of aspiration and also a Britain of mutual obligation'.

Nowhere in the UK can match the diversity of ethnic background found in East London. Aspiration is central to this book largely because it lies at the heart of our account of the hopes and plans articulated by the respondents – particularly those from minority ethnic groups. It is not, however, a core concept in social science and it is also an easy one to sneer at, being a good example of what some Marxists once termed 'false ideology'. Too often, to aspire is to have hopes and plans, only for them to be cut off by the structural realities of capitalist society before they reach fulfilment. Despite this, many of the respondents entertained serious hopes for the future, often to be realised through their children and, in spite of the disappointments of the last 10 or 15 years, many felt that they have at last been making slow but definite and discernible progress in pulling themselves off the bottom ranks of society to which they, their parents and often their grandparents had been consigned since coming to Britain in the 1960s and 1970s from the Caribbean, South Asia or East Africa. Many of these migrants had often enjoyed a relatively high social status in their home country and had witnessed a decline in their social and occupational status when they arrived in Britain.

## Aspiration and minority groups in East London

The discrimination experienced by the parents and grandparents of the minority ethnic respondents in East London's labour and housing markets and within education and the rest of the welfare system arguably constituted what the Macpherson Report (1999) (in relation to the police) labelled a process of 'institutional racism'. Even trades unions and other supposedly progressive organisations that might have been presumed to have been there to open up opportunities for them let them down – in some cases badly, but always misguidedly (Modood, 1997). Given the importance of state employment in East London, these forms of institutional racism held many minorities back despite their relatively high levels (in relation to whites) of educational qualification.

Since the 1990s, predating the 1997 Labour election victory, there has been an opening up of a 'rights agenda' which has slowly forced an awareness of such forms of overt and covert discrimination further up the social, political and cultural agendas and made it less acceptable – not just with respect to minority ethnic groups but also to other groups such as sexual minorities and people with disabilities. With the Human Rights Act 1998 becoming enshrined in EU and UK law, this helped make employers and others aware of a wide range of discriminatory practice and the sometimes high cost of non-compliance.

What we have seen over the last 15 or so years in East London appears to represent something of a 'sea change' which we outlined specifically in relation to housing in the previous chapter. We summarised this as a process of 'minority ethnic suburbanisation' in which the desire to move out from the inner London boroughs of initial settlement, such as Hackney, Tower Hamlets and Newham, represented more than simply an improvement in some individual respondents' economic circumstances which permitted them to buy a better (usually semi-detached) house in a 'better area'. More importantly, however, it symbolised and crystallised the flowering of a whole set of aspirations about who they were and what they might achieve and, as such, was indicative of a feeling of collective self-confidence that these hopes were realisable both for themselves and, crucially, in the expectations that they might harbour for their children. This was to be realised through meritocratic achievement in the education system with the expectation that, if they did well, it would be recognised in professional or managerial employment with high levels of social esteem and material well-being. In this scheme of things, suburbanisation was a 'win–win–win' situation: better housing in a better area, better educational opportunities for one's children and getting away from areas that were perceived as increasingly problematic because of both the arrival of new migrant groups and ongoing evidence of social and physical decline. The move out from inner London therefore is representative of a wider strategy of aspiration as well as being indicative that people had some confidence that it was achievable.

For many in the better-established of East London's minority groups, the last 10–15 years have provided an unprecedented opportunity to exercise what have often been long-held, well-nurtured but essentially mothballed aspirations which they have slowly been able to begin to shape into realisable strategies for social and economic advancement. Although the frustrations and setbacks may have outnumbered the successes, we believe that it is important to recognise that the last decade has provided the context for what many of our respondents would see as a period of time in which they stopped – at best – treading water and finally began to feel they were swimming with the current. This sense, by at least some of the respondents, that they were moving up the social hierarchy, is partly a consequence of changes in the wider structure of occupations, particularly the growth of lower middle-class jobs in the private and the public sector, partly a result of their own often considerable efforts and partly a consequence of the emergence of new sources of marginality, notably the residualisation of some parts of the white working class who did not suburbanise to outer East London and beyond, and who appear to have sunk further into the depths of economic non-activity. New groups of migrants have also replaced these long-established minority groups; this has engendered a feeling of no longer being at the bottom of society. In much of East London, not being white has become 'ordinary'; for members of minority ethnic groups this upward move is slow and fragile and possibly temporary; the fear of falling back is always there and, inevitably, the recession may put all this in jeopardy. Their aspirations and hopes for real mobility, however, are invested in their children and specifically their children 'making it' through the higher echelons of the university system into the managerial jobs or – preferably – the professions. There is an acknowledgement that their achievement of this is still some way off but there is nevertheless a belief in the possibility of progress among this group of respondents.

We do not want to suggest that East London has become a glossy success story of high-aspiring minority ethnic groups translating their dreams for the future into solid material achievement. East London remains the most deprived sub-region of London, its majority population remains solidly white and most are lower middle and working class. Nevertheless, compared to what it used to be, the changes are dramatic and, we would argue, suggestive of the kinds of change that might eventually embrace large parts of London – in which no ethnic group can assume that it is in the majority or that its cultural norms are inevitably the societal norms. For this reason, examining people's educational aspirations for their children and their reasons for moving to the areas where they currently live, gives us real insights not just into the behaviours of upwardly aspiring members of relatively long-established, although previously downtrodden, minority ethnic groups, but also into the changing nature of the white middle classes. There is a process of replacement going on across East London in which different groups are taking the place of those who, for whatever reason, have died or moved out.[1]

So far, we have focused on the minority groups pursuing a suburbanisation strategy out of inner London but there are also the more familiar processes of inner-city gentrification and working-class 'white flight' going on within many of the same places. The houses becoming vacant in Redbridge are, generally speaking, those of a white lower middle class and a working class who have either retired, died or who aspire to move to Essex with its perceived ethnic homogeneity and educational excellence (achieved by a ruthlessly selective grammar school system). The 'urban-seeking' (Lockwood, 1995) middle classes in our study are represented by the affluent professionals heading for Victoria Park or, in the case of their somewhat less affluent colleagues, for the terraced streets of Newham, whose mainly Asian owners have often been keen to sell in order to move into Redbridge. We are not suggesting a healthily functional housing market that allocates places to different groups by matching their aspirations with what is available, but we are suggesting that there is a dynamic within the housing market and the structuring of residential choice that reflects a complex of class and ethnic backgrounds in the context of a rapidly changing city whose social structure has changed out of all proportion in a relatively short period of time. As we show in the remaining chapters, a key structural imbalance in all of this is the provision of education places, the endowment for which the area's working-class past has left it massively underprovided.

It was a contemporary sociological cliché to characterise the difference between the middle and working classes in the postwar decades as between 'immediate' and 'deferred' gratification in which the middle-class child deferred moving into the labour market to gain qualifications. To be upwardly mobile out of the working class required the 'grammar school boy' [*sic*] of old to adapt to a set of middle-class beliefs and behaviours (Jackson and Marsden, 1962). An alternative characterisation was to draw a distinction between 'individual' and 'collective' notions of social mobility (Goldthorpe and Lockwood, 1963). Today, we would argue, following decades of sociocultural change, that more individualised notions of aspiration are widespread and have become normalised. In this environment, education and the attainment of qualifications – particularly at degree level – have become the common factor for entry to the higher professional and managerial occupations (Savage et al, 1992). In this situation (despite the recent evidence on the contemporary slow-down in rates of social mobility) there is a widespread perception that educational qualifications are crucial both to the intergenerational maintenance of privilege and to the fulfilment of aspirations that one's children should progress into middle-class jobs. This is particularly the case among some ethnic groups that have particularly high records of educational attainment even when social background is held constant, which we discuss later in the chapter (Hamnett et al, 2007). These groups were never part of the postwar consensus in which both collective and individual mobility strategies were legitimated through the state. De-industrialisation, the decline in the organised working class and its institutions, the rise of neoliberal forms of governance based around league tables and performance indicators, have tended to reinforce a 'culture of aspiration' – nowhere more than in the field of education. In our interviews in East London, which included all the major ethnic groups, this came across particularly strongly among those respondents from black and minority ethnic (BME) backgrounds.

As we saw in Chapter Three, the size of the BME middle class in the UK grew spectacularly between 1991 and 2001 from a small base, and its absolute size in relation to the middle class as a whole has remained relatively insignificant. Indeed when this growth is normalised (that is, taking into account the relative sizes of the minority middle class to the middle class as a whole), most BME groups have experienced a lower rate of upward mobility than the white population, although there are exceptions, notably among Indian groups (Butler et al, 2008). There is, however, a 'London effect'. London is not only an increasingly middle-class city but it is also one in which the rate of growth of the middle classes is higher than elsewhere and in which the BME middle-class populations are both larger and faster-growing than elsewhere in the UK. This constellation of ethnicity and class also has a distinctive geography within London that has developed over the past half century since the start of its de-industrialisation and the coming of mass immigration from the New Commonwealth and Pakistan, discussed in Chapter Three.

## Organisation of the chapter

This chapter is organised around the voices of the respondents and their articulation of their aspirations. We do this by looking, first, at their wider educational aspirations and, second, at how these aspirations have become 'spatialised' by seeing where people are now in relation to where they would like to be or where they used to be. This involves them in 'narratives' about decline and decay from which they hoped to distance themselves matched against ones of ambition and achievement. Where they live becomes symbolic of who they and their children might become: for some, staying where they are or where they used to be runs the risk of being swallowed up by a fear-inducing underclass whose jaws were forever snapping. We begin our account by building on the material introduced in Chapter Three, with a focus on the educational aspirations expressed by respondents (including those 'who have made it' as well as those who see themselves as 'on the way up'). We then explore this in the concept of familiar narratives of fears over security and crime and the breakdown of a sense of belonging and community that many associate with the rise of the 'buy to let' phenomenon.

## Educational aspirations in East London

Almost all the respondents, of all ethnic backgrounds, regarded education as extremely important, primarily as a key to upward social mobility; almost all had aspirations for their children to do well at school and, if possible, to go on to university, which they saw as being key to getting a good job and gaining social recognition. Not surprisingly – largely for the reasons outlined above – the central importance of education to social mobility was most strongly voiced by minority ethnic respondents who saw it as the way upwards, but such views were also very clearly articulated by successful university-educated professionals living in the gentrified areas around Victoria Park:

> 'Oh, the single most important thing that a parent can give to their children in life is a first-class education and I have no doubts about that whatsoever. It [education] only comes second to a secure family home.'

> ['What aspirations do you have for your children? Can you tell me about any aspirations you have in terms of progression on to tertiary education or certain career paths?']

> 'Good, solid education in primary, secondary and tertiary. [...] So, I'm looking for ... my educational aspirations are that not only do they learn to read and write, but also that they have depth to their education which is something that they take through into their college years and nourishes them throughout their lives ... that they understand and are enthused by a joy of learning.' (White British, male, Victoria Park)

Equally, however, respondents who had not themselves had a good education saw it as very important. They wanted to ensure that their children maximised their opportunities and avoided some of the difficulties they themselves had experienced and, for this reason perhaps, they were more narrowly focused on performance. In response to a question about the importance of education and whether she expected her daughter to go to university, the following Barkingside respondent had this to say:

> 'I hope she does. Yes, well yes, I kind of expect her to. She kind of expects herself to, and that's maybe something that I've instilled into her, I don't know. But education's incredibly important to me for her. I want her to enjoy school because I want her to want to carry on learning. I didn't particularly enjoy school and I did half a year of my A-levels and dropped out. And I don't want the same thing to happen to her. I don't want her to have to claw her way up into, you know, a half-decent job like I had to because I

don't have the qualifications to immediately get a good job. So to me it's incredibly important. However, saying that, you know, I want her to have a well-rounded education and that includes sports and after-school activities and mixing with her friends.' (White British, female, Barkingside)

However, aspirations for a good education were not restricted, either on the one hand, to the successful middle classes wanting to reproduce their advantage in their children or, on the other, to minority groups who had been previously unable to progress educationally. The following respondent (white and in a routine job) was very clear about the need for education in a society where educational qualifications were more important than 'in her day':

> 'I think it's important because I missed out, leaving school at 16 with just a handful of CSEs, it got me by, but in today's day and age it doesn't. I think children are [now] expected to attend university, you can't do [university] without qualifications, and I just feel that if they miss out now, you are going to be a burden on me for the rest of your life and ... trying to tell a child that they do need to get the exams to go forward in your life can be quite hard.' (White British, female, Barkingside)

## My son, the doctor...

Education was seen as particularly important by most minority ethnic respondents who saw it as the key to upward social mobility and a passport to a better life. This view was strongly articulated by many Indian respondents, but it was by no means restricted to this group.

> 'In my community Indian people or Hindus we value education as the base for success because if a person is not educated the chances of success is very limited. So education is most important.... For example if you've got £50 in your pocket I could slap you and take your £50, right. But if you've got education nobody can take education from you and it's the background that helps success in life. That's how I see it....' (Ugandan Indian, male, Barkingside)

Another Indian respondent talked about the way in which Indians tend to push their children educationally, and the importance of qualifications and the professions as a key marker of achievement and status. The old Jewish joke about 'My son, the doctor' is a very real phenomenon among the Indian community in London.

> 'I think Indians especially, they do push their children, you know, they do push their children quite a lot and I think it's unfair on children really to push them that much 'cos ... my mum's kind of got that mindset of, you've got to go study – if my son's playing piano or going swimming or playing in the forest, it's like, well shouldn't he be studying, shouldn't he be working? So it's all work and no play kind of attitude, 'cos he's got to do well at school, 'cos he's got to get to university, then he'll have a good job, then you kind of give back to your parents. And I think that is the mentality of a lot of Indian people who have come to this country.'

> ['Why do you think it's particularly pronounced in Indian families?']

> 'Because education is seen as the way to get out of, you know, to take yourself higher basically. That is the stepping-stone ... when I was growing up, I remember my parents, you know, they want me to be, kind of this typical Indian mentality that you either be a doctor or a lawyer or an engineer – that's the three professions you know you're set up for life. You're a doctor, you know you'd always get work as a doctor, or an engineer or a lawyer, so ... so they kind of convince their children they want them to go into a profession which ... you know, so ... as I say, you ask most Indian parents what they want their children to be, and at the top of the list will be the doctor.' (Indian, male, Central Redbridge)

These aspirations focus very much on the achievement of traditional *professional* outcomes:

> 'In our culture to be a doctor or a lawyer or engineer, that is considered a prestigious qualification, people can get good jobs if they achieve those qualifications.' (Pakistani, male, Central Redbridge)

Such views were repeated over and over again by the Asian respondents, who spoke of the strong sense of future orientation in the Asian, and particularly Indian, community in Britain in which education is seen as an investment in, and stepping-stone to, the future.

There is a deeply embedded sense of emotional capital and achievement in terms of being the first in the family to have achieved an education and a wish to hand this on which represents more than simply wanting to embed relative privilege in terms of one's children. The next respondent talks eloquently and movingly about the importance of education when he compares his achievements to those of his uneducated father:

> 'I was talking with my wife the other day, and basically my gift to my children … you could say inheritance, what I pass on to them, is that they've all achieved a university education. If they've done that then I'll feel I've done my bit as a parent. I want them to be good, well-rounded citizens, but I want them to get a university education because my dad told me – my dad is not educated, he can't put two letters together – but he said to me, son, look, you can get a job and you can lose a job. But if you get an education no one can ever take that away from you. And that's been in the back of my mind for years and I look at people, they leave school aged 16 or 17 and they go get a job and, fine, at the time it's fine because they are earning, but I just feel to be a well-rounded citizen they need to have a good university education. I was the first in my family to get a university education. My dad was uneducated but when he went to my graduation ceremony his feet didn't touch the ground and, you know, he felt that he could actually hold his head up high among all the other relatives. A lot of them are doing very well in terms of business, finance, shops – money-wise they are doing well – and my dad, you know, he's just a labourer, but the fact that his son achieved against all the odds and went on to university, that was it for him, that was it, and in terms of support from my parents, they offered me – they said, go on son, study.' (Pakistani, male, Newham)

Such respondents did not want their children to have to work their way up through a set of manual jobs; they wanted them to be professionally qualified.

'Some people, they don't bother. They are not bothered about their kids' study. They think that after school their children will get a job in the supermarket. I don't want my kids to work in the supermarket. I want my sons to become a doctor, or a pilot or something like that. You have to think about it like that. I am a civil engineer but I am working in a different field. When I came here I didn't have any qualification at all. When I came here I thought I have to study and study and study. I worked in a petrol station when I was a student. I came home from uni and went to work, then went to uni. I finished the degree, an honours degree, and I am qualified. But I don't want my kids to … every morning, every morning, every morning, I am asking my two kids when I am taking them to school, how are you going to study after [school]; what are you going to do when you finish your studies? Now I am telling him he is to be a doctor. I have to look after him now so that he will look after me [in the future].' (Sri Lankan, female, Newham)

It wasn't, however, all about professional jobs and a totally instrumental approach to schooling and education, as the following respondent indicates:

'I think it is extremely important and the realisation came from the belly rather than it being the last position, as far as I was concerned, or my wife was concerned, because she had been a completely disillusioned student when we were in Pakistan…. She found the education over here interesting, she got involved in it. She built the foundations for herself, scraped some GCSEs enough to be admitted into AS-levels then did enough at A-levels to get into a good university and managed to complete her degree. And did it on time and got an acceptable grade. So there's a wealth of satisfaction there and I think that was quite important. It was important to her because she got cousins, one who's graduated from Harvard, another one graduated from university in Canada. So yes, there was quite a tradition … so that was very important for her.' (Pakistani, male, Barkingside)

Not every Asian respondent saw education and the professions as a given – family disputes often arise over aspiration whose origins lie between the two sides of the family:

'What I want them to do? My boy I'd like to see – it's like me and Mrs have had an argument about this – I want him to become a taxi driver, a black cab because my brother is a black cab. I think he can earn good money there but she says, like, I want him to be a doctor, because her family is all doctors – her cousins and her dad and everybody.[...] But apart from that, yes, I wouldn't mind if he gets qualifications, I'd be proud of him.' (Pakistani, male, Central Redbridge)

The stress on the importance of 'education as aspiration' was by no means confined to Asian families. Many black respondents were also very clear about its value, as the following respondent makes clear:

'For me education is all important and I think because I have two boys, black boys have a very hard time, I'm very lucky, I wouldn't say I'm very bright but I was brought up in Oxford where I was one of seven or eight black children, but I was the sort of person who kept their head down and didn't get into trouble, I think it is quite different these days and I think that black boys and men have it very hard, it's probably easier for a black woman to get further ahead.'

['Will you encourage your children to aim for university?']

'Yeah, I want them to understand that education means they have the option, this is how society measures you, it's the way you get your foot in the door and unless you really apply yourself and get the foot in the door there will be no other options. But I think university is being watered down and that there are too many people in the workplace with qualifications that don't mean anything.' (Black Caribbean, female, Central Redbridge)

The common concern among minority respondents in Newham about the consequences of not pushing your children is well expressed in this excerpt:

'I want them to all go to uni, all three of them ... most parents – I've been at this school for a couple of days now [the respondent's eldest child has only just started school] and basically I've been watching how parents drop their kids off – they just drop them then go! They are not interested in what the child is there to do. With me, I want to see what my child is going to do over the day sort of thing. Basically I like to have a plan what my kids are doing anyhow.' (Ghanaian, female, Newham)

Some white respondents were more relaxed about education, and they did not see it as all consuming. They saw it as important, but they did not want to push their children to achieve at all costs and were happy for them to do what they wanted in life. This is in marked contrast to most of the minority ethnic groups we interviewed. Compare the clearly stated set of ambitions over the preceding pages with that of this white but upwardly mobile Newham respondent:

'I'd like her to go to university but if she didn't it wouldn't be the end of the world. I'd like her to have choices about what she did. And whatever she ends up doing I want it to be a positive choice, "I'm doing this because this is what I'd like to do", not "I'm doing this because I can't do anything else or because I'm stuck". So whatever she wants to do is fine with me. Whatever choices she wants to make in terms of GCSEs, that's fine, do what you want, do what interests you, but whatever you do you have to do the best you can. And I wouldn't say "oh, you have to do this because its got fantastic career opportunities", you know, that's not me but I just think that, you know, the more you do and the more qualifications you have the more options you have and the more choices you have….' (White British, female, Newham)

The following Redbridge respondent's laissez-faire approach would be total anathema to many of the Asian respondents living in the same research area:

['What are your aspirations for your children's future? What do you hope they will do when they're older?']

'I just want them to be happy and to enjoy their life and obviously, yes, do well at school but so long as they're happy. As far as I'm concerned, as long as they're happy and they enjoy … at the end of the day as far as I'm concerned, life is too short to worry about a hell of a lot of things. You need to be enjoying what life you have. I want them to do well, I do.' (White British, female, Central Redbridge)

A somewhat similar response came from a white respondent in Victoria Park:

> ['How important do you think schooling and education is to you ... both as an individual and as a family?']
>
> 'I think it's reasonably important. I wouldn't put it up there as really top ranked just because, you know, I think there's more important things in a child's life. As long as your child is well adjusted and doesn't suffer in school I think, you know, the school is appropriate.' (White European, female, Victoria Park)

The white respondents who valued happiness, choice and satisfaction above attainment were in an overall minority, however, especially when compared to the Asian and Black respondents who clearly saw education as the key to success in later life. But, as we shall see, the extent to which parents were able to realise their educational aspirations for their children was variable and the educational system was a source of considerable frustration to them. In much of East London the schooling system remains structured by its working-class heritage; despite current efforts to make improvements, it struggles to realise the dreams of its aspiring populations. The changes in selection policy and the tightening up of admissions procedures are indicative of attempts to make the system fairer. Such changes, however, are essentially cosmetic rationing devices and will not be able to meet most people's aspirations and preferences; the respondents were very clear about this. Most recognise the possibilities but have long been schooled in the realities of disappointment.

## Education and residential strategies

Across East London different patterns emerge in how respondents are adapting to the possibilities and the structural constraints of the education system; these are often an outcome of different 'push' and 'pull' factors. These adaptations were not only linked to the wider question of aspiration mapped out at the start of this chapter but also to perceptions about the local area and how respondents perceived other areas. As intimated in Chapter Three, residential strategies were commonly part of a wider strategy of upward social mobility which often – for both white and non-white groups – involved moving further out to the suburbs or beyond. There is thus a strong and persistent link between aspiration, education and spatial mobility, but it is one that varies and mutates depending on the groups concerned, their resources and where they live.

Unsurprisingly, despite the generally upbeat assumptions underlying a sense of aspiration, there is – for those who have lived in East London for some time – a general sense of unease surrounding the very recent history of rapid social change. Inevitably, much of this is narrated in familiar discourses about fear of crime and security and a wider feeling about a loss of community – ironically even by those from minority ethnic groups who were marginalised within the white working-class communities in which they had lived.

## Reasons for moving

At the most mundane level, respondents told us that their main reason for moving was that the new property was affordable and they liked the particular house. This, however, needs to be contextualised within the broader point made at the start of this chapter about having the confidence to move; for years many minority respondents had not only not been able to afford to move up the housing ladder but they *may* have also felt constrained by the broader social norms from moving out of their immediate areas of residence. Our data confirm that generally the white middle-class respondents tended to be reluctant outmovers while for other groups this represented an 'aspirational' move. Perhaps surprisingly, particularly given the points made above, relatively few respondents *offered* schools and schooling as the main motivation for moving, unless linked to a larger discourse about suburbanisation. However, *when we raised the issue of education*, it was clear from the survey, and even more so from the follow-up in-depth interviews, that this was *the* major concern for the respondents (who all had children), but that they often needed some encouragement to talk about it.

At a more general level, the survey data reinforce our findings on social change, discussed in Chapters Two and Three, by suggesting that there is simultaneously an inward and upward trajectory among the (almost exclusively white) higher professional groups which complements an outward movement among the (mainly black and Asian) group of respondents keen to leave the inner city for the suburbs. There was a third (and again almost exclusively white) group of 'outmovers' who were largely motivated by a desire to find better schooling but who were divided over the issue of ethnic mix and diversity. One group, being unable to afford to buy larger housing for an expanding household in their preferred inner London location, often settled on areas like the Leytonstone research area as combining the elements of the inner city and the suburbs, while the other group, mainly concentrated in Barkingside, articulated a 'white flight narrative' about getting away from 'the Asians'. Most of the latter were keen to move eastwards – particularly to Essex – in search of a better standard of living, bigger houses and a more tranquil life while the former did so with considerable reluctance.

Respondents often referred to a long-term relationship with East London. In many cases, respondents were born in the area in which they currently live and/or continued to have relatives living in East London. This was significantly less the case in Victoria Park, which was much more representative of a middle-class incomer model of gentrification (Butler, 1997). The dominant narrative, however, was one involving the rapid change in the social composition of residential areas and respondents' perceptions of, and responses to, those changes. Grievances centred around dirt and litter, the presence of gangs and antisocial behaviour among younger elements, immigration and perceptions of social fragmentation as well as the erosion of neighbourly and street-level social interactions between residents – something people from this part of London in particular have prided themselves on in the past (Watt, 2007). Generally speaking, those who had lived in East London the longest, and the most able to recall 'the good old days', voiced the most intense dissatisfaction. Comparisons were made not only between the East London of today and the one they grew up in, but also the one of five years ago, such is the perceived rate of change. While the nature and consequences of transformation is hotly debated, most respondents mourned the loss of a distinctive way of life, in which neighbours were known to one another and committed to their area; these features were traditionally seen as a fulcrum of East London social identity. In this respect, there is a remarkable parallel with the findings of Young and Willmott 50 years ago (Young and Willmott, 1962), although the circumstances and the character of the neighbourhoods have changed dramatically (see also Dench's account of the new East End; Dench et al, 2006).

### The area's going downhill: perceptions of neighbourhood change in East London

'I have been happy in the immediate area I live in but recently I have become a bit unsure as to whether the new tenants or owners who are moving in are, you know, in a similar category as I am, which is, you know, bringing up children with discipline, not letting them roam the streets, not unnecessarily, not at night and not disrupting people and causing damage to property ... there's been a lot of local youths about, coming from Hainault, you know, and other areas, and doing bad things in there, behind the garages, drugs and sex and all that.' (Malaysian, female, Barkingside)

One of the key factors driving outward migration was a very widespread perception that large parts of inner East London had deteriorated and gone downhill in recent years. The nature of the changes identified were complex, involving increasing residential instability and turnover associated with the rise of buy-to-let rental housing and waves of migrants, an increase in congestion, dirt and crime, and a decrease in personal safety. Many respondents held these views, irrespective of their ethnicity. A concern for the increasing amount of litter, vandalism and graffiti was expressed, especially in Newham, Waltham Forest and Redbridge:

'If you look, Ilford has gone down, environmentally it is just *filthy*, it really is, I just think, god, the streets are littered with rubbish.' (Black Caribbean, female, Central Redbridge)

The declining physical appearance of East Ham was one reason given by another Black Caribbean respondent for moving to Newbury Park in Redbridge. She directly linked this to an increasingly transient local population who took little care in their surroundings. When asked what she was looking for from her move, she responded:

'Obviously a better area than East Ham, I think it has become overcrowded ... it became dirty, it wasn't clean. I think it was just a case of finding a better area.'

['In your eyes, what were the factors underpinning those changes?']

'... to me it was just, cleanliness, it just seemed dirty, everyone's rubbish was on the High Street or in the garden, and I don't think anyone took pride in their homes.... I know quite a few people moved out [for the same reasons]. A lot of houses were purchased by Asians, you did find older whites were moving out and you didn't get new whites moving in ... people were renting out their properties and you were never sure who your neighbour was. They just haven't got the responsibility.' (Black Caribbean, female, Barkingside)

The increase in buy to let appears to be having negative consequences on social cohesion. As well as the associated decline in the physical appearance of streets, having rental properties next door or nearby brings with them a sense of the unknown:

'[Ilford] is gradually going downhill because there's a lot more litter ... people keep dumping things ... you get everything from cars to washing machines.... Eleven years ago it was much different – much cleaner, and there were a few more families here that aren't here now, they've moved. Most of them have anyway. But [they] kept us here, we had very good neighbours.' (White British, female, Central Redbridge)

This respondent continues:

'... It's not that we're worried about what sort of ethnic background they come from, it's just that we're worried about what they're going to be like if you know what I mean. Because you don't know who is going to be in there ... it tends to be [this way] with buy to rent ... we've found that it can be a bit of a problem, with noise and cars and that sort of thing.'

This resident gives the impression of a neighbourhood teetering on the brink of transience in which the ability of homeowners effectively to 'choose' whom they live next to – traditionally one of the key advantages of owner-occupation in a market economy – has been threatened by the penetration of buy-to-let renting into East London streets that were, in the relatively recent past, solidly home-owning. A Pakistani living in south Ilford commented on the transient nature of his area:

['Do you feel this area is getting worse?']

'Yeah, crime-wise very much [so]. You see prostitutes on every corner of this area. New people are moving in, so it's like a cycle – people are not living here for a long time, they keep changing, and changing and changing. An influx of another community makes you feel alienated, and some people move out, especially the white people, they move out for certain reasons, because of cultural differences or habits.' (Pakistani, male, Central Redbridge)

One Ilford resident likened the tenure cycle in his neighbourhood as having gone full-circle back to a 'rented area' after a period in the 1980s and 1990s in which owned homes outnumbered rented properties on his street. Another Barkingside respondent noted how East Ham had deteriorated:

'East Ham, I had been there for just over 30 years so it was a place where I grew up and I could see the changes and everything – becoming more congested, more traffic – the volume increasing – just the state of the place, you know, deteriorating. I needed something different, a change.

It was the crime rate, increase in crime rate. I think neighbours as well. Although we had really nice neighbours it was like, they were always changing so we didn't really get to know all the people … so, and just the roads, the streets – they were getting really bad. And children, they were changing, their behaviour was changing, they were becoming more rough, the way they spoke as well, it was just picked up – it was street talk or whatever. And it was just that our kids used to bring a lot [of that] home. There wasn't a change from school life to home. And we thought we just needed something completely different to bring them out of that area.

That was the change in neighbours as well. We realised that a lot of people *were* moving out and renting their old properties out and then moving out because of, you know, congestion in the street. But about how each street is kept, I have been there since the '70s and then looking at how I was living as a parent now compared to how my parents were living – completely changed. We don't know each other and we lived in the same road for how many years, we didn't know each other. And the way people kept their houses as well. Not inside, on the outside, you know, inconveniencing other people as well: putting their rubbish out, putting their old furniture out, and not having any consideration of keeping a clean street….What I perceived was just no respect for each other. There was no respect.

People would come to this country for less than a year, they would live and just treat the place. I don't know, how it was back home or … I just didn't see any consideration.' (Tamil, female, Barkingside)

East Ham received particular attention in this regard; it functions as a source of non-white residential dispersal in East London with many upwardly mobile families leaving in search of a better living environment in outer London.

Another reason this respondent gave for moving to (what was) predominantly white Barkingside was to put some distance between herself and a co-ethnic community whose competitive nature she was beginning to find 'suffocating' ("everyone wanted to know your business"). Such imagined class differences between minority ethnic 'elites' and a more unorganised and anarchic minority ethnic 'other' was apparent elsewhere. Not everybody, however, wanted to leave East Ham. One Asian respondent felt it was ideal for him:

'I know with a lot of families that as they get more aspirant and financially well-off they tend to move out towards Ilford, Gants Hill, and the nicer sort of suburbs, em, but, and people often say to me "why don't you move out? East Ham is becoming a bit of a dump, because you're getting people … refugees and other people moving in to the area and it's going to bring the tone of the area down?" … that is a factor there, but as far as I'm concerned in terms of what it offers it is just ideal for me. I have been a West Ham supporter all my life and the football ground is just a stone's throw away. Green Street, High Street North, tube station … everything! I mean, I think I'm in the centre of the universe.' (Pakistani, male, Newham)

Overcrowding is an important theme, not least because of its associations with immigration and the physical deterioration of neighbourhoods. The frequency of the overcrowding theme – often associated among respondents with 'buy to let' – is indicative of a more general negativity surrounding tenure change within the study areas. More specifically, the fragmenting clusters of what were once solidly owner-occupied housing in streets to which people once aspired are now, as a consequence of the penetration of rental properties and subdivision of once grand detached and terraced period properties, considered less attractive places to live.

Many respondents saw a clear distinction between the East London of old and the East London of today, between a romanticised past of streets laden with house-proud and loyal residents committed to their local area and a modern narrative of insular neighbours and mess. This cannot be reduced to the stereotypical immigration-centred caricature of an old, stuffy and xenophobic white working class blaming non-whites for everything, as such views were as prevalent among non-white respondents as among whites. It is instead a more generational and class-based form of expression among a multi-ethnic interviewee group with children in local schooling who felt concerned enough on issues relating to local schooling to take part in the research. Whatever the analysis of these views, overcrowding is a reflection of local trends in property development in which single-family homes are converted to more profitable multiple-occupancy dwellings to cash in on a strong demand for rental properties. As one Forest Gate respondent put it:

> 'But now you are getting more and more [examples] where they are buying the property and never living in it! They buy it and do it up, and the minute it's done up the To Let sign goes up! And it does concern me that you get people who are not committed to the house and therefore they might not take good care of it, and there's not the same commitment to the area, they are just in there.' (White British, female, Newham)

To the dismay of a large proportion of this area's older residents, the tenants in many buy-to-let flats are often economically marginal members of migrant groups from the new EU entry nations and refugees and asylum seekers who are felt to have little apparent investment in the area. Entrepreneurial Asian landlords are common agents in the buy-to-let market in this part of London. Indian Sikhs especially are heavily involved in the private building industry and a walking tour of the area reveals the frequency of ongoing renovation works, with skips and scaffolding a common sight alongside paved-over front gardens with old bathroom and kitchen suites awaiting disposal. These are commonly the ex-homes of the old white population who have now either died or moved to the eastern fringes to locations like Romford, Hornchurch and Upminster, or ex-urban commuter towns in rural Essex such as Brentwood and Chelmsford. The Indian builder cited earlier spoke of the success with which Asians have applied themselves to local property development:

'At this point I don't have enough money to buy another house here, but we were talking this morning about how if I had the money and wanted to secure my kids' future I would buy, and that's what people are doing, it's the Asian mentality.' (Indian, male, Redbridge)

Unsurprisingly, much of this change is perceived and articulated as a loss of control when people feel that they don't speak for their neighbours, that they aren't 'people like us'. This often became seen as an issue of crime and, in particular, the source of 'panics' about drugs and prostitution:

'Actually, Leyton was a very good area before. But nowadays there's so many, you know, [of] the drug-dealing people coming in to this area. We are very fed up in this area – especially this area, the flats. So being in the centre here, you know with the shopping centre and Tesco's, more and more people come around and there is too much drug dealing. This is a big problem.' (Pakistani, male, Leytonstone)

Where, of course, all this comes together is in relation to children; people intimate that they could tolerate the sort of changes going on but that they could not accept them in terms of their actual, or more often potential, impacts on their children – not simply in terms of received behaviour but the influence they feared other children would be having on their own children.

What this adds up to, looked at from those who see themselves as having been able to escape, is the breakdown of a sense of 'community' and 'belonging' which may have been mythical but its absence played strongly on respondents' fears as they constructed ideas of who they wanted to be and become, which inevitably crystallised around where they did not want to be and where they aspired to live.

## Aspiration: suburbanisation *and* education

The classic attraction of the suburbs to the middle classes lies in it being a trade-off between access to urban labour markets and 'quality of life' that was assumed to be higher in non-urban areas. It is also one against which many of the established middle classes, many of whom were brought up in such environment, have rebelled. Savage et al (2003) have suggested that the middle classes of the postwar period were seeking 'security' in the suburbs as an antidote to the insecurity of the era in which they had been raised – the tumultuous years of the depression and political extremism and those of war time – whereas many of their children could not wait to get away from the suffocating sameness of this security and live the excitement of inner city and its accompanying frissons. Studies of gentrification have emphasised this suburban childhood aspect to the 'social formation' of early gentrifiers (Williams, 1986; Butler, 1997).

For many of the respondents, however, particularly those from minority ethnic groups, the suburbs represent the classic route to social aspiration – an escape from the cage of the inner city with its associations with poverty, deprivation and failure. Among many of East London's minority ethnic groups we are currently witnessing an outward move to the eastern suburbs in which whole reference groups based around family and friendship appear to be moving *en masse* to the suburbs, and in so doing recreating the same ethnic enclaves but on their own terms rather than those of force of circumstance. For white respondents, however, there appears to be a more painful pull between suburbia and its urban counter attractions; this was particularly poignantly expressed by respondents who had become devotees of the inner city. This next respondent lives in Victoria Park and toys with the problems of inner-city schooling and suburban living:

'We are thinking of moving to Bromley or Beckenham, South London. Or, the other way; up the M11 towards Bishops Stortford – out that way.'

['Are schooling factors behind these decisions?']

'Yeah, that's one of the main reasons really. Because here, where we are, the nearest [secondary] school is Morpeth, which is a good school with a great reputation but last year from Chisenhale [primary school], I think only one or two pupils got in because it's so heavily populated, I mean, the catchment is getting smaller and smaller so the chances of us even getting in to the local secondary school are not guaranteed. And also to be honest, the other major reason why we are thinking of moving is because of the size of the housing ... and the number of children [laughs]....
I think mostly people like the fact that it's so central. I mean, it is a nice area to live – there are nice parks and a mixture of businesses, a mixture of people. We'll miss things like that, the cosmopolitan feel because we'll end up in

suburbia somewhere, we'll end up in a semi ... we won't have the cultural mix we have here which makes things so interesting.' (White British, female, Victoria Park)

Leyton, as we have seen, is something of a 'half-way house' between the city and suburbs by which some have avoided the urban–suburban dilemma: it has affordable terraced housing (unlike Victoria Park), 'urban grit' (in spades, according to many) and an ethnic mix while being near enough to the suburban boroughs to take advantage of their schooling.

In effect, what respondents are doing is attempting to optimise a number of sometimes conflicting, sometimes not, aspirations and lifestyles for their households. For many of the Asian respondents the move to Redbridge was 'win/win', as it was for the upper professionals in Victoria Park able and willing to buy education in inner London's elite schools; for others there were compromises (in Leyton with the urban environment; in Newham with schooling, as in Victoria Park for those not in the charmed streets around Lauriston Primary or having to contemplate the secondary transition to local schools). Most, as we have seen, had come to terms with their decisions and were generally at ease with the various outcomes – these were the result of both 'push' factors (a deterioration in the urban environment and poor schooling) and 'pull' factors (the attractiveness of housing, the social and ethnic mix and particularly the reputation of accessible schools). In the next three chapters we explore how these strongly held aspirations – particularly around education – are structured, rationalised and experienced.

## Conclusions

As we argued in the introduction to this chapter, the role of aspiration was an important tool in the New Labour political repertoire. This differentiated them from the pre-Blairite, Labour Party of old, which was more focused on equality and redistribution than aspiration. The key point, however, is that the idea of aspiration is one which has resonated very strongly with a significant part of the British population, in an era where the stress has been more on individual success than the collective struggle to improve welfare and opportunities (Mattinson, 2010). Indeed, Gordon Brown stated in 2010 that New Labour wanted to create 'an age of aspiration'. He also added that he wanted to ensure that this was linked to strong bonds of community and collective endeavour. While this may be seen as no more than political rhetoric, the important point is that the 'politics of aspiration' is now a key strand of Labour policy, however (in)effective New Labour may have been in putting it into practice. We have argued in this chapter that nowhere has the idea of aspiration been stronger than among some of the minority ethnic groups who, in the last 20 years, have begun to make significant advances in terms of educational attainment and upward social mobility. While first-generation immigrants laboured to keep their heads above water economically and to avoid or overcome overt or implicit discrimination, some of them and their children have now moved up into middle-class jobs. These are often lower middle class public sector administrative jobs but a few have made the jump into senior professional and managerial jobs, and many of their children are now moving ahead in the educational system. While many minority ethnic groups now aspire to, and some have achieved, home ownership and a move out to a better living environment, for many of them their aspirational goals are focused on their children, whom they commonly want to get a good education, go on to university and get a good job. For some groups, particularly among the Indians, the importance of education appears almost 'hardwired', and they provide a social and familial context for continuous striving to better themselves and their children. This is strongly manifested in the significance given to professional qualifications: whether medical, dental, pharmaceutical, engineering, financial or legal. This group, as many of the respondents demonstrated, have arguably taken over the ethos of 'my son/daughter, the doctor'. While this is perhaps the most marked example of aspiration, it is also clear that other ethnic groups also value the importance of education as a key to social mobility and success, particularly in an era where a much greater proportion of the population is going to university and where a degree is now often a pre-requisite to a good job, if not necessarily the good jobs of yesteryear. It is therefore not surprising that many parents are keen to move into, or have already moved into, boroughs where educational quality and attainment is seen to be high and there is considerable competition to get their children into what are seen to be good schools. We consider these issues in more depth in the next three chapters.

## Note

[1] The choice of the word 'replacement' is deliberate; much of the discourse on gentrification centres round the use of the term 'displacement'. While we do not deny that this was central to much gentrification, it does not adequately describe the more apparently voluntaristic moves being described here.

# FIVE

# Social reproduction: issues of aspiration and attainment

'I was talking with my wife the other day, and basically my gift to my children ... you could say inheritance, what I pass on to them, is that they've all achieved a university education. If they've done that then I'll feel I've done my bit as a parent.' (Pakistani, male, Newham)

## Introduction

Nowhere is the changing ethnic composition of East London shown more dramatically than in its schools. We discuss two key issues in this chapter – those concerning aspiration and attainment – which we introduced in the previous chapter. In this chapter, we focus on how they are operationalised, delivered and achieved on the ground in relationship to education and the schooling system. Our starting point is that there is a strong sense of aspiration among the middle classes, broadly defined, of East London, which is particularly marked among some minority ethnic groups for whom education is the key to upward social mobility and the realisation of often long-held aspirations, as outlined in the previous chapter. The problem is that the education system in London and particularly East London has long been characterised by low expectations and low attainment – partly, but not exclusively, as an outcome of its history as an area of long-term working-class settlement. There are important differences in educational attainment across London boroughs including in East London where some are top performers but the overall level is poor, thus reflecting the more general west–east division of advantage/disadvantage. Differences also exist in attainment according to ethnicity and social class. Ethnic segregation in schools is also a particular issue in parts of East London, while in other parts there is an unusual degree of ethnic mixing. The means of achieving educational aspirations are therefore mediated by class, ethnicity and geography.

In this chapter we draw on two main data sources to examine these issues: first, official educational statistics produced either by local education authorities (LEAs) or central government (the Department for Children, Schools and Families [DCSF], or its predecessors and successor) and, second, data derived from the Pupil Level Annual School Census (PLASC) and the related National Pupil Database (NPD) to which we were granted access for schools in our East London study area. In subsequent chapters we develop this analysis and draw extensively on our own survey and interview data to indicate the extent and different ways in which parents 'strategise' to achieve this.

## Location, education and aspiration

The key finding that emerges from our questionnaire and the follow-up in-depth interviews with parents across our East London study area was an overwhelming concern for their children's education; many BME respondents (particularly Asian) had either moved, or were thinking of moving, to the suburbs in order to get their children into better schools. This aspiration to move out is paralleled – albeit to a lesser extent – by a significant minority of white respondents living in one of the outer London study areas who aspire to move to Essex which they perceive as offering high-quality education and attractive housing. Such respondents routinely invoked (as we saw in Chapter Three) the influx of Asian groups from inner London into the area as a reason for considering a move to Essex in an often barely disguised racist 'white flight' narrative. The Asians replacing them came mostly from Newham and, in their turn, expressed a desire to distance themselves from newer waves of migrants into that borough from elsewhere – the Horn of Africa, the Balkans and, more recently, the so-called 'A8' EU accession states. Other white respondents (living in Victoria Park, Newham and to some extent Leytonstone) offered a countervailing 'urban-seeking' gentrification narrative. This better-established and professionally qualified group was also concerned about education but had differing strategies for dealing with its perceived shortcomings in inner London, although some were reluctantly considering a move out of London as their children approached the secondary school transition age.

These broad trends identified here (the discussion of which forms the basis for much of the rest of the book) therefore provide fascinating accounts of processes of ethnic and class 'sorting' in our East London study area focused around a common concern with social reproduction. A sense of place – both in terms of where to live and where to school one's children – is an outcome of that sorting and the sources of variation can be related to ethnicity and parental class which underpin the different ways in which the respondents articulated their aspirations for their children and their hopes for achieving further upward social mobility. Broadly speaking, leaving to one side the 'white flight' group, there was a clear ethnic divide between the 'urban-seeking' white middle classes and the 'urban-fleeing' minorities (Lockwood, 1995). The white respondents may have been divided by social class and material wealth, the more positively advantaged seeking out places like Victoria Park, which lies firmly within the traditional inner London gentrification belt, while the less advantaged (often lower professionals working in the public sector) were attracted to Newham and Leytonstone, which combined an 'inner-city feel' with still affordable terraced housing.

These largely white professional groups were mostly already established on their career trajectories and were not anticipating significant changes in their occupational status; they had, for the most part, gained higher educational credentials that would sustain them through to retirement. They were able to take a somewhat more relaxed view of passing these advantages on to their children, largely because they possessed the financial capital (via private schooling) and/ or cultural capital and social networks to enable this to happen. By contrast, the minority ethnic respondents were not, for the most part, established on the career trajectories to which they aspired. Many had taken the first step by having gone to university (more often than not the local 'access university') and remained anxious to make further progress. Their main concern was, however, for their children's future. For them, the terraced housing of Newham, Stratford or Leytonstone had little of the cachet or attraction it offered to the white middle classes. Its schools often posed a direct threat to their aspirations for their children from which they could see no alternative but to move.[1] The semi-detached housing of outer suburbia was a positive attraction, in contrast to the 'living nightmare' it represented to the white inner-city gentrifiers (Butler, 1997). The minority ethnic groups actively contrasted such housing to the often multi-occupied terraces of inner London that they, their parents or grandparents had been forced to share when they first came to London. A semi with a place for the car in what was once the garden was an indication particularly among many of the Asian respondents from Newham and East London of having 'made it' – or at least of being on their way.[2] Lacking the kinds of capital possessed by the white professional middle classes to negotiate what was seen as the nightmare of inner-city schooling, the mix of selective, high-performing and well-disciplined non-selective schools in Redbridge made the move out very attractive particularly for Asians, as we witnessed through the words of several of our interviewees at the end of Chapter Three.

**5.1: A paved-over front garden in Redbridge, providing private off-street parking for family cars**

In the remainder of this chapter we examine the underlying reality of, and particularly the structural constraints to, these perceptions about education and schooling in East London and the ways in which social background and ethnicity structure provision, access and attainment. We show that the perceptions of educational failure and success are symptomatic of a deeply flawed system of education in London that is especially problematic in East London.

## Class, ethnicity and education in London

London has become an increasingly unequal city over recent decades and, by the early years of this century, following a continued upsurge in the financial services industries, it has become an increasingly gentrified middle–class city (Hamnett, 2003). By 2001 the largest social class grouping in London was the middle class (broadly defined as the top two SECs), which comprised roughly one third of the population aged 16–75. Approximately a further third are economically inactive (which includes students, the retired and home makers as well as those with disabilities or incapacities) with the remaining third being divided between the 'working class' (that is, mainly manual occupations) and 'intermediate' occupations (Butler et al, 2008). Thus contemporary London, as we saw in the previous two chapters, is a very different city compared to the one of 40 years ago, which was numerically and, in many respects, culturally, dominated by manual working-class occupations.

It could, of course, be argued that some of today's non-manual middle and intermediate occupations fulfil roles similar to those performed by the manual working classes in its days as an industrial city; undoubtedly many white-collar workers including many in professional and managerial occupations could be characterised as the new 'proletariat' of a post-industrial economy, having suffered a process of 'deskilling' similar to that which befell much of the skilled working class in the latter part of the 20th century. Harry Braverman (1974), who coined the term 'deskilling', argued that the same fate would befall white-collar work and that the spread of information technology is leading to a similar and contemporary reorganisation of the labour process among non-manual white-collar workers. What is clear is that the social consequences have been dramatic, leading to new levels of wealth and income for those at the top end of the professional elite (in law, banking and associated private sector services), and the rapid and substantial growth in the lower middle classes (new NS-SEC 2 or the old SEG 5 classifications) discussed in Chapter Three. This has largely been at the expense of the traditional manual working class. It would, however, be entirely mistaken to assume that this new white-collar middle classes have taken on the social characteristics traditionally associated with the white, male, manual working-class culture of an industrial city.

The new middle class in London comprises many new entrants, often from minority ethnic groups and often the first in their families to experience higher education, with ambitions for themselves and especially for their children. As argued above, unlike the established ranks of the white middle classes (higher and lower) who largely make up London's gentrified population, these groups are not well established on chosen career trajectories and their aspirations for a continued upward trajectory come across very strongly in the interviews. As argued in Chapter Four, this notion of aspiration meshes strongly with the dominant political narratives of recent decades articulated by Thatcherism and New Labour alike (Jessop et al, 1988). These narratives are markedly different from those in the post-(Second World) War years in which a sharp divide between middle- and working-class culture was articulated both by sociologists and cultural commentators (Zweig, 1952; Hoggart, 1958).

East London, in common with the rest of London but more so, inherited an education system in which it was assumed that its working class would mostly fail (Willis, 1977; Harrison, 1985). Despite efforts to change the culture of expectations and boost attainment such as by the introduction of city academies, the structure of schooling in East London is little changed. The aspiration and desire for upward social mobility, on the one hand, and the structures for achieving it, on the other, are therefore in danger of becoming dangerously ill-matched. We next turn to the performance of the schooling system in East London.

## Educational attainment in London

Education in inner London, as in many of Britain's big cities, is commonly thought to be in serious crisis. Its educational system faces major problems of low aspirations and poor attainment which have generated considerable academic, political and media debate for over 20 years. While attainment figures are undoubtedly low, with boroughs such as Islington and Greenwich among the poorest performers in the country, perceptions of the performance of schools are worse and are regularly reflected in newspaper articles. For example, in an article in *The Times*, Mary Ann Sieghart (1998) asserted that:

> Standards at state secondary schools in London are shockingly, disgracefully bad. This world class capital city has third class education.

She went on to argue that:

> Although London has many of the richest and poorest people living side by side, they are not educated side by side. Instead, almost anyone who can afford it (and that includes desperately thrifty Asians and blacks) opts out.... Instead of the ideal of the comprehensive ... there is educational apartheid.

According to Sieghart, what is needed is a more meritocratic selective system that would prevent middle-class parents buying into private schools and would, instead, provide an attractive standard of socially mixed education. While approximately 5% of children nationally are educated privately, some estimates for the proportion in inner London put the number at nearer 20% (Machin and Wilson, 2005), although most recent official figures estimate the proportion as being just over 11% and declining as the recession bites.

The problem, as Sieghart pointed out, is that in a city with low levels of attainment in its secondary schools, members of the middle classes seek to ensure the educational success of their children by either moving out of inner London, seeking out a state school with high standards or 'sending their children private' (Butler and Robson, 2003). There have been a number of high-profile opt-outs which have generated considerable media debate. The leading Conservative Party politician, Oliver Letwin, caused controversy when he stated at the Conservative Party conference in 2003 that he 'would rather beg on the street than send his children to the local [Lambeth] comprehensive'. Shortly afterwards, Diane Abbott (Labour MP for Hackney North and Stoke Newington) announced that she was sending her son to the private City of London School for Boys because educational provision in Hackney, particularly for black boys, was so poor.[3] The educational problem in inner London, which Sieghart identified, is the product of a long history during which poor educational attainment was largely taken for granted given its mainly working-class catchment. As indicated in the previous section, it is only in recent decades, with the gentrification of inner London and the shift from a selective to a comprehensive system, where all classes and abilities are educated together, that the problem of standards has become an issue for the middle classes. Previously, a select network of grammar schools with high attainment standards catered to the relatively small middle class who did not use private schools; the rest went to 'secondary moderns', which ensured the problem was one of working-class failure and could therefore be safely ignored (Butler, 1999). However, increasing demands are being put on the system by a steadily growing middle class in the context of a changing labour market with a greater emphasis on educational qualifications. The dominant regime of publicising school performance through the publication and widespread dissemination of league tables has been putting the education system under increasing strain and subjecting the few high-performing schools to ever greater competition for places.

## Differences in educational attainment and their causes

The significant variation in GSCE achievement levels between and within local authorities across Britain has been well known for the last 20 years. In general, large cities perform less well and their inner areas particularly poorly compared to suburban areas (Gordon, 1996). In 2009, the national average of pupils who passed 5+ GCSEs grades A*–C was 50.7%; within London there was a range from 66% in the top suburban boroughs to 40–50% in such inner London boroughs as Hackney, Islington, Haringey, Newham, Southwark and Tower Hamlets (see Figure 5.1).

**Figure 5.1: Percentage pupils achieving 5+ GCSEs grades A\*–C, by borough, 2009**

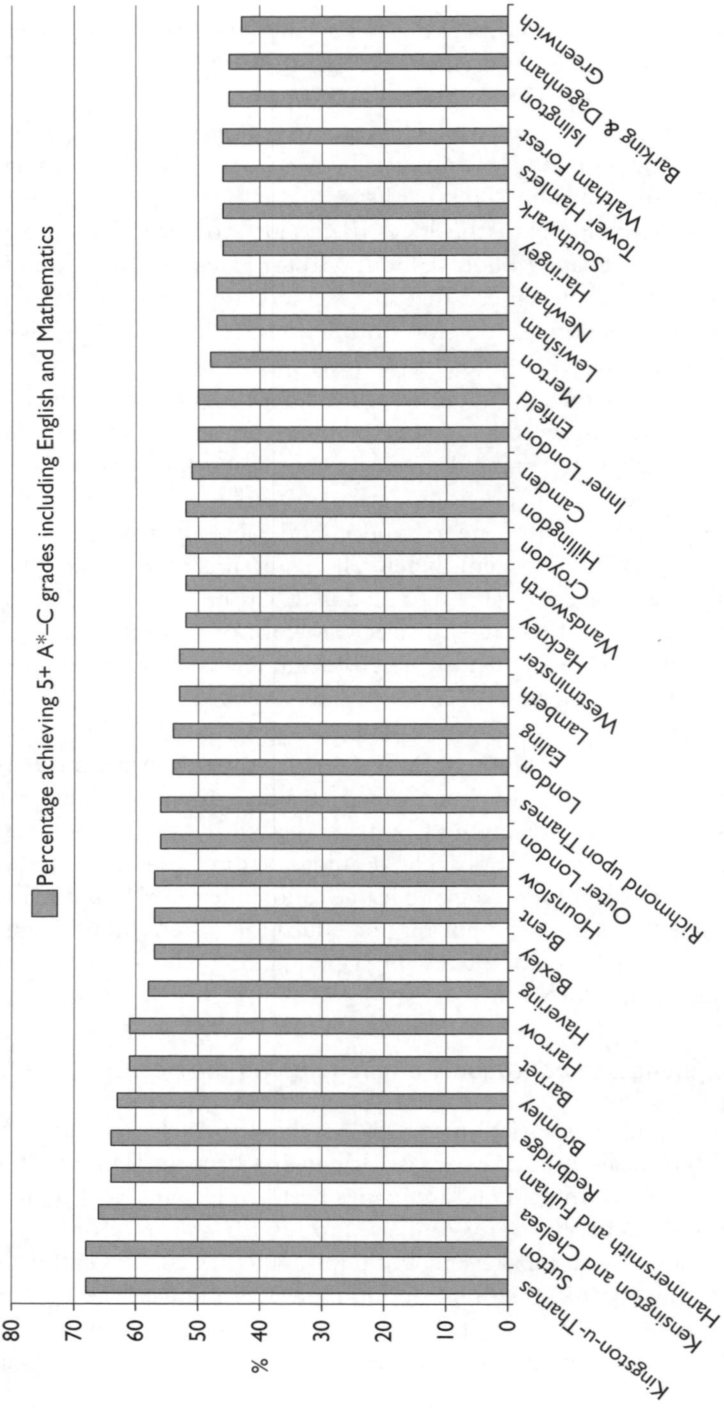

Percentage achieving 5+ A\*–C grades including English and Mathematics

There has been considerable media and political debate over the nature of the poor level of educational attainment and its causes. However, the borough-level differences mask even more marked differences between schools. Figure 5.2 shows percentages of pupils gaining 5+ GCSEs grades A★–C for individual schools in East London ranked by borough. Two things stand out; first, that there are very major differences between boroughs, with Redbridge and Havering at the top, with some schools scoring 100% and many others over 80%, compared to Barking where the highest-ranked school scores just over 60%. Second, there is a major variation within boroughs, with some schools having less than 40% of pupils gaining 5+ GCSEs grades A★–C. While there are a few such schools in Redbridge and Havering, there are many more in the other boroughs.

Contrary to what the previous Labour government seems to have believed regarding so-called 'failing' schools, the performance of individual schools can be explained, in large part at least, by their recruitment patterns. A considerable amount of scholarship has pointed to the ways in which the middle class strategise to get their children into high-performing schools with a high proportion of children from similar social backgrounds (see, for example, Ball, 2002; Power et al, 2003). Much of this work has argued that it is not only home

**Figure 5.2: School attainment, 5+ GCSEs grades A★–C, by borough, East London, 2006**

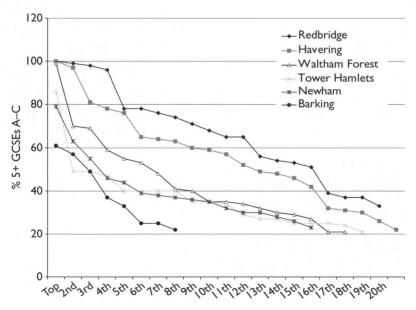

background that matters but that there is also a 'school composition effect'; when a critical proportion of children from (dis)advantaged backgrounds occurs, it has been suggested that a 'tipping point' is reached and schools become either desirable or to be avoided.[4] Nick Davies (2000), in a powerful critique of educational policy in *The Guardian*, showed how the middle class abandoned an ex-grammar-school-turned comprehensive in Sheffield when streaming was abolished. This suggests that class effects on educational attainment work at school level and help explain how some schools become perceived as highly desirable in the eyes of active middle-class 'choosers' while others must be avoided at all costs. Webber and Butler (2007) provide quantitative confirmation for how social backgrounds and their peer group effects operate *within* schools.[5] Social background is, however, not the only factor in explaining variations in the level of educational attainment; Gordon (1996), for example, has pointed to the proportion of single-parent family households. Another source of the variation in educational performance in London can be attributed to differences in ethnic composition across the city given the variations in educational attainment between different ethnic groups. We discuss these issues below.

## Ethnic segregation in schools in England and in London: the background

Johnston et al (2004) note that in England as a whole, over 87% of pupils are of white ethnic origin, with about 3% of black ethnic origin and 6.6% of Asian ethnic origin. There is a substantial variation in the presence of minority ethnic groups, however, with some LEAs, particularly in London, having very high proportions of minorities. Nonetheless, research by Ron Johnston, Simon Burgess and Deborah Wilson suggests that school ethnic segregation is not a major issue in England as a whole (Johnston et al, 2004, 2005b, 2006a, 2006b; Burgess et al, 2005; Burgess and Wilson, 2005). Johnston et al (2006a), on the basis of a classification of all state-maintained secondary schools in England, showed that 80% were in schools where whites comprised over 80% of students, and a further 11% were in white majority schools, while only 2% were in schools where non-white ethnic groups constituted over 70% of students but no single group dominated and a further 2% were in similar non-white schools, in which members of one group formed the majority. Thus, schools where non-whites comprised more than 50% of all pupils in the school only accounted for 9% of all non-white pupils. However, the distribution of minority ethnic pupils has a distinct geography with a particularly marked concentration in London; Johnston et al (2006a, p 982) note that of the 374,000 non-white secondary school students in England, some 165,000, or 44%, lived in Greater London:

> Whereas nationally around 90% of all white students attended schools where whites predominated and virtually none attended schools with white minorities, in London only 75-80% were in white majority schools. In a city with a large non-white population many white students attended schools with a substantial ethnic minority although relatively few attended schools with non-white majorities.

Johnston et al (2005b, p 48) also note that:

> Of the sixty-three [type IV] schools, in which non-whites formed at least 70% of the total enrolment but in which no single group predominated, forty-five were in London LEAs with seventeen of them in three East London boroughs – Newham, Redbridge, and Waltham Forest: in all but three, Asians formed the largest group, with various mixtures of Bangladeshis, Indians and Pakistanis.

But Johnston et al (2006a, pp 982-3) go on to point out that:

> For non-whites however, in London as in the country as a whole, residential segregation was less than school segregation. With large non-white populations, spatial polarization was greater in the capital city than elsewhere in the country especially in schools. This is particularly the case with Bangladeshis, among whom 45% of all primary school students and 41% of those attending secondary schools were enrolled in schools with a substantial non-white majority, with one ethnic group 50% or more of the non-white total.

Given differences in birth rates and the age distribution of the minority ethnic and mixed ethnicity populations, the percentage of minority ethnic pupils in the school population is substantially higher than the overall population. While the percentage of minority ethnic secondary school pupils in Greater London as a whole was 40%, in 1999 the figures for individual boroughs varied from a high of 77% in Brent, followed by Tower Hamlets (71%) and Newham (70%), to lows of 10% in Bexley and Bromley and just 5% in Havering. In 1999, 14 boroughs had over 50% of secondary school pupils of minority ethnic background, almost all of them in inner London. The data for 2009 show that the proportions of minority ethnic groups have increased markedly across all boroughs; this was particularly marked in those boroughs which had a lower proportion of minority ethnic groups in 1999. By 2009, 22 boroughs (a majority of London boroughs) had more than 50% minority ethnic pupils.

The ethnic composition of the East London study area changes dramatically as it radiates out from the innermost boroughs, with large (70–80%) minority ethnic secondary school populations (Tower Hamlets, Newham, Hackney) via the more ethnically mixed boroughs of Waltham Forest (59%) and Redbridge (66%) to Barking & Dagenham (40%) and Havering (17%), which remain predominantly white in overall population terms. The distribution of minority ethnic secondary school pupils across London and how this has changed between 1999 and 2009 is clearly indicated in Figure 5.3. Newham and Tower Hamlets both saw the percentage of minority ethnic pupils rise from 70% to 81%, and in Hackney the percentage rose from 64% to 70%. The changes in ethnic composition were particularly marked in the three boroughs of Redbridge, Barking & Dagenham and Havering in outer East London. In Redbridge, the percentage of minority ethnic pupils rose from 47% to 66%, in Barking & Dagenham from 14% to 40% and in Havering from 5% to 17%. It is clear that minority ethnic groups now comprise a clear majority of pupils in secondary schools across much of East London, with the exceptions of Barking & Dagenham and Havering, but even here the proportion of minority ethnic school children is considerably higher than in the population as a whole. The percentages are likely to increase further in the coming years given the high BME birth rates in some London boroughs.

The proportions of minority ethnic pupils in individual schools within boroughs can differ even more markedly. The schools in East London vary from, at one extreme, those that are virtually exclusively Asian, primarily Bangladeshi, in Tower Hamlets and, to a lesser extent, in Newham, to schools in Havering and Barking & Dagenham that are over 90% white. Of the 99 secondary schools in the study area for which we have data on ethnicity, three schools (all in Tower Hamlets) had over 95% Asian pupils, six had over 80% and 10 over 70%. Of these, seven schools were in Tower Hamlets, two in Newham and one in Redbridge. At the other end of the scale, there were six schools with

# Figure 5.3: Non-white secondary school pupils by borough, 1999 and 2009

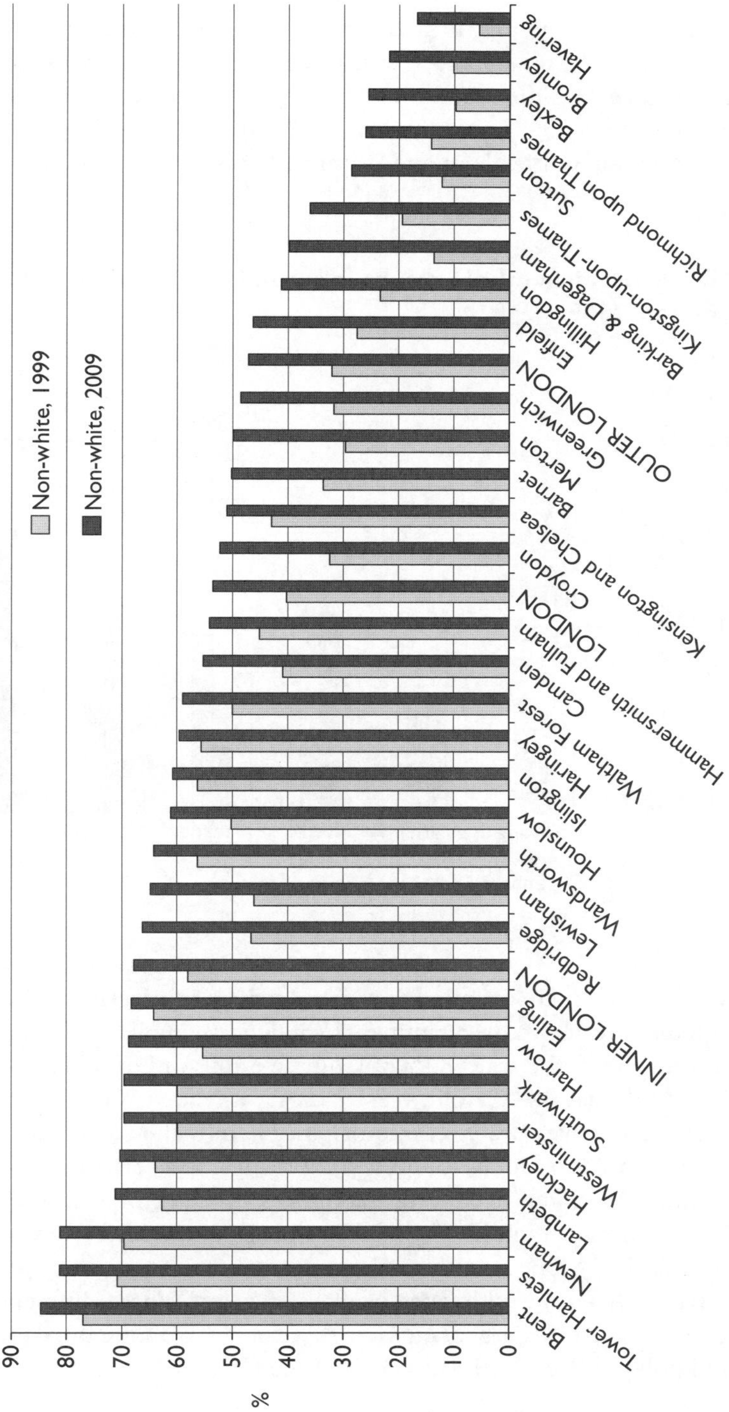

over 90% white pupils, 17 with over 80% and 20 with over 75%, most in suburban Havering and Barking & Dagenham and two schools in Redbridge. The concentration of black pupils is less marked, with two schools of over 50% and 10 of over 40%, mainly in Hackney and, to a lesser extent, in Newham and Waltham Forest (see Figure 5.4).

**Figure 5.4: Main ethnic groups in secondary schools in East London, 2009**

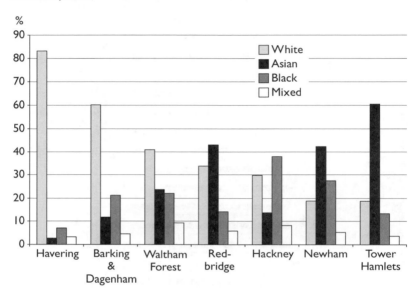

We now turn to examine how this structure of class and ethnic difference relates to the attainment by individual pupils (see Figure 5.5). At one end of the scale, 80% of Chinese pupils in London gained 5+ GCSEs grades A★–C, followed by those of Mixed White and Asian, Indian and Asian Other ethnic origin. There is then a middle group with scores of around 45–50% comprising those of Irish, Pakistani, White British, and Mixed White and Black African ethnic origin. At the bottom are those pupils of Mixed Caribbean and White, Black African and Black Caribbean ethnic origin. Boys in these last groups perform particularly badly, with rates of 30% or below. These differences of gender and particularly of ethnicity have generated substantial political and policy debate (DfES, 2003; GLA, 2004).[6]

**Figure 5.5: Percentage pupils achieving 5+ GCSEs grades A\*–C, London, 2003, by ethnic group**

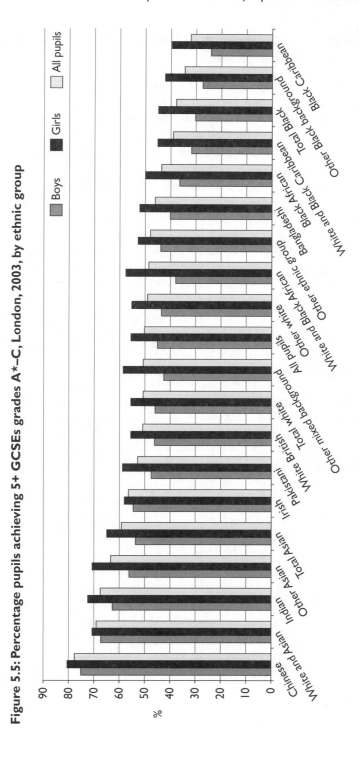

## Educational attainment in East London: social (class) background and ethnicity

Some boroughs have much higher levels of educational attainment than others, and this is even more true at the school level. We also know that some ethnic groups do much better than others in GCSEs and that social class is an influence on educational attainment: the higher the social class, the higher the educational attainment. Different boroughs and schools have different class and ethnic compositions so, not surprisingly, their attainment levels vary considerably. The key questions therefore become: what is the relative contribution of class and ethnicity to attainment and what difference does it make to attainment going to a school with different types of social mix? The previous government took what many saw as the 'easy' approach to this by labelling schools with low attainment as 'failing' schools. It is much more likely that they had an 'unfavourable' social mix in pupil recruitment based around the factors outlined above.

There is no comprehensive data source that enables us to link social class, ethnicity and educational attainment at an individual pupil level. The best available data set is the PLASC, which contains data on, *inter alia*, pupil ethnicity, whether a pupil receives free school meals, home postcode and school address and to which is added information on pupil attainment (at Key Stages 1 to 4) from the NPD. PLASC is constructed from data gathered annually from every English state school on each pupil registered at the school on the census date in January. Using PLASC and NPD allows educational attainment to be measured at the pupil level which can then be aggregated up to the level of the school, education authority or nationwide. A significant weakness in PLASC is the lack of an indicator for pupil social background, other than whether a pupil receives free school meals. PLASC is unable to distinguish between pupil family backgrounds that are not sufficiently deprived to make the child eligible for free school meals. In order to obtain some measure of the effect of home background on pupil attainment at a more fine-grained level we linked pupil home postcodes from the PLASC dataset to the geodemographic codes provided in the Mosaic database of neighbourhood types. This has enabled us to classify the social area background of pupils[7] and thus analyse the relative influences of social status, ethnicity and gender on attainment.

There are 11 major Mosaic 'groups' which are set out in Table 5.1 below; these are then further subdivided to give 61 individual 'types'.[8] Although the Mosaic group names are chosen for marketing reasons (and are somewhat blander in the public sector version!), they nonetheless

## Table 5.1: The Mosaic groups

| | |
|---|---|
| A | Symbols of success |
| B | Happy families |
| C | Suburban comfort |
| D | Ties of community |
| E | Urban intelligence |
| F | Welfare borderline |
| G | Municipal dependency |
| H | Blue collar enterprise |
| I | Subsisting elders |
| J | Grey perspectives |
| K | Rural isolation |

provide a powerful measure of the social characteristics and social status of residential areas. The classification is of neighbourhood spaces and should not be seen as a hierarchical ranking such as provided by more conventional notions of social class; there is, however, as Table 5.1 demonstrates, an implied ranking of household income and social status. Postal code areas classified under Mosaic groups A, B and C have the highest proportion of what would normally be termed middle-class households, whereas those classified under groups F, G, H and I have relatively few middle-class residents and more low-income households.

The analysis is based on seven East London boroughs (Barking & Dagenham, Hackney, Havering, Newham, Redbridge, Tower Hamlets and Waltham Forest). The data set includes 17,891 pupils at Key Stage 4 (that is, GCSE) in 2003. They attended a total of 285 secondary schools scattered across London and South East England. However, we have excluded all schools beyond the boundaries of the seven boroughs. This restricts the number of schools inside the study area to 115, but these schools account for 90% of pupils resident in the study area[9] (Table 5.2).

Across the seven East London boroughs,[10] pupils from the least affluent groups (Mosaic groups F, G, H and I) account for approximately

## Table 5.2: The distribution of pupil schools within and outside the study area

| | No. of schools | % | No. of pupils | % |
|---|---|---|---|---|
| Outside study area | 164 | 57.5 | 1,464 | 8.1 |
| Inside study area | 115 | 40.4 | 16,181 | 90.0 |
| Unidentified | 6 | 2.1 | 336 | 1.9 |
| Group total | 285 | 100.0 | 17,981 | 100.0 |

one third of all pupils while those from the most affluent groups (Mosaic groups A, B and C) account for a further third. However, there are some very striking disparities in the distribution across boroughs of pupils according to Mosaic group. Redbridge and Havering are clearly the most affluent boroughs with a much higher proportion of pupils from the most affluent backgrounds (73% and 68% respectively) and the lowest proportion of pupils from the least affluent backgrounds (8% and 20% respectively). They also appear towards the top of London boroughs in terms of overall attainment (see Figures 5.1 and 5.2). Waltham Forest occupies an intermediate position with a quarter of pupils from the most affluent Mosaic classifications and a roughly similar proportion (22%) from the least affluent groups. At the bottom end, Barking & Dagenham, Newham, Tower Hamlets and Hackney have the lowest proportions (19%, 8%, 2% and 1% respectively) from the most affluent backgrounds (Mosaic groups A, B and C) and much higher proportions (67%, 27%, 54% and 58% respectively) from the least affluent backgrounds (Mosaic groups F, G, H and I) (see Table 5.3).

**Table 5.3: Proportion of children according to Mosaic classification of home postcodes[a]**

| Borough | Affluent A, B, C (%) | Intermediate D, E, J, K (%) | Deprived F, G, H, I (%) |
|---|---|---|---|
| Redbridge | 72.7 | 18.5 | 8.5 |
| Havering | 67.2 | 11.4 | 21.2 |
| Waltham Forest | 24.0 | 53.3 | 21.9 |
| Barking & Dagenham | 21.7 | 10.6 | 67.3 |
| Newham | 7.7 | 62.6 | 26.0 |
| Tower Hamlets | 1.8 | 42.0 | 53.5 |
| Hackney | 1.2 | 40.6 | 57.0 |
| % | 30.0 | 35.3 | 33.3 |
| n | 5,376 | 6,309 | 5,954 |

Note: [a] 1.4% or 253 pupils were unclassified for various reasons.

## Ethnicity, class and schools: impacts on attainment

Education is not – and should not be – simply concerned with attainment in public examinations; nevertheless, with the encroachment of neoliberal forms of governance which require that most services be understood in a market-compatible language in which there are inputs and outputs, it is hardly surprising that output measures such as attainment have taken on such importance with politicians and parents alike. Citizens (consumers) receive a product (education) in a market whose quality is marked by how well it is delivered (attainment) which then translates into demand (popularity). We discuss this further in the next chapter when we consider how parents make choices about where to school their children. In order for markets to operate, those involved in them need as much knowledge as possible and that knowledge needs to be freely available to those participating in the particular market. One of the striking developments of recent decades has been the increasing public availability of knowledge that was previously tacit or restricted to those 'in the know' – professionals such as teachers and doctors. The availability of this knowledge has been facilitated by three factors: the increasing hold of neoliberal approaches to governance with its focus on performance measures, targets and choice; the technological ability to gather, process and store large quantities of such information reliably and relatively cheaply; and, finally, the ability to disseminate it widely, quickly and seamlessly via the internet. However, as we have seen, in relation to school attainment it only tells a rather crude story based, as it is, on raw data. Producing more nuanced and context-sensitive findings that take into account the social background of pupils – the so-called value-added measure – is something that governments have struggled with using such measures as the IMD to provide context. Webber and Butler (2007) used a different approach drawing on Mosaic and PLASC/NPD to examine the performance that might be expected from a school with a given Mosaic profile of pupils based on the national average of GCSE results obtained by each Mosaic group, which is then measured against the actual results obtained. This allowed them to make judgements about whether such schools were performing above or below what might be expected in relation to their actual score (see Butler et al, 2007).

When we applied this methodology to the East London study area, we expected to see a steady improvement in the raw capped GCSE scores[11] as we moved away from the centre; however, when we plot the actual scores the picture is less clear, although results do improve with distance from the city (Butler et al, 2007). When we normalise this in terms of a measure of over/underperformance, the picture becomes much more complex. There are some very good performances by individual schools in Redbridge and Havering and also in Waltham Forest but the rest performed less well than might be expected given the home background of pupils. The largest group of 'over-performing' schools, however, is in Newham, while Tower Hamlets has the highest number of schools that are performing as might be expected. We omitted Hackney from this analysis given the exceptionally high proportion of pupils being educated outside the borough, something we discuss in the following chapter.

This finding might seem to contradict what most of the respondents and the raw attainment data were telling us – that education improved the further you moved out from the centre. In particular, Redbridge was the educationally aspirational location for many of the respondents, especially those living in Newham. However, the results were less surprising when we consider that most people measure benefits in absolute rather than relative terms. What mattered to many of the respondents was whether the school attainment results are better in Redbridge than Newham and it is that which fuels the desire to move to Redbridge and leave Newham. They are simply not interested in the fact that Newham schools are doing a good job given the social background of their pupils. This cuts little ice with ambitious parents wanting their children to do better and fearing that they might be 'pulled down' by local demographic factors. In the next section, we consider the impacts of socioeconomic background (using Mosaic classifications) and ethnicity on attainment across East London.

## Pupil attainment at GCSE

Almost one third of pupils in the East London study area receive free school meals and, according to our analysis of PLASC, such pupils obtain, on average, almost seven GCSE points less than pupils who do not. However, as we have noted, using free school meals is a comparatively crude measure that is unlikely to capture the more fine-grained influences acting on pupil attainment; not surprisingly, our analysis confirms that pupils living in higher status Mosaic areas[12] obtain a higher average GCSE score: the range is from 45 for Mosaic code A to 31 for Mosaic code G, a difference of 14 points. This is substantially greater than the variation using the proportion of children on free school meals as a measure. Pupils from the most affluent backgrounds (Mosaic groups A, B and C) tend to achieve better scores than those from the least affluent backgrounds (Mosaic groups F, G, H and I) (see Table 5.4).

Turning to pupil attainment by ethnicity we also see a clear hierarchy of performance (see Table 5.5): 'Asian Other' and Indians are at the top (with a mean score of 37.0 and 36.4 respectively). White pupils fall in the middle (34.9) and Black Caribbean, 'Black Other', Black African and Bangladeshi pupils in that order from the bottom (32.8; 32.7; 32.6 and 32.1 respectively) with a range of 4.9 points. This is in line with the figures reported nationally (DfES, 2003). The range of scores according to social background is therefore greater than for ethnicity.

**Table 5.4: GCSE scores according to Mosaic group (at pupil level)**

| Mosaic group | Count | Actual mean score | Difference from group total |
|---|---|---|---|
| K | 14 | 43.9 | 9.6 |
| A | 582 | 42 | 7.7 |
| J | 156 | 38.6 | 4.3 |
| C | 4,274 | 38.1 | 3.8 |
| B | 520 | 36.5 | 2.2 |
| D | 5,042 | 33.5 | −0.8 |
| E | 1,097 | 33.1 | −1.2 |
| I | 237 | 32.7 | −1.6 |
| H | 1,698 | 32.4 | −1.9 |
| U [unclassified] | 253 | 32.2 | −2.1 |
| G | 338 | 31.2 | −3.1 |
| F | 3,681 | 31.1 | −3.2 |
| Group total | 17,892 | 34.3 | 0 |

**Table 5.5: GCSE scores according to ethnic group (at pupil level)**

| | Count | Actual mean score | Difference from group total |
|---|---|---|---|
| Asian Other | 462 | 37.0 | 2.4 |
| Indian | 1,410 | 36.4 | 1.0 |
| Unclassified | 959 | 35.9 | 0.8 |
| White | 7,968 | 34.9 | 0.3 |
| Other | 541 | 34.4 | 0.0 |
| Pakistani | 1,147 | 34.2 | 0.0 |
| Chinese | 118 | 33.7 | −0.1 |
| Black Caribbean | 1,441 | 32.8 | −0.4 |
| Black Other | 220 | 32.7 | −0.5 |
| Black African | 1,562 | 32.6 | −0.5 |
| Bangladeshi | 2,064 | 32.1 | −0.7 |
| Group total | 17,892 | 34.3 | 0.0 |

The mean pupil scores according to each Mosaic code may, however, be influenced by differences in their ethnic composition and vice versa. If, for example, some ethnic groups live disproportionately in more or less advantaged Mosaic areas, the scores for these areas will be influenced by their ethnic composition. We therefore controlled for both pupil social and ethnic background. The results of this calculation show the differences between the actual and expected GCSE score range from +8 points for Chinese pupils to −2.6 points for 'Black Other' pupils, a total difference between the largest and smallest difference of 10.6 points. Chinese, 'Asian Other', Indian, 'Other' and Black African pupils perform better than expected after social background has been controlled for. While Black Africans and Bangladeshis perform (according to their actual GCSEs) below average, when social background is accounted for they actually do better than expected. At the other end of the spectrum, 'Black Other' and Black Caribbeans perform worse than expected, while Pakistani and White pupils do slightly worse than expected. This suggests that while pupils from some ethnic groups perform better than other ethnic groups, much of this can be explained by their more advantageous social position. We also investigated what happened to the social background effect when ethnicity is controlled for. The range in the difference between actual and expected scores is equal to 12.5 capped points, which suggests that social background is a slightly more important explanatory variable in educational attainment than the ethnic group of a pupil. Figure 5.6 shows mean capped GCSE score plotted against Mosaic group for each ethnic group, suggesting that there is a consistent pattern for all ethnic groups, with a general decline in mean score from those pupils living in the highest Mosaic areas to those living in lower areas. In other words, an advantageous social background has a strong positive effect on GCSE performance for all ethnic groups.[13]

Finally, we considered the effect of 'school composition' in order to see, among other things, whether there was any evidence to support the commonly expressed concern of the respondents that their children

**Figure 5.6: Mean capped GCSE score by ethnic and Mosaic group**

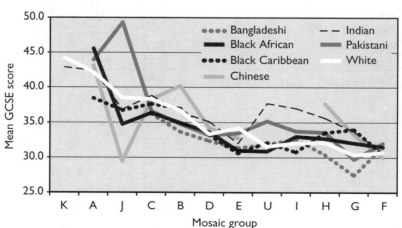

were being 'dragged down' by disadvantaged children in their schools and would be pushed along by the relatively privileged composition of schools in Redbridge. Our findings broadly confirm that the 'better' the social composition of the school, the better pupils do above and beyond their own social background, ethnicity and gender. For the purposes of the exercise above, when examining data at the pupil level, we assumed that gender was equally distributed (roughly 50/50) according to variables such as geography, Mosaic group and ethnic group. Therefore at the pupil level there was little need to introduce gender into the equation. However, at the school level, gender concentration varied considerably (from the extreme of an all-boys school to the other extreme of an all-girls school) and was likely to be a significant factor determining school performance.

We know that girls tend to outperform boys at all stages including Key Stage 4. In our study area, using regression analysis, we found that girls outperformed boys by approximately four capped GCSE points. Hence when analysing data at the school level we need to control for the proportion of girls/boys at each school in order remove gender impacts from any potential 'school effect'. The data contained in the PLASC dataset were accordingly ranked by Mosaic group, ethnicity and gender, to predict the mean GCSE score for each pupil. For each pupil, the added score was calculated by subtracting the expected score from the actual. These differences were then aggregated up to the school level to give a school added score. If there were no 'school effects' we would expect the added score to be the same regardless of school.

In fact, the range of added scores varied from +13 points (for two selective schools in Redbridge) to −8.[14] This indicates that school attainment is not simply the product of the pupil composition, or rather the social background, ethnicity and gender of the pupil. Some schools do better than would be expected given their pupil composition while other schools do worse.[15] This suggests there are school effects above the social composition effects discussed above. A pupil going to a school with a high academic performance is more likely to do better than predicted according to his/her social/ethnic/gender background and vice versa. This suggests that a pupil, regardless of her/his individual social background, ethnicity or gender will tend to perform better at GCSE level if s/he attends a better performing school than a poor performing one. When we disaggregated the actual mean GCSE scores by the proportion of pupils from specific clusters of Mosaic residential areas, we found that the schools with the highest added score tend to consist disproportionately of pupils from the most affluent Mosaic groups, A, B and C. The overall implication is that a pupil, regardless of his/her social background, tends to do better in a school composed of a larger proportion of pupils from Mosaic A, B and C backgrounds. Conversely, ranking schools by the proportions of pupils from the lowest Mosaic clusters (F, G, H and I) reveals that schools with the largest proportions of pupils from these backgrounds tend to have a lower added score. This suggests that in schools consisting of a large proportion of pupils from Mosaic groups F, G, H and I, a pupil is likely to achieve GCSE results lower than would be predicted by his/her own social and ethnic background.

The evidence suggests therefore that school effects are related to pupils' social background. Although schools in Newham and Tower Hamlets, which as we have noted are the two most disadvantaged areas in terms of the distribution of Mosaic codes, do rather better than we might predict from their enrolment, parents in such areas are right to believe that their children would be advantaged by going to schools where there are high proportions from Mosaic A, B and C backgrounds. In East London, these are largely found in Redbridge, Havering and, to a lesser extent, Waltham Forest. Interestingly, pupils from schools with large proportions of Mosaic D and E groups perform less well than predicted by their residential social and ethnic background. This is of some interest given that some white middle-class respondents living in Newham were committed to schooling their children in socially mixed local secondary schools. Work by Diane Reay et al (2007) argues that some middle-class parents living in the inner city place emphasis on a child's social skills and their ability to mix with all classes and ethnicity over and above outright attainment. Being educated in an inner-city state school, for some middle-class parents, has the premium of augmenting the child's wider social understanding and better preparing them for the reality of life in a socially mixed, multi-ethnic and multicultural city.

In summary, the evidence shows how the social composition of a school can have an impact on school performance or added score by reinforcing the effects of ethnicity and social background on the performance of the individual pupil – for better or worse. This, we suggest, supports the recognition of a 'peer effect', by which we mean a situation where a pupil is surrounded by a large proportion of a particular group of pupils, perhaps high achievers or peers of the same ethnic or social group, which can encourage, or support, a pupil to do well. This also works in reverse, for example where a pupil is surrounded by poor-performing pupils, or among a large proportion of pupils of a different ethnicity, s/he might be discouraged or held back. However, it should be stressed that we cannot simplistically model this for all situations, and nor can we ignore the 'ecological fallacy' in which group behaviour is imputed to individual performance. On top of the composition effect, and any peer effect, may be included other school effects such as inspirational leadership, good quality teaching staff, small class sizes, good facilities and resources. It is clear that the social composition of a school can have both a positive and a negative cumulative effect over and above the characteristics of individual pupils. Finally, if a more meritocratic education system is to be achieved, government policy must seek not only to address resource imbalances between schools but also the whole process of pupil selection by schools. Generally speaking, we read this evidence to reinforce parental perceptions about the quality of their child's schooling and the various risk factors that affect school choice and allocation. We take up these issues in the following two chapters.

## Notes

[1] One of the attractions for black (Christian) families of living in inner London was that the 'faith option' enabled them to send their children to Church of England or Roman Catholic schools some distance from home as these schools were often located in the outer London boroughs of Redbridge and Havering. Our impression was that, unlike Asian respondents, black groups felt a greater affinity for inner London living but worried about the bad influence of its local 'rude boys' on their children, so faith schooling some way distant was a 'win-win' solution.

[2] A generation back, one way it was possible to identify a house in inner London that had been bought by people from the Caribbean was to note how the bricks had been painted red and the mortar picked out in white paint.

[3] Ironically, if her son had been a year younger, she would probably have been able to evade this particular dilemma by sending him to the new Mossbourne Academy which replaced Hackney Downs School, once demonised by the government as 'the worst school in Britain' despite its results being no worse than average and its alumni, who included Lord Maurice Peston, Michael Caine and Harold Pinter.

[4] The economist T. Schelling discusses this view of a 'tipping point' and we are grateful to Kathleen Noreisch for drawing our attention to this work (see Schelling, 1971, 1978).

[5] There is no evidence that we are aware of, however, which supports the view that streaming improves school performance.

[6] Not surprisingly, there are a wide range of views regarding the underlying causes of these variations in attainment by ethnic group, ranging from cultural explanations, through those that stress differences in class composition of different groups and areas, to a focus on institutional racism in schools (see Harpin, 2005). Thus, it has been argued by William Atkinson, the (black) headmaster of a school in West London, that the roots of the problem lie in a growing culture of failure among some ethnic groups, notably the black and white working class (Garner and Pyke, 2002). Similar views have been expressed by Trevor Phillips, chair of the Commission for Racial Equality (2005). On the other hand, Lee Jasper, who was Ken Livingstone's policy director for equalities and policing at the GLA, has argued that black boys do poorly at school because of the racism of white teachers. A flaw with this argument about white institutional racism is that some minority ethnic groups come out at the top of the attainment hierarchy.

[7] When we refer therefore to social background, we are imputing this from the Mosaic classification of the pupil's home background. We recognise that this is not based on individual level data such as might be used to classify households by social class; nevertheless we believe that, in the context of our discussion on how home background influences educational attainment either directly or through the peer group effect, this is an appropriate shorthand term to describe the kind of area in which the pupil lives. It should be noted that the Mosaic data provide a classificatory measure of the neighbourhood within which a pupil lives rather than the particular individual households that make it up, which is the traditional way in which social scientists have measured social class. Mosaic data on the home postcode of each pupil therefore provides an indirect measure of the pupil's social background, taking into account such variables as social class, tenure, age structure and income composition of the area, drawing on a range of private and commercial data sources. Used in this way, Mosaic classification does not provide a measure of a pupil's individual household affluence but a measure of the affluence of the neighbourhood in which the pupil lives. This must be borne in mind when interpreting our findings. It is worth noting that there are, on average, approximately 11 households for every postcode in London. Furthermore, as Webber and Butler (2007) have shown, the Mosaic classification is a powerful predictor of educational attainment at a national level. Furthermore, Butler (2007) has compared results from survey data to the Mosaic classifications and concluded that they provide a good descriptive match of areas of inner-city gentrification.

[8] The Mosaic classification system is based around postcode clusters that are grouped within a particular 'type' or group (see Table 5.6 overleaf). Each group is described in terms of the dominant social characteristics, a large part of the information being extracted from census data, and other data on income, labour market status, occupation, social class and a number of consumption indicators (such as holidays, preferences for alcoholic drinks, newspapers, food and cars). The means by which these classifications are derived are based on a set of principles set out by Harris et al (2005).

[9] It should be noted that Hackney sends a disproportionate number of its secondary school children outside the borough because of a shortage of schools within the borough.

[10] The distribution of pupils by borough is given as follows:

| Borough | No of schools | No of pupils | % |
|---|---|---|---|
| Newham | 15 | 3,052 | 18.9 |
| Redbridge | 19 | 2,874 | 17.8 |
| Tower Hamlets | 19 | 2,488 | 15.4 |
| Havering | 19 | 2,409 | 14.9 |
| Waltham Forest | 21 | 2,375 | 14.7 |
| Barking & Dagenham | 10 | 1,843 | 11.4 |
| Hackney | 12 | 1,140 | 7.0 |
| Group total | 115 | 16,181 | 100.0 |

[11] For every pupil this totals the number of points according to each GCSE (or GNVQ equivalent) grade. An A* grade is awarded the maximum eight points while the lowest grade, G, is awarded one point. The score is limited, or capped, to the pupil's eight best grades so the maximum score a pupil can achieve is 64. So, for example, a pupil's best eight exam results of one A* grade, two As, two Bs, and three Es will score a total of:

$$1(8) + 2(7) + 2(6) + 3(5) = 49$$

[12] In some cases the capped GCSE score of the pupil is unknown. In these unknown cases the pupil has been removed from the subsequent analysis. This leaves a total of 17,209 pupils whose capped GCSE scores are known.

[13] The detail of this together with more statistical tests that confirm the above analysis can be found in Hamnett et al (2007).

**Table 5.6: Mosaic classifications**

| Mosaic groups | Mosaic types | | | | | | |
|---|---|---|---|---|---|---|---|
| A: Symbols of success | Global connections | Cultural leadership | Corporate chieftains | Golden empty nesters | Provincial privilege | High technologists | Semi-rural seclusion |
| B: Happy families | Just moving in | Fledgling nurseries | Upscale new owners | Families making good | Middle rung families | Burdened optimists | In military quarters |
| C: Suburban comfort | Close to retirement | Conservative values | Small time business | Sprawling subtopia | Original suburbs | Asian enterprise | |
| D: Ties of community | Respectable rows | Affluent blue collar | Industrial grit | Coronation Street | Town centre refuge | South Asian industry | Settled minorities |
| E: Urban intelligence | Counter cultural mix | City adventurers | New urban colonists | Caring professionals | Dinky developments | Town gown transition | University challenge |
| F: Welfare borderline | Bedsit beneficiaries | Metro multiculture | Upper floor families | Tower block living | Dignified dependency | Sharing a staircase | |
| G: Municipal dependency | Families on benefits | Low horizons | Ex-industrial legacy | | | | |
| H: Blue-collar enterprise | Rustbelt resilience | Older right to buy | White van culture | New town materialism | | | |
| I: Subsisting elders | Old people in flats | Low income elderly | Cared for pensioners | | | | |
| J: Grey perspectives | Sepia memories | Childfree serenity | High spending elders | Bungalow retirement | Small town seniors | Tourist attendants | |
| K: Rural isolation | Summer playgrounds | Green Belt guardians | Parochial villagers | Pastoral symphony | Upland hill farmers | | |

[14] This excludes schools catering for pupils with special educational needs (SEN).

[15] See Webber and Butler (2007) and the associated database for all schools in England (http://education.guardian.co.uk/schools/specialreport/page/0,,1719371,00.html).

# SIX

# The limits to parental decision making under conditions of constrained choice

'You know what, I'm in denial. I don't know yet. If we are still here – and that's no guarantee, we could go abroad … we will consider moving out of London, partly for schools, but also just for the awfulness of having your applications rejected. It's so horrible that part of me wants to just go and move next to a school that would be local to us – a comprehensive. And, honestly, it's such a finger-burning experience, even at primary level, and I have seen a good friend who applied for four or five secondary schools get not even one of them, and the awfulness of what she went through.... I don't want to put my child through that, so I'd consider moving to avoid it. And I'm just not prepared to lie or cheat like other people.' (White British, female, Victoria Park)

## Introduction

In this chapter we develop the theme of 'choice' about schooling in East London, reflecting the importance placed on schooling and the difficulties faced in getting their children into a favoured school articulated by the survey respondents and interviewees. The parents were undoubtedly responding to increasing pressures (moral as well as strategic and instrumental) to maximise their children's opportunities by getting them into a good school – 'doing the best for one's child' is now a top imperative for being a 'good parent'. A good school, as we have already intimated, is often judged by its attainment, although most of our parents pursued a more sophisticated optimisation strategy in which they balanced a number of criteria – attainment, educational ethos, social mix, physical accessibility and, crucially, judgement about whether they were likely to succeed in getting their child into their favoured school. As we shall show in this chapter, parents often chose the school that they felt they had the best chance of getting their child into rather than their 'preferred' school. Their chief fear was failing in their preferred choice and then finding themselves allocated to a school they felt was completely unacceptable. The overarching theme of this chapter is a consideration of the 'choice agenda', which now dominates school selection in East London, in the light of the very real constraints on achieving that choice. Our conclusion, which is shared by many of the respondents, is that increasingly choice is constrained by where you live and that you may make a choice about which secondary school you would like your child to go to but, unless you live within its catchment area, you are not going to be successful in that choice. Indeed, for some of the most popular schools you may live in the catchment area but, unless you live sufficiently close to the school gate measured by a geographic information system (GIS) (150 metres in the case of one popular primary in one of our research areas), you may not get your choice. Places in popular schools are increasingly rationed by distance and many parents feel let down by the system of rationing, having thought they had chosen correctly when moving into the catchment area of a popular school only to find out when the results of the following September's secondary school allocation were announced in March that they had not moved close enough.

In the previous chapter we reviewed the educational achievement of the various East London boroughs and we referred to the differences between individual schools that vary even within educationally successful boroughs. In this chapter we look in more detail at how this has an impact on the way individual families are 'playing' this emerging educational market, which almost invariably means making decisions about where to live. This, in turn, has an effect on local housing markets, driving some who cannot afford particular roads in a catchment area to take a risk and hope that demand from those living nearest to the school will be sufficiently low this year for them 'to get lucky': often, as we shall see, they do not. Others, not understanding the allocation system and/or unable to afford housing in the catchment areas of the more popular schools, buy elsewhere in the borough and then discover that they are offered a place in what they understand to be an unpopular school. Ultimately, as we shall show, 'geography matters'; however, ''twas ever thus', as we indicate in the second section of this chapter. In the third section we consider how the relatively autarchic system of education in East London – with relatively few cross-boundary movements – is changing to one that is becoming yet more focused around individual distance to school catchment areas. In the fourth section we consider the extent to which the tripartite division within boroughs between very popular, average and 'unacceptable' schools is related to attainment or whether it can be explained by wider fears about educational failure and success. Finally, we turn to the issue of how our respondents interpret the educational map of school choice in East London and how they navigate their way through it by drawing on the 100 in-depth interviews we carried out across our study areas.

## Structuring of school choice in East London

The respondents had children at school across the seven boroughs of the study area and also scattered further across the rest of London and South East England (Figure 6.1 shows the location of every school attended by the respondents' children). At the time we undertook the survey work, in 2006, a sizeable minority of the approximately 300 parents surveyed were sending their children into schools well beyond their own boroughs of residence. This should be no surprise; some were fee-paying schools but in other instances parents were taking advantage of the provisions of the Education Act 1988 which formally recognises the right of parents to choose schools for their children outside the narrow area of where they live and indeed outside their LEA area. There is a long history of middle-class parents seeking out educational opportunities for their children well beyond their immediate area of residence.

The private sector, particularly boarding schools, has always operated on a regional or national basis, but so has the state sector, with grammar

**Figure 6.1: Location of schools attended by respondents' children**

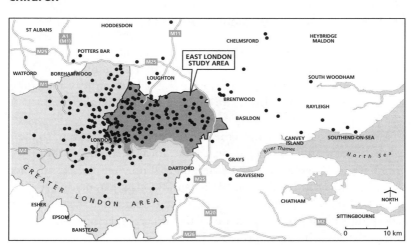

schools traditionally serving a sub-regional market. Following the move to comprehensive schools in the 1970s – a process led by the Inner London Education Authority (ILEA) – many middle-class parents sought 'out of borough' solutions, either in the selective grammar schools of some outer London boroughs or counties like Essex and Kent, which retained such schools with entry by competitive examination. This was largely in response to what they saw as inadequate local (comprehensive) secondary schooling. They also cast an envious eye – often with a measure of success – over some of the more successful non-selective comprehensive schools 'out of area'. Since we undertook our survey in 2005–06, the system has been 'tightened up' to remove the discretion for primarily middle-class 'user choosers' to seek out the best schools across a sub-region or even wider afield. This was often achieved by, for example, holding multiple offers in different LEAs and playing them off against one another, often with the tacit connivance of headteachers happy to see bright well-motivated children on their roll. This is much less likely now following two related moves by LEAs in London. First, in 2006 it was agreed that there would be a single application system in London for secondary schools that would allow every parent to make up to six choices – at a stroke this cut off the multiple application strategy. Second, schools were required to publish their entrance criteria, which reduced considerably the discretion previously enjoyed by headteachers to take pupils who they wanted but who were not, strictly speaking, eligible. Increasingly, as we show below, with limited exceptions for schools that select by faith or ability testing, this comes down to how far you live from the school gate, or how far your elder sibling did.

## Inter-borough secondary school movements in Greater London

There is a long-standing history of school choice in London with distinctive traditions between inner and outer London. From 1963 until its abolition in 1990, education in inner London (not including Newham and Haringey) was run on an integrated basis by the ILEA (see Figure 6.2).

While most children within the ILEA (and elsewhere) went to their local primary and continued on to the local secondary school for which it was a 'feeder', it was not difficult to send your child to another school within the ILEA area. Many middle-class parents in recently gentrified areas did precisely this where they did not like the secondary schooling – particularly after many of the old grammar schools became comprehensive. In outer London, LEAs were coterminous with the

**Figure 6.2: ILEA area**

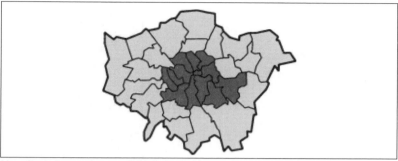

*Note:* Shaded central area = ILEA. Individual boroughs are identified in Figure 2.3 (p 38).

county boroughs and there were fewer inter-borough flows although quite a few children crossed the boundaries in and out of the adjacent ILEA area; in 2007 the great majority (78%) attended schools in their own borough in outer London and this reflects a long-standing tradition. There are, however, major inter-borough variations and geographical patterns which merit analysis.

The proportion of children attending private school in London is approximately 2.5 times the national average of 5% (although the numbers are disputed) and, as Figure 6.3 shows, this is not geographically evenly spread across London. The DCSF provides data for the number and percentage of pupils living in each borough who go to (state) secondary schools within their own borough, in other boroughs or outside London. The data analysed here are for 2007. It is important to note that there is a substantial variation in the size of the secondary school population resident in different London boroughs, ranging from suburban Croydon with almost 20,000 pupils at the top to Kensington & Chelsea with just under 3,000 at the bottom.[1] These figures reflect not just the demography (age, family status, etc) of the population but also the proportion attending private schools; this is particularly high in some of the inner and outer west London boroughs such as Kensington & Chelsea and Richmond. In general, the suburban outer London boroughs tend to have many more pupils than those in inner London. Four East London boroughs – Newham, Havering, Redbridge and Waltham Forest – were among the 12 largest in terms of pupil numbers in London (see Figure 6.4).

With the important exception of Hackney, all of our East London study area boroughs have a high proportion of their children being educated within the borough in which they live (see Figures 6.5 and 6.6). Hackney has such a high proportion of secondary age pupils (44%) going 'out of borough' for largely historical reasons.

**Figure 6.3: Number of pupils attending independent schools in named LEAs, 2007**

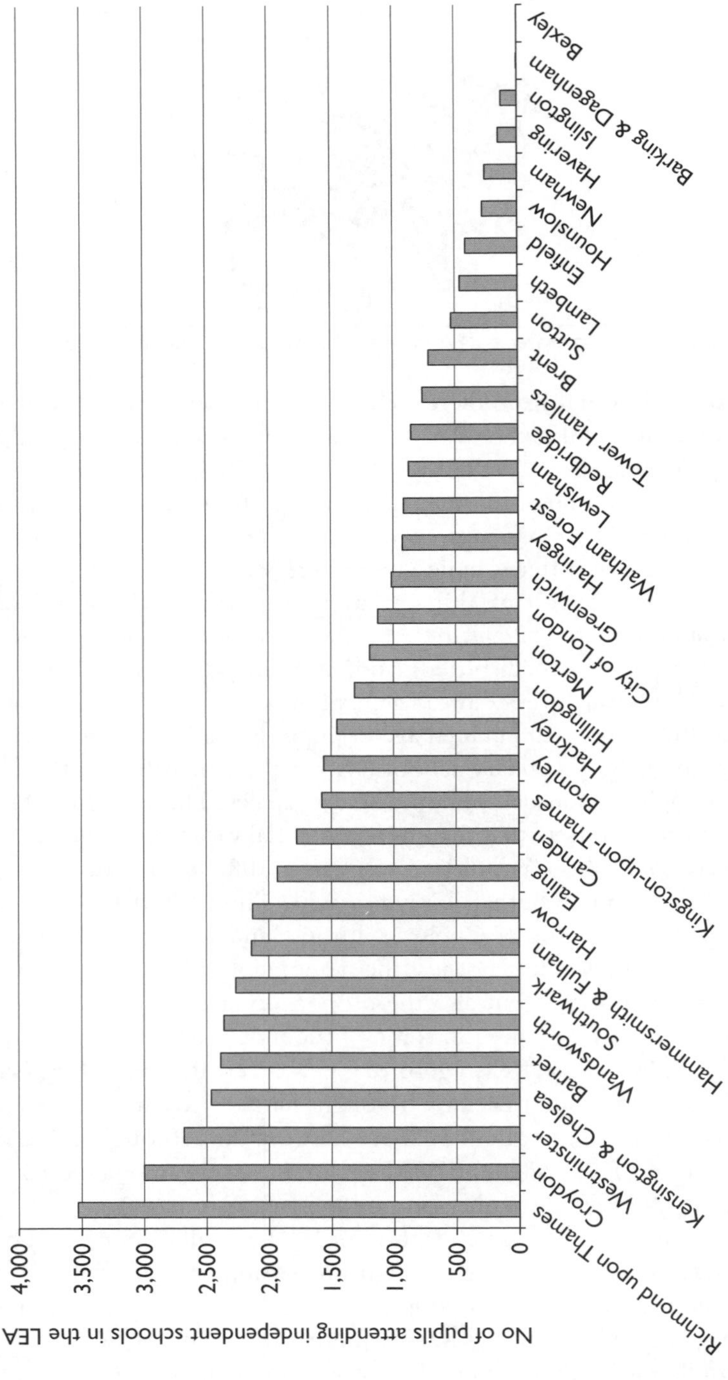

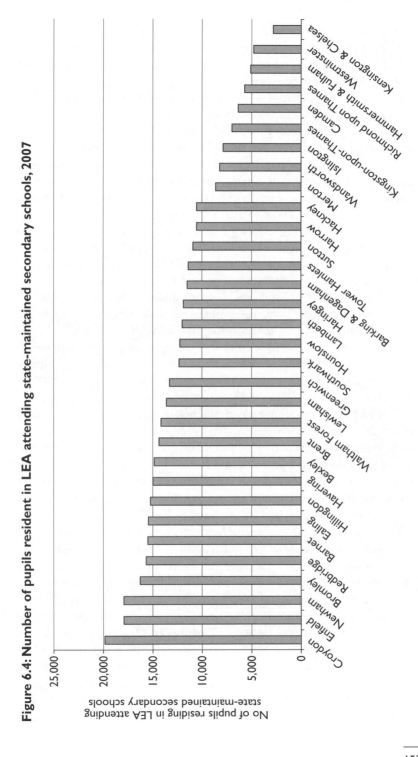

Figure 6.4: Number of pupils resident in LEA attending state-maintained secondary schools, 2007

Twenty-five years ago, when Hackney was still part of the ILEA, Paul Harrison (1985) noted its poor levels of educational achievement in which many parents – not just from the middle classes – sent their children to secondary schools elsewhere in London (Butler, 1997). This contributed to an under-provision of secondary school places in Hackney which, combined with an ongoing perception of poor attainment, has continued to fuel an 'out of borough' exodus at the secondary transition. Of the 10,400 pupils residing in Hackney only 6,800 pupils were at secondary schools maintained by the borough in 2007. The 3,600 shortfall is reflected in the fact that 4,580 Hackney pupils went to schools outside the borough as opposed to 980 pupils from outside Hackney who were at schools in Hackney. Most of the children not being educated in Hackney attend the numerous secondary schools on the Islington/Hackney borders while those in Islington go west to Camden and beyond or into the private sector (Butler and Robson, 2003; Hamnett and Butler, forthcoming).

In the two adjacent inner London boroughs of Tower Hamlets and Newham, 94% and 92% respectively of resident pupils attend schools in the borough. The explanation for such a high figure may lie in the very high (80%) minority ethnic secondary school pupil population in both boroughs that, the evidence suggests, tend to favour ethnically segregated schools (Burgess and Wilson, 2005; Johnston et al, 2005b). This has not been the case in Hackney, where the large Black African and Black Caribbean minority ethnic groups often go to school 'out of borough'. Elsewhere in our study area, the percentages being educated outside the borough are between 12% and 16%, which is at the low end of the scale even for outer London. Turning to the pattern of *inflows*, that is, the percentage of pupils attending schools within the LEA but resident elsewhere, the lowest figures in London are for Newham (6%) and Barking & Dagenham (10%), both in East London.

The outer East London boroughs form a system of tightly integrated educational autarchies with relatively small two-way cross-borough flows. As already noted, the most self-contained boroughs are Tower Hamlets and Newham, which had just 6% and 8% respectively of pupils going to schools 'out of borough'. The cross-borough flows are summarised in Figure 6.7, showing a locally specific network of cross-borough flows between Barking & Dagenham, Havering, Redbridge, Newham and Tower Hamlets, with small numbers of pupils going to Essex schools. Hackney is different, as we have seen, in that a significant proportion of its children go to school in Islington, Haringey and Camden. In this respect, it is more linked into a different North London network of schools compared to the other boroughs

Figure 6.5: Percentage of pupils attending secondary schools within and outside borough of residence, 2007

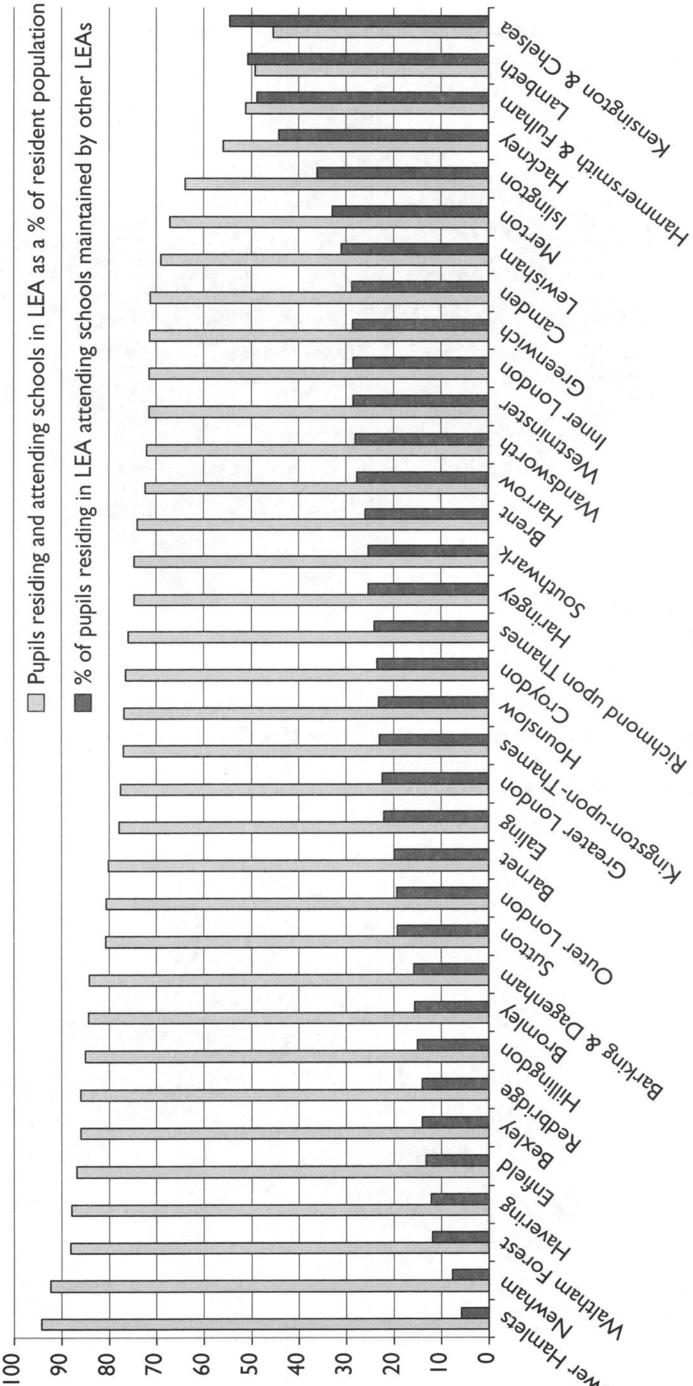

**Figure 6.6: Percentage of pupils attending school in LEA of residence, 2007**

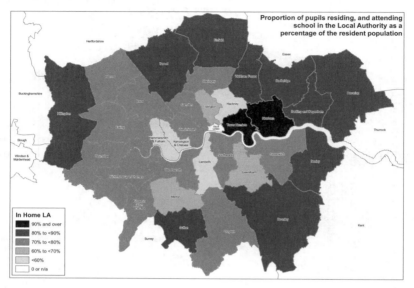

**Figure 6.7: Inter-borough flows for the East London study area**

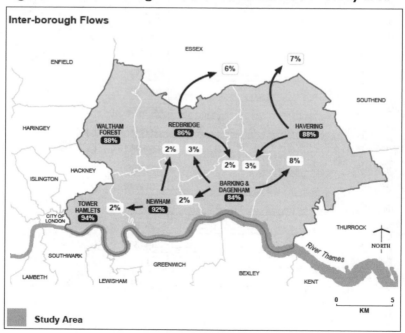

in our study area. For this reason we have excluded it from much of the subsequent analysis – the respondents in Victoria Park were also much more likely to be drawn from the higher managerial and professional middle classes and also to send their children to private schools, especially those located in the City of London.

The overall picture for our East London study area is therefore one where – with the important exception of Hackney – the majority of children are being educated in their borough of residence, and what movement there is occurs between adjacent boroughs including Essex, with its high-performing selective schools. This broadly confirms our findings about where the respondents' children were going to school. Figure 6.1 indicated that children were being widely educated across the sub-region but mainly within the East London boroughs. Given the deliberately more middle-class composition of our sample, in otherwise non-middle-class boroughs, we would expect most 'user choosers' to come from this group. As we indicate, this has been a fast-changing landscape and our survey involved parents who had children already in the system when it was easier, with some knowledge and planning, to circumvent the rules favouring local children – this would of course also mean that younger siblings had privileged access to such schools even with the more restrictive new regulations.

We demonstrate in the next section the existence of a local circuit of schooling in East London in which (a) the highest-attaining schools recruited from the most affluent areas and parent group, and (b) these schools were *both* local and sub-regional in recruitment. The poorest schools, on the other hand, had an almost entirely local clientele.

## Local circuits of schooling in East London: the best and the worst and how they recruit

We decided to look at East London as a whole (ignoring local authority boundaries) in order to investigate broad sub-regional patterns of school recruitment and attainment drawing on the PLASC/NPD data described in the previous chapter, leaving out Hackney for the reasons given above.

We selected the top six and bottom six schools in the study area according to their rank position on the average capped GCSE points score for those children with no SEN. These schools collectively account for 13% of the 96 schools attended by pupils in the database. Figures 6.8 and 6.9 show the home postcode sectors and associated Mosaic groups (see the discussion in the previous chapter and especially notes 7 and 8) for those children attending the best- and worst-performing

## Figure 6.8: Location of the six highest performing schools and Mosaic codes of their pupils

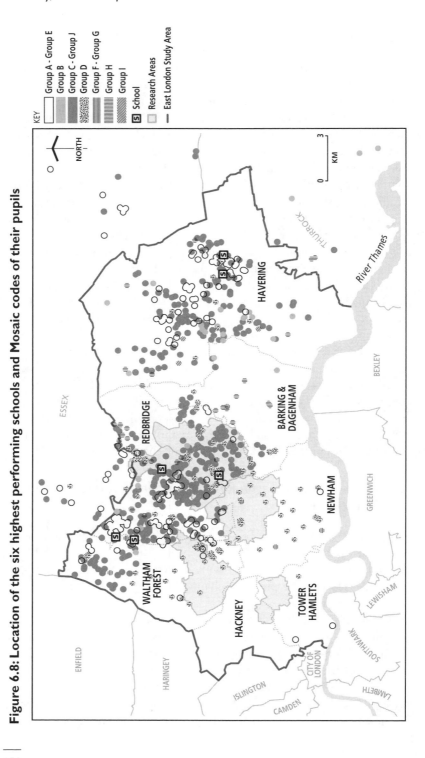

**Figure 6.9: Location of the six lowest performing schools and Mosaic codes of their pupils**

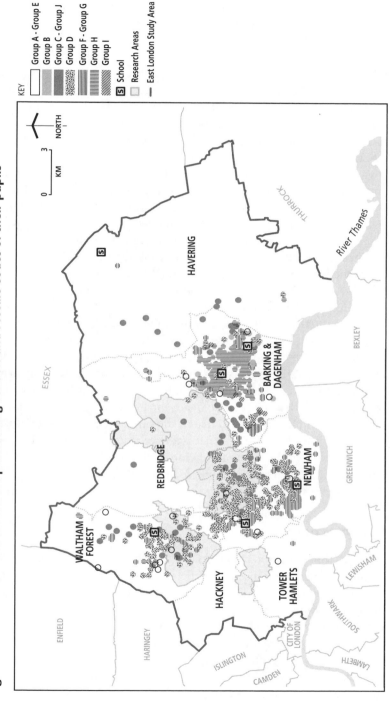

six schools respectively in our study area – what is significant is how they respectively draw from the most advantaged/disadvantaged Mosaic classifications. The findings indicate that there are both geographical and social background factors at play in the social composition of educational attainment and these are probably interrelated. For the six best schools, pupils are clearly recruited from an advantaged set of home postcodes while pupils attending the six worst schools come from the least advantaged Mosaic codes. The pattern in Figure 6.9 is one of highly localised catchment from the most deprived Mosaic codes. In Figure 6.8, the picture is more complex largely because three of the schools (two selective grammar schools in Redbridge, and Coopers' Company and Coborn School in Havering) have a wider geographic catchment than normal. They recruit almost exclusively from two kinds of area: those characterised by advantaged postcodes; and predominantly Asian postcodes in Newham which are within the catchment areas of both Redbridge selective schools. We undertook further modelling which confirmed this pattern of recruitment (Butler et al, 2007).

We argue, therefore, that there is a pattern to school choice in the East London study area (leaving out Hackney) in which either a small but undoubtedly middle-class minority live cheek-by-jowl with high-performing schools or conversely such schools recruit both locally and widely, unlike the poor-performing schools which have a mainly local catchment. Thus far, we have confined ourselves to comparing boroughs and to some extent individual schools and have shown in respect of both that the balance of advantage/disadvantage in terms of home background appears to match the one between high-achieving and low-achieving schools. What we have not yet considered is how this is working at the level of individual schools and for the individual families making choices about where their children should go to school. We therefore turn next to look at this aspect of the choice system.

## Making choices

One of the defining characteristics of New Labour's policy on secondary education has been the stress on expansion of parental choice (Tomlinson, 2003; Ball, 2008; Clarke et al, 2008), a policy being continued with vigour by its successor the Conservative–Liberal Democrat coalition government. This represents an attempt to introduce quasi-markets into education and health (Le Grand and Barlett, 1993) and build on the open enrolment system embodied in the Education Act 1988 enacted by the Conservative government at that time. The idea is that by empowering 'consumers' to make choices, providers will be forced to improve their offer, and the overall quality of provision will improve as consumers gravitate to good choices and away from poor ones and thereby act to raise standards by changes in demand. The view was clearly set out in the subsequent New Labour government's 2005 White Paper, *Higher standards, better schools for all* (DCSF, 2005). As former Prime Minister Tony Blair stated in the Foreword:

> Many other countries have successful experience with *school choice*. There is increasing international evidence that *school choice* systems can maintain high levels of equity and improve standards. International experiences with *school choice* suggest that fair funding which follows the pupil, good information and support for parents, fair admissions, and rapid intervention where schools are failing are all important in delivering *choice*. (DCSF, 2005, p xx; emphasis added)

Ruth Kelly, the then education minister, added in the Introduction that:

> ... we will ensure that ... the system as a whole is increasingly driven by parents and by choice and the White Paper itself states that: "This will be a system driven by parents doing their best for their children. If local parents demand better performance from their local school, improvement there should be. If local choice is inadequate and parents want more options, then a wider range of good quality alternatives must be made available. If parents want a school to expand to meet demand, it should be allowed to do so quickly and easily. If parents want a new provider to give their school clearer direction and ethos, that should be simple too. And if parents want to open a school, then it should be the job of the local authority to help them make this happen". (Section 1.35)

The maximisation of parental choice in education may at first seem an attractive idea, which contrasts well with the idea of standardised provision by the state where there is limited choice and parents get what they are given, irrespective of quality – exemplified in Alistair Campbell's crude characterisation of the 'bog standard comprehensive'.[2] The problem with the free market ideology of consumer sovereignty is that choice is unevenly distributed and asymmetric and is usually available only to those with the knowledge and the resources to make choices. At a wider level, the notion of choice fits well with the move away from a 'provider model' of welfare services to a more consumer-oriented 'purchaser' one in which (ironically, many may argue) resources are allocated to those that are most successful. In the case of education, there is a clear output measure of success in public examinations and it has thus perhaps become the 'pathfinder' for such experiments in quasi-market social policy. Choice, however, is also crucially dependent on the structure of available provision. In practice, given the constraints of the supply of school places and the inheritance of past performance and perceptions of achievement, 'school choice' seems to offer little except the 'choice' of the local school within a tightly defined catchment area. In this sense, the term 'choice' is a misnomer. It is perhaps more correct to use the term 'preferences', some of which will be met, others not, and those preferences will be largely contextualised by the operation of local housing markets.

Thus, parents are often 'choosing' within a system characterised by a shortage of 'good'[3] schools relative to demand, and the nature of the bureaucratic allocation process is such that many parents and children are denied their favoured choice(s) and are, instead, allocated a place at a school which they may find unattractive. The result for many parents and children is not the widening of school choice but an increase in the level of anger and frustration at being denied their choices. There is no easy solution to this problem, caused as it is by a, perceived or real, difference in performance between schools and a shortage of desirable schools. As the 2005 White Paper recognised:

> The affluent can buy choice either by moving house or by going outside the state system. We want to ensure that choice is more widely available to all and is not restricted to those who can pay for it.... There are two keys to success: First, we must ensure that there are more good places and more good schools.... Second, we must ensure that all parents have a decent chance of securing places for their children at the school they want. Some schools will inevitably be oversubscribed and will not be able to offer places to everyone who would like one. We must be sure that the process for deciding who secures a place is open and fair and that the less affluent are not disadvantaged.... (DCSF, 2005, Section 3.2)

The fundamental problem, however, remains the very uneven geographical distribution of social class, housing and school quality and their interrelation. Some areas have poorer performing schools than others, not because they are inherently 'failing' schools but because of the nature of their catchment area and their intake and the perceptions that are held of them. It is thus possible to argue that 'good' schools can, to an extent, be seen as 'positional goods' (Hirsch, 1976), that is, goods which are in short supply and whose value is, in part, a reflection of their desirability in comparison to alternatives. As Tony Blair noted in his Foreword to the White Paper:

> While parents can express a choice of school, there are not yet enough good schools in urban areas; such restrictions are greatest for poor and middle class families who cannot afford to opt for private education or to live next to a good school, if they are dissatisfied with what the state offers.

## Structuring of school 'choice', allocation and attainment in East London

Since 2006, all London boroughs have participated in a pan-London allocation process designed to prevent parents applying simultaneously for school places in more than one London borough and thereby being able to accept multiple places in different boroughs. All parents are now permitted six choices of schools (across boroughs if they so desire) in rank order, which are evaluated by the LEA in sequence using an equal preference scheme whereby all preferences for a school are considered at the same time and are measured against the oversubscription criteria if necessary, until they can be matched with a school for which they meet the entrance criteria and which has places. If, therefore, it is not possible to offer a place for the first choice school, the second choice is then considered and so on down the list. When allocating places for comprehensive schools (other schools manage their own admissions within the overall framework) most London boroughs have very similar criteria. Most give first priority to children with a statement of SEN, followed by children in care and children with special medical, psychiatric or social needs – in all such cases there needs to be a convincing statement by the parent or carer about why this is the most appropriate school for their child. The next criterion is usually siblings at the school and then, finally, distance, although some schools reserve a small percentage of places for children with particular aptitudes (for example in music) and these usually come before the application of the distance criterion. Table 6.1 provides a summary of the criteria for boroughs in East London.

**Table 6.1: Ranked secondary school admissions criteria, East London boroughs, 2008**

| Borough | First criterion | Second criterion | Third criterion | Fourth criterion | Fifth criterion |
|---------|-----------------|------------------|-----------------|------------------|-----------------|
| Barking & Dagenham | Children in care | Distance to school | n/a | n/a | n/a |
| Hackney | Children in care | Medical/social | Siblings | Distance | n/a |
| Havering | Children in care | Medical/social | Siblings | Distance | n/a |
| Newham | Statement of SEN | Children in care | Siblings | Distance | n/a |
| Redbridge | Statement of SEN | Children in care | Medical | Catchment + distance | Siblings |
| Tower Hamlets | Children in care | Medical/social | Distance (firstborn) | Siblings | Distance (not firstborn) |
| Waltham Forest | Statement of SEN | Children in care | Medical | Siblings | Distance |

*Source:* Borough guide on transfers to secondary school

Although the distance criterion comes third or fourth in the list, it is effectively the most important as the proportion of children with a statement of SEN, in care or with other special needs is generally very small – below 10% of the total and often far less. Siblings at the school is an important criterion but, as most siblings reside with their brothers and sisters, this is indirectly linked to distance as one child must already have a place at the school – although families may have moved in the meantime away from the immediate area of the school. Most LEAs and schools publish data on maximum distance to school for successful applicants for the previous round of admissions and the proportion of places offered on the distance criterion. This can vary from 90% to zero, but is generally over 60%. Where no places have been offered on the distance criterion, this is generally an indication of low school popularity and of a very low ratio of applications to places. There are usually one or two unpopular schools of this type in each borough, where distance is not a significant factor as surplus places are filled by the LEA making offers to parents who did not list the school as a preference or gave it a low preference. By contrast, for the most popular schools, that is, those with a high ratio of applicants to places, the distance criterion 'kicks in' quickly and, generally speaking, the higher the ratio of applications to places, the tighter the distance criterion which is applied using some form of GIS-based system from the designated school entrance to the front door of the pupil's home – observing all official pedestrian crossings!

Religious or faith schools are allowed to set their own criteria for admission and, in the majority of cases, the key criterion is that the parents are active members of the faith in question. This is most rigorously applied by Roman Catholic schools, which demand high rates of church attendance and participation, and priests will generally only sign the required letters of recommendation for those who have been active members of the congregation over a sustained period of time. Foundation schools and academies are also permitted to frame their own admissions policies, but the popular ones also tend to operate a distance criterion to ration places.

There is another issue that is also of considerable importance. Parents who place a very popular school at the top of their preference list but who do not live within the catchment area stand a high chance of being rejected. It is then possible for their child to be allocated to a far less popular school, possibly on the other side of the borough. It may thus be a more sensible option to list as their top preference a school of middling popularity reasonably close to where they live, as they may have a greater chance of gaining a place. There is thus a high element of risk involved in the school preference decision, in that parents who opt for a 'riskier' strategy stand a higher chance of failure and of getting an allocation to an unpopular school unless they live within the catchment area.

## Redbridge

Redbridge is interesting educationally, not least because of its diversity of provision; it contains two grammar schools (Ilford County for boys and Woodford County for girls), the only ones in East London, nine non-denominational comprehensive or foundation schools and four denominational comprehensive schools (three Catholic and one Jewish). It has a reputation for high quality education that is supported by its school results, which are the second best overall in London. Like all other London LEAs, Redbridge has a very clear admissions policy for its comprehensive and selective schools. Entry to the two grammar schools is by selective examination from those living in an extended catchment area which takes in parts of surrounding boroughs, and entry to the two foundation schools and four faith schools is determined by the governors. For the nine community comprehensive schools the list of admissions criteria that sequentially determine the allocation of places is shown in Table 6.1. The fourth criterion is: 'children living in a catchment area based on the distance from their home to the school's main gate, using the shortest reasonable walking route by public roads and footpaths'. With the exception of children with special needs, it is the catchment area and then, within that, distance, which is the determining criterion for admission in the majority of cases. Indeed, Redbridge is unique in East London in publishing a detailed, street-by-street, map of its school catchment areas (see Figure 6.10).

The number of applications to schools and, importantly, the ratio of applications to places, shows a marked variation between schools – from highs of 8.7 and 7.7 applications per place for the highly popular Seven Kings and Valentines comprehensive schools and around 7 for the two grammar schools to a low of 1.4 for Hainault Forest and the Jewish faith school King Solomon (see Tables 6.2 and 6.3) (www.redbridge.gov.uk). The fact that the grammar school figures are slightly lower than those for the two most popular comprehensives probably reflects the fact that there is a degree of self-selection in terms of pupil ability. The low figure for King Solomon may reflect the rapidly declining Jewish population of the catchment area. The second point shown by the data

**Figure 6.10: School catchment areas in Redbridge**

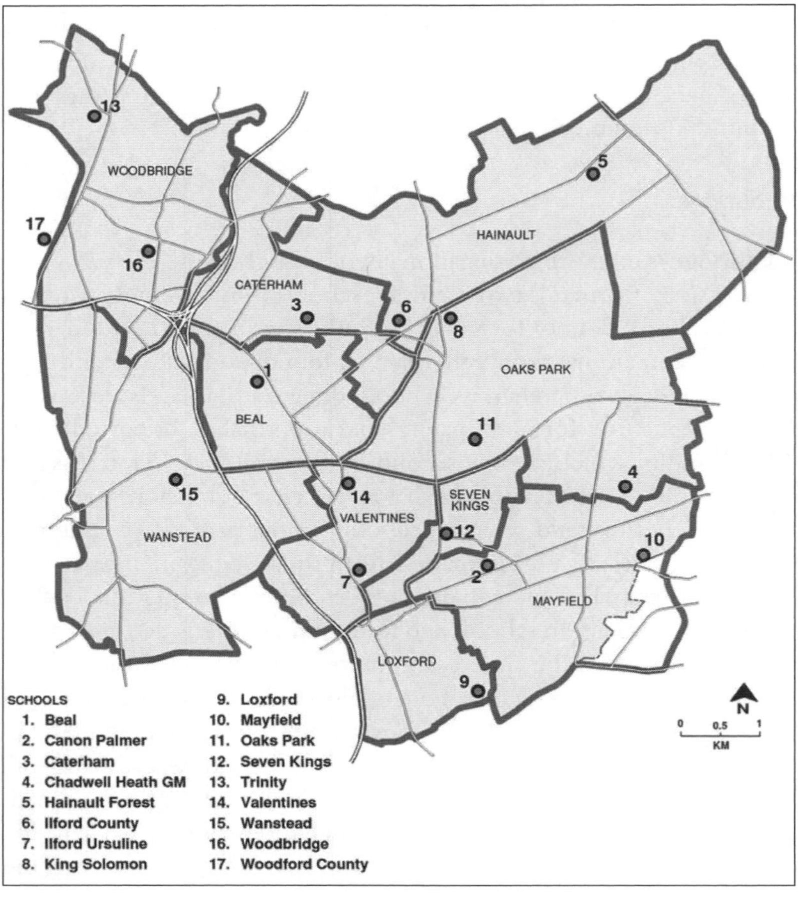

WOODBRIDGE
CATERHAM
HAINAULT
OAKS PARK
BEAL
SEVEN KINGS
VALENTINES
WANSTEAD
MAYFIELD
LOXFORD
SCHOOLS
1. Beal
2. Canon Palmer
3. Caterham
4. Chadwell Heath GM
5. Hainault Forest
6. Ilford County
7. Ilford Ursuline
8. King Solomon
9. Loxford
10. Mayfield
11. Oaks Park
12. Seven Kings
13. Trinity
14. Valentines
15. Wanstead
16. Woodbridge
17. Woodford County
N
0 0.5 1
KM

**Table 6.2: Redbridge: applications/places (A/P) ratio, 2008, and percentage of places allocated on catchment/distance criteria**

| | Places | Appli-cations | A/P ratio | Catch-ment | Dis-tance | % catch-ment | % distance |
|---|---|---|---|---|---|---|---|
| Seven Kings | 210 | 1,829 | 8.7 | 182 | 9 | 86.7 | 4.3 |
| Valentines | 180 | 1,378 | 7.7 | 138 | 2 | 76.7 | 1.1 |
| Ilford County | 120 | 855 | 7.1 | | | | |
| Woodford County | 120 | 817 | 6.8 | | | | |
| Beal | 240 | 1,399 | 5.8 | 201 | 16 | 83.8 | 6.7 |
| Ilford Ursuline (Catholic) | 120 | 544 | 4.5 | | | | |
| Chadwell Heath | 180 | 806 | 4.5 | | | | |
| Oaks Park | 240 | 891 | 3.7 | 204 | 13 | 85.0 | 5.4 |
| Canon Palmer (Catholic) | 192 | 685 | 3.6 | | | | |
| Wanstead | 240 | 841 | 3.5 | 171 | 44 | 71.3 | 18.3 |
| Caterham | 183 | 568 | 3.1 | 100 | 52 | 54.6 | 28.4 |
| Mayfield | 240 | 635 | 2.6 | | | | |
| Trinity Catholic (Catholic) | 240 | 612 | 2.6 | | | | |
| Woodbridge | 240 | 609 | 2.5 | 158 | 51 | 65.8 | 21.3 |
| Loxford | 240 | 565 | 2.4 | 234 | 1 | 97.5 | 0.4 |
| King Solomon (Jewish) | 150 | 233 | 1.6 | | | | |
| Hainault Forest | 171 | 244 | 1.4 | 96 | 65 | 56.1 | 38.0 |
| Total | 1,170 | 7,628 | 6.5 | 521 | 27 | 44.5 | 2.3 |

**Table 6.3: Redbridge: schools, applications and places**

| | Applications | Places | A/P ratio | GSCE 5+ A*–C |
|---|---|---|---|---|
| Seven Kings | 1,758 | 180 | 9.77 | 71 |
| Valentines | 1,233 | 180 | 6.85 | 51 |
| Ilford County (selective) | 796 | 120 | 6.63 | 98 |
| Woodford County (selective) | 763 | 120 | 6.36 | 99 |
| Beal | 1,296 | 240 | 5.40 | 68 |
| Oaks Park | 901 | 240 | 3.75 | 53 |
| Ilford Ursuline (Catholic) | 446 | 120 | 3.72 | 74 |
| Chadwell Heath | 600 | 180 | 3.33 | 76 |
| Canon Palmer (Catholic) | 636 | 192 | 3.31 | 65 |
| Wanstead | 743 | 240 | 3.10 | 56 |
| Caterham | 510 | 183 | 2.79 | 33 |
| Trinity (Catholic) | 609 | 240 | 2.54 | 78 |
| Mayfield | 581 | 240 | 2.42 | 39 |
| Woodbridge | 574 | 240 | 2.39 | 54 |
| Loxford School | 541 | 240 | 2.25 | 37 |
| King Solomon (Jewish) | 314 | 150 | 2.09 | 65 |
| Hainault Forest | 221 | 171 | 1.29 | 37 |

*Source:* Calculated from London Borough of Redbridge Education website

on the number of places offered to applicants within or outside the catchment area is that there is an inverse relationship between the ratio of applicants to places and the percentage of places offered to applicants from outside the catchment area. Seven Kings, Valentines and Beal, the most popular non-selective schools, only offered 4%, 7% and 1% of places respectively to non-sibling out-of-catchment applicants. At the other end, Hainault Forest offered 38% of places to out-of-catchment area applicants. Like many less popular schools in other boroughs, this school tends to function to fill places from unsuccessful applicants to other schools in the borough. The more popular the school, the less the chance of places being offered to applicants from outside the catchment and vice versa.[4] What is very clear in Redbridge is that if pupils do not live in the catchment area of one of the most popular schools, their chance of being offered a place at one of these schools is minimal and this is reflected in the appeal statistics for the borough (see Table 6.4). In 2006, the school with by far the highest number of appeals (70) was the most popular Seven Kings, of which only two were successful. The second highest number of appeals (23) was for Valentines, the second most popular school, of which just three were successful; other schools had fewer appeals (Table 6.4).

**Table 6.4: Redbridge: appeal statistics, 2007**

| School | Appeals heard | Appeals dismissed | Appeals allowed |
|---|---|---|---|
| Seven Kings | 70 | 68 | 2 |
| Valentines | 23 | 20 | 3 |
| Wanstead | 17 | 13 | 4 |
| Oaks Park | 14 | 12 | 2 |
| Beal | 13 | 12 | 1 |
| Loxford | 11 | 8 | 3 |
| Caterham | 6 | 5 | 1 |
| Woodford County | 3 | 2 | 1 |
| Ilford County | 1 | 1 | 0 |

*Source:* Calculated from data on the London Borough of Redbridge Education website

## Havering[5]

Havering has 11 co-educational community comprehensive schools (CCS), one single-sex CCS (Royal Liberty), two foundation schools (Abb Cross and Frances Bardsley) and four voluntary-aided schools, of which two, Campion (boys) and Sacred Heart (girls), are Catholic schools and St Edward's is a Christian school. Coopers' Company and Coborn is a historic prestige school established by the Coopers City Livery Company. The borough admissions policy prioritises children in care or with special medical or educational needs, then siblings, but the key criterion once more is distance to the school, measured on a straight-line basis. There are no catchment areas, although the distance criterion effectively delineates catchment areas in that the nearer to the school a child lives, the greater the chance of being offered a place.

As in Redbridge, and most local authorities, there is a hierarchy of preference for schools (see Table 6.5). At the top is Coopers' Company and Coborn, with six applications for every place. At the bottom are King's Wood and Bower Park, with 1.3 and 1.4 applications per place respectively. In general, the closer a pupil lives to Coopers' Company and Coborn or the other top popular schools, the greater the chance of gaining a place, although there is a historic exception to this in that Coopers' was located in Bow in the inner borough of Tower

**Table 6.5: Havering: the distribution of places by school preference, 2009**

|  | % of places by preference | | | |
| --- | --- | --- | --- | --- |
|  | 1st | 2nd | 3rd | Other |
| Coopers' Company and Coborn (voluntary-aided) | 97.8 | 1.1 | 1.1 | 0.0 |
| Sacred Heart (voluntary-aided) | 97.5 | 2.5 | 0.0 | 0.0 |
| Campion (voluntary-aided) | 95.3 | 4.0 | 0.7 | 0.0 |
| Abb Cross (foundation) | 94.0 | 4.8 | 0.6 | 0.6 |
| Chafford | 90.8 | 3.6 | 2.6 | 3.1 |
| Marshall's Park | 89.8 | 6.4 | 3.2 | 0.6 |
| Redden Court | 87.2 | 10.4 | 1.6 | 0.8 |
| Hall Mead | 84.9 | 13.5 | 1.6 | 0.0 |
| Brittons | 78.7 | 14.7 | 4.0 | 2.7 |
| St Edward's (voluntary-aided) | 76.2 | 12.4 | 8.1 | 3.3 |
| Frances Bardsley (foundation) | 75.0 | 14.1 | 5.5 | 5.5 |
| Albany | 66.7 | 21.0 | 7.5 | 4.8 |
| Royal Liberty | 64.2 | 17.5 | 2.5 | 15.8 |
| Bower Park | 63.3 | 13.3 | 1.7 | 21.7 |
| Emerson Park | 63.0 | 24.0 | 7.8 | 5.2 |
| Sanders Draper | 59.5 | 24.7 | 8.9 | 7.9 |
| Gaynes | 50.5 | 24.0 | 18.8 | 6.3 |
| King's Wood | 34.5 | 5.3 | 1.8 | 58.5 |

*Source:* Calculated from London Borough of Havering (2009) website

Hamlets until 1971 when it moved out to Havering in outer London. Interestingly, its admissions policy states that after children in care/ need, siblings and children of a Christian denomination or associated to any of the other major world faiths have been offered places, the criterion used to fill the remainder of the places or as a tie-breaker for religious criterion places is:

> 70% of the remaining places will be allocated to children on the basis of proximity to the school. The remaining 30% will be allocated from the School's historical catchments in Essex, East London and Thurrock. These 30% will be allocated to those from outside Havering who live close to the historic school site at Tredegar Square, Bow, or, for the other catchment areas, on the basis of proximity to the School in accordance with the traditional intake proportions from these areas.

Thus, while religious faith appears to be the key criterion, distance is still the major factor for allocation, even though this incorporates a historic element. Distance/proximity to the school is the most important basis for allocation of places for all the non-denominational and non-voluntary-aided schools. When the number of pupils allocated on the basis of distance and siblings (which, as argued above, is effectively a proxy for distance in that older siblings had to gain a place at the school) are added together, they dominate the allocation except for two less popular schools: Bower Park and King's Wood.

As elsewhere, the main educational losers in Havering are those children who live a long way from the popular schools. In the case of King's Wood and Bower Park the shortage of demand for places is topped up by local authority allocations from elsewhere in the borough. They are effectively functioning as a reserve pool, where pupils who do not get places at their first choices are offered places. In this respect, they have a similar role to Hainault Forest in Redbridge. The most popular schools – Coopers' Company and Coborn and the two Catholic schools, Sacred Heart and Campion – are filled with almost 100% of first preferences, while for the least popular school, King's Wood, only 35% of its intake had listed it as first preference and it received 58% of its pupils from those who did not rank it in the first three and who were allocated by the LEA. Bower Park and Royal Liberty also had 22% and 16% of places allocated by the LEA to pupils who had not placed it in their first three preferences.[6]

## Barking & Dagenham

In Barking & Dagenham, the criteria for allocation are very simple and in line with those of other boroughs: the first is children in care, and second is distance to school. As with other boroughs, Barking & Dagenham, as Table 6.6 shows, exhibits the classic structure of one or two unpopular schools with low applicants-to-places ratios (Eastbrook 1.6 and Dagenham Park 1.2). Borough allocational data show that the bottom three schools have a significant proportion of pupils allocated to them by the LEA who have not applied to the school: 51% in the case of Eastbrook and 67% in the case of Dagenham Park, whereas for the four most popular schools the figure is zero. Distance is the central rationing device for school allocation and this is particularly crucial for the most popular schools. By contrast, some children attending the less popular schools come from over 11 miles and up to 28 miles away, although these are the furthest distances for individual pupils and are not representative of all pupils.

**Table 6.6: Barking & Dagenham: schools, applications and places, 2008**

|  | Applications | Places | A/P ratio | % distance | % local authority allocation | Maximum distance (miles) |
|---|---|---|---|---|---|---|
| Barking Abbey | 1,294 | 270 | 4.8 | 88.1 | 0 | 2.07 |
| Robert Clack | 1,431 | 300 | 4.8 | 90.3 | 0 | 1.93 |
| Jo Richardson | 1,099 | 240 | 4.6 | 90.4 | 0 | 1.76 |
| Eastbury | 695 | 300 | 2.3 | 91.3 | 0 | 5.01 |
| Sydney Russell | 687 | 300 | 2.1 | 88.3 | 5 | 27.88 |
| Warren | 478 | 240 | 2 | 67.9 | 19.6 | 12.12 |
| Eastbrook | 474 | 300 | 1.6 | 43.7 | 51.3 | 22.26 |
| Dagenham Park | 263 | 220 | 1.2 | 27.2 | 66.8 | 11.54 |

*Source:* Barking & Dagenham school place allocation statistics, 2008

## Hackney

Hackney is one of London's most deprived boroughs, and education has traditionally been seen as a problem and, as we have seen, it is atypical of the rest of the East London study area – we have offered some explanations for this above. While much has improved since Paul Harrison (1985) labelled the educational system in the borough as 'schooling for failure', the borough still ranks low in attainment rates. Hackney has a major shortage of school places relative to the number of pupils resident in the borough that probably boosts popularity figures for the schools somewhat artificially. The borough guidance document on transfer to secondary school explicitly states that: 'Hackney schools have become increasingly popular with a limited number of places available resulting in more pupils applying than places available'. The borough, until recently, used a 'banding' system whereby all pupils were tested for verbal, quantitative and non-verbal skills and split into a number of bands in terms of ability. In order to try to ensure a mixed ability intake comprehensive schools have to take a specific proportion of children from each band and the allocation criteria operate within this. As with the other boroughs in East London, Hackney has some schools that are far more popular than others and these have a high ratio of applicants to places and a high level of appeals, most of which are unsuccessful. The three most popular schools are all new academies – Mossbourne, Bridge and Petchey – with applications-to-places ratios of between 6.1 and 7.6. This compares with ratios of 2.1 and 1.6 for Clapton Girls Technology College and Haggerston School for Girls. The latter only offered 59% of its 180 places and was subsequently filled with unsuccessful applicants for other schools. Not surprisingly, it has no distance barrier for pupils, who come from all over the borough. The academies, by contrast, have very tight distance bands for allocating places. Mossbourne Academy, the most popular of the three, has distance cut-offs of between 0.23 miles for accepting band D pupils and 0.47 miles for band A pupils. Bridge Academy has distance cut-offs for successful applicants ranging from 0.38 to 0.69 miles from the school, and Petchey Academy has distance cut-offs ranging from 0.52 to 0.74 miles for different bands. These are remarkably tight cut-offs and indicate their popularity.

The impact of the interaction of the differences in demand and the distance criteria on the distribution of successful and unsuccessful applicants is shown in Figures 6.11 and 6.12 for two academies. It is clear that if potential pupils do not live within a very short distance of each of the academies, their chances of admission are minimal. By contrast, successful applicants for Clapton Girls Technology College and Haggerston School for Girls, Cardinal Pole and Hackney Free School come from all over the borough and there appear to be virtually no unsuccessful applicants for these schools. These maps are very revealing about the geography of acceptance and rejection for schools places in Hackney and highlight very clearly the crucial role of place of residence and distance to school on acceptance.

**Figure 6.11: The spatial distribution of successful and unsuccessful applicants, Bridge Academy, 2008**

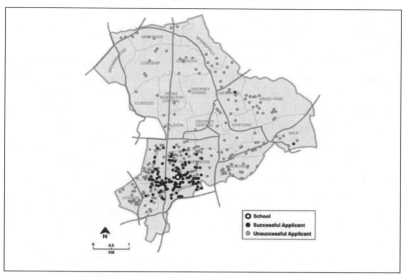

**Figure 6.12: The spatial distribution of successful and unsuccessful applicants, City Academy, 2008**

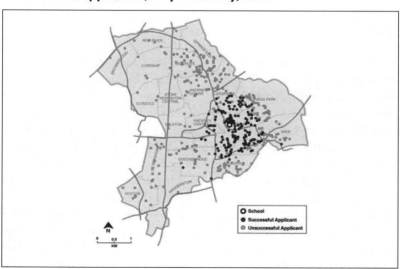

## Waltham Forest

In Waltham Forest the applications-to-places ratio is generally not widely dispersed, with most schools having a ratio of between 3.0 and 3.8, and just two schools with a ratio of over 4, and two of under 2. This, however, should not be taken as evidence of a better-managed system; it is notable, for example, that the three least popular schools made fewer offers than they had places and a number of places were allocated by the LEA on a 'top-up' basis for those who did not achieve their preferred schools. In the case of these schools, as in the other boroughs we have discussed, there was no distance cut-off. By contrast, four schools – Connaught School for Girls, Walthamstow Girls, Kelmscott and Highams Park – had a distance cut-off of around 0.7 miles compared to figures of two to four times that for other, but somewhat less popular, schools. The distance cut-off for the more popular schools in Waltham Forest has remained low and stable over time, varying from around 0.6 to 1 mile, whereas other schools can rise to 3+ miles, and sometimes have no distance cut-off, indicating that pupils were taken irrespective of the distance they lived from the school. Once again, distance to school is the key rationing mechanism for the more popular schools and indicates how the applications/places ratio and distance from school data need to be read in close conjunction with each other.

## Newham

Newham is one of the most ethnically mixed areas in London, with 60% of the borough population and 72% of secondary school children belonging to minority ethnic groups in 2001. As noted previously, Newham (and Tower Hamlets) educate around 94% of their children within the borough. As in the other boroughs analysed there is a hierarchy of schools in terms of the applications/places ratio, ranging from Stratford (5.8) at the top to Rokeby (1.8) and Eastlea (1.9) at the bottom. Two Catholic schools, St Angela's (80%) and St Bonaventure's (64%), have the highest percentage of GCSE grades A*-C in the borough. Excluding these two schools, which only cater to a small proportion of the borough pupil population, there is a broad relationship between popularity and distance, with Stratford and Forest Gate the most popular schools in terms of the applications/places ratio and having the shortest maximum distance to school (0.43 and 0.79 miles respectively). It is significant that the four least popular schools, Kingsford, The Royal Docks, Eastlea and Rokeby, had no distance cut-off for places, indicating that they take children from all over the borough (see Table 6.7). Thus the general principle of the most popular schools having the tightest catchments holds even in such an ethnically mixed borough.

**Table 6.7: Newham: schools, applications and places, 2008**

| | Applications | Places | A/P ratio | Distance (miles) |
|---|---|---|---|---|
| Stratford | 1,035 | 180 | 5.75 | 0.434 |
| Forest Gate | 851 | 210 | 4.05 | 0.789 |
| St Angela's (voluntary-aided) | 635 | 180 | 3.53 | n/a |
| Brampton | 1,057 | 300 | 3.52 | 2.769 |
| Lister | 951 | 270 | 3.52 | 1.874 |
| Sarah Bonnell | 818 | 240 | 3.41 | 1.195 |
| Langdon | 1,217 | 360 | 3.38 | 1.567 |
| Plashet | 887 | 270 | 3.29 | 0.894 |
| St Bonaventure's (voluntary-aided) | 586 | 180 | 3.26 | n/a |
| Cumberland | 969 | 300 | 3.23 | 1.688 |
| Little Ilford | 782 | 270 | 2.90 | 0.888 |
| Kingsford | 752 | 300 | 2.51 | n/a |
| The Royal Docks | 556 | 240 | 2.32 | n/a |
| Eastlea | 468 | 240 | 1.95 | n/a |
| Rokeby | 330 | 180 | 1.83 | n/a |
| Total | 11,894 | 3720 | 3.20 | |

## Tower Hamlets

Tower Hamlets is the only LEA in the study area still to operate a banding system for all its community schools, whereby children are tested and then allocated to one of four bands in terms of ability. The borough then attempts to ensure that a quarter of the places in each school are allocated to each of the bands, with the allocational criteria coming into play when schools are oversubscribed. The criteria differ slightly from those in other boroughs in that, after children in care and those with special medical or social grounds, they take: 'children living nearest to the school who are the first born of their sex in the case of a single-sex school or the eldest child in the case of a mixed school. The number of children admitted under this category will then be selected up to 25% of the children in each band'. This is followed by siblings, and then distance to school comes into play.

What this rather convoluted formulation means is that places are offered to the first-born children using the banding rule on the basis of distance, then siblings are offered places, and then distance comes into play again. In addition to 11 community schools, Tower Hamlets has two voluntary-aided Christian foundation schools (Sir John Cass and Raines Foundation) and two voluntary-aided single-sex Catholic schools (both called Bishop Challoners), all of which operate their own admissions criteria. Sir John Cass has 180 places, 36 of which are 'foundation' places offered to families who are 'faithful and regular worshippers in a recognised Christian Church'. The remaining applicants are allocated on the usual care, sibling and distance grounds, with a preference to children living in specific parishes. All places are subject to the Tower Hamlets banding system. Given the very high number of Bangladeshi pupils in Tower Hamlets (58% of the total), what this means, in effect, is that these four schools mainly take white and black pupils from a Christian background. Sir John Cass is the clear favourite in terms of the applications-to-places ratio, with a number of schools having a ratio of less than 2, which is low compared to elsewhere in East London. This may reflect the very specific ethnic composition of the borough.

## School popularity, allocation and attainment: a 'chooser: loser' model?

The conclusions of this analysis are quite simple. All the boroughs in the East London study area have a clear hierarchy of schools in terms of popularity. Given that the number of applicants at the most popular schools exceeds places by a considerable margin, they all operate what is effectively a system of rationing places in terms of distance to school. We discount the sibling rule as it is a function of the spatial relationship between home and school, albeit at one step removed. The findings show that it really does matter where pupils live in terms of effective school choice and this has become more acute in recent years.

Across East London, the most popular schools tend to have higher rates of GCSE success, and vice versa, although the relationship is far from perfect. A correlation analysis of the applications/places ratio with the percentage of pupils gaining 5+ GSCEs grades A$\star$–C showed that borough-level correlations range from a low of 0.15 in Newham (a borough where there are few high performing schools) to 0.875 in Barking & Dagenham (with even lower performing schools), with most correlations in the area of 0.4–0.5. When faith schools, which tend to get higher GSCE pass rates but which have a lower applications/places ratio because of their faith-specific criteria, are excluded, the correlations increase slightly, to 0.6–0.7.[7] Given that the correlations are far from perfect, school popularity clearly involves other factors apart from school attainment, important though this undoubtedly is. As noted above, faith schools with high GSCE pass rates[8] tend to have lower applications/places ratios as only children of the specific faith are permitted to apply. In general, however, the top two to three schools in each borough in terms of GSCE pass rates tend to be the most popular, and the bottom one or two schools the least popular. Given that parents do not simply apply for places at schools on the basis of their GSCE pass rates, but take into account a variety of other factors, not least their location and convenience, as well as their general reputation and ethos, it can be argued that it is parental perceptions of the school that matter in terms of applications and popularity, rather than simply GSCE results. In such narratives, while there are successful and poorly performing schools, the large number in the middle are also important. At the top and bottom ends of the attainment spectrum there seems to be a stronger relationship with popularity that reinforces parental perceptions and therefore reputation. The more strongly motivated parents may consistently list top–performing schools as one of their top preferences, while avoiding schools with a poor reputation. To this extent, parental perceptions and preferences will reinforce reputations, helping to strengthen the reputations of the popular schools and weaken those of the less popular schools simply in terms of the differential number of applications. This is a particular problem for less popular schools which, because of their low applications-to-places ratio and the fact that they are allocated pupils by the LEA who have failed to get into their preferred schools, can serve to reinforce their negative images.

In this sense, it might be argued that the 'choice agenda' is, somewhat ironically, making schools with acceptable results less popular or at least not doing as well as they might because they are not highly favoured. It is entirely possible therefore that, in such a situation, this will create a perception that there is a reciprocal relationship between popularity and GSCE pass rates in which the success of the most popular schools is reinforced by strong reputation and competition for places, and the lack of success of the least popular schools is reinforced by a poor reputation and low numbers of applicants. It may be that the poor performance of some schools is partly a result of the league table system that encourages more motivated (and usually socially and economically advantaged) parents to apply for schools with higher pass rates. However, the social composition of catchment areas is also of considerable importance, influencing, as it does, the overall ability level of pupils and school examination results. To argue, as the New

Labour government did, that so-called 'failing' schools are primarily the result of management failures is to ignore the well-documented role of social variations in the catchment area and school intake on results (Hamnett et al, 2007; Gordon and Monistorious, 2007).

What this demonstrates is that in educational terms it increasingly does matter where you live. Those fortunate enough to live in proximity to the most popular schools are more or less guaranteed a place. Those who do not have to hope they can secure a place at one of their other choices, which could be located almost anywhere in their borough; these parents will often feel that they have therefore been allocated to, at best, second-best schools. In many cases, parents may have to choose the least bad school for their children. This, of course, is at odds with the comprehensive model of equality of educational opportunity.

The implications of this are three-fold in an era of increasing political stress on parental choice, league tables and attainment. First, it is highly likely that demand for the popular schools will intensify as some parents move into their catchment areas but, where such areas exist, they may still fail to achieve their choice on the distance to school criterion. Second, the marginalised status of the less popular schools is intensified, as they effectively become stigmatised and parents do not put them on their list of preferences – even though they may perform reasonably well and children attain their potential. Third, given that only a proportion of parents and children will be successful in their preference for a popular school, the operation of the whole system, it could be argued, will increase parental discontent with the realities of choice, although it is difficult to see any easy alternatives given the shortage of popular schools. The choice model inflates the notion of a popular school and so helps create unpopular schools. When any allocational system rests on a shortage of the most popular and desired items, and an oversupply of less attractive items, dissatisfaction is guaranteed. What can be done is to avoid designing public policy in such a way as to create such schools. What most parents want is a school which will teach their child to their full potential and in which a good educational ethos is sustained by a strong social ethos. What is very noticeable is that parents do not want to choose; indeed, many aspire to live in Redbridge precisely because they are attracted to the idea of a 'good' comprehensive school in a catchment area where they know their child will get a place. What they find perplexing and unacceptable is that they are forced to make choices and then, having so done, can find their choices denied. They then have to engage in damage limitation in order to avoid what they see, often with some justification, as the worst-performing schools, and are left with a sense that they have had to settle for second best.

They are also likely to become victims of people playing the system, as happens with the Seven Kings School in Redbridge, or else get forced into playing that game themselves. As one respondent noted:

> 'Seven Kings is quite a big school but it has a very small catchment so you have to be in specific roadsets, it's not like borough wide or anything, it's tight, and you do find there are loads of people who are moving in, buying flats etc, specifically to get their kids into the school. Obviously the prices of the houses rise and it has a knock-on effect.' (Pakistani, male, Central Redbridge)

It is clear then that parents living in different boroughs face different opportunities and challenges in relation to choices about schooling; they are also able to draw on different resources in confronting these dilemmas. As we saw in the discussion of suburbanisation and education towards the end of Chapter Three, there was a widespread belief throughout the study area that the quality of schools in Redbridge and Havering was superior to those elsewhere in East London – a belief, as we have seen, which is backed up by published attainment data. Respondents, in effect, confirmed that at some level there existed a single sub-regional education market in East London; you might have to move house to access it and it might contain interlocking 'circuits of schooling' but, with the important exception of Hackney, and possibly Tower Hamlets, there was an East London schooling hierarchy with Redbridge sitting at its apex. There was also an acute awareness by parents of the role played by geography, as we have already seen witnessed in respondent narratives and official data, that – crudely – the further you moved eastwards from the centre of London the better the educational provision:

> 'I think this area is a lot worse ... school wise. I think that further out – in Woodford where everyone wants to move – they certainly have better schools there. So it's kind of, the further out you go in certain areas, the schools are better. Definitely.' (White British, female, Victoria Park)

## Limits of choice and the role of resources

*First* and most obviously, respondents identified a general set of constraints in terms of the overall range of schools which were available.

> 'There's plenty of choice if you are prepared to pay for it, yes. If you either can't or won't pay for it then there isn't much choice at all, I think.' (Indian, male, Victoria Park)

Hackney and Tower Hamlets were perceived as having very poor secondary schools and only a small number of primary schools that were seen as acceptable to most respondents.

> '... the state provision in Hackney doesn't remotely equate to the standards that I myself enjoyed that I wish my children to have. And so the answer is that it's never even really been on the map of possibilities – sending my children to state schools in Hackney.' (White British, male, Victoria Park)

Even in Redbridge, as we have seen, there was a north–south divide in the borough, with some of the schools serving the council housing estates in the north being seen as 'sink schools'.

Parental assessments of local schooling thus immediately involved them in questions of 'choice' between a faith, selective, private or local comprehensive school. These choices are clearly constrained by the resources parents are able to deploy and, as we shall see, the 'rules of engagement' in how they went about making their choice. With the exception of the mainstream schools, all the others were not uniformly available and – if they were – involved risk: choosing a selective school and failing the selection process could prove to be a major error as you then, in effect, went to the back of the queue.

The *second* factor in determining choice was the resources that respondents were able to deploy. Private schools required a large and secure set of financial resources and faith schools generally required a considerable investment over a long period of time in the local church. If parents have not 'got faith', or do not want their children to go to a faith school and do not have the financial resources or do not want to send their children to a private school, their options are largely determined by geography:

> 'Secondary schools ... there's supposed to be freedom of choice – the choice we have is religion or not religion. If you haven't got religion, you've got further choices. You've got, can they pass the 11 plus or can't they, or can you pay. So if you haven't got religion, if you haven't passed your 11 plus and if you can't pay for private education, you're

stuck with the local comprehensive, and there isn't a choice.' (White British, female, Barkingside)

'If you haven't got the religion, you haven't got the money – you haven't got the choice. So you would just go to the local school.' (Turkish, female, Leyton)

The financial resources required for private education are so great that they are restricted to those with high incomes (or family resources); in terms of the respondents, these were largely confined to those living near to Victoria Park. Such middle-class respondents had come to terms with the fact that, if they wished to continue living in this area of inner London (and indeed much of inner London), they would have to educate their children privately. In fact, several would do so out of preference wherever they were living – this emerges from the following exchange with a Victoria Park respondent. He would consider Lauriston Primary School but also conjectures that the difficulty of getting into the private secondary sector ("not just getting

**6.1: The old Lauriston Primary School in Victoria Park, just across the road from the new school**

*Note:* The building has been converted into apartments, many of which are rented specifically for the purpose of gaining entry to the school and thus displacing many already living in the area from this favoured school.

money out of your wallet"), means that you are probably constrained into private education from an earlier stage:

['Were state schools ever considered?']

'Never considered, no.'

['Why not?']

'Because they wouldn't remotely [stress] be able to provide the level of educational input and attainment that I as a typical middle-class parent would aspire my children to have.' (White British, male, Victoria Park)

For the most part, respondents simply did not have the resources or social capital to consider sending their children to private schools. For many in this situation, faith schools rapidly became the favoured option:

'I think people are gravitating towards faith schools because you haven't got much choice between the bad and the bad!' (White British, female, Leyton)

Faith schools were seen as desirable because of the personal values and higher standards that they were seen to offer. However, getting a child into a faith school is not an easy matter, particularly for Catholic schools where parents were required to demonstrate a very high level of commitment in terms of church attendance and religious observance; even those who were practising Catholics could find the entry requirements extremely tough. As one parent perceptively commented:

'It's a difficult one because it's quite hard to fiddle being Catholic, you either are or you aren't, whereas with C of E [Church of England] you can just keep turning up and get your kids christened automatically and that's OK. So if you didn't happen to be Catholic, you could just turn up regularly at the C of E church and hopefully there aren't enough Catholics [applying] to bump you out. There are a series of admission criteria and it starts with: Catholic; going to one of the two local churches – there are two parishes linked to the school, so that would be the top criteria. So you fill two classes … then you go down a series of criteria, Catholic go to local church, Catholic but do not go to local

church, baptised Catholic ... and, you just keep going down
the list.' (White British, female, Victoria Park)

There were, however, some interesting differences between areas.
In Victoria Park, the 'faith choosers' were often parents reluctantly
reverting to their fall-back positions, who had failed to get their children
into Lauriston and didn't like the alternative (Orchard), whose intake
was described by the following respondent as the 'mirror image' of
Lauriston:

> 'Although [husband] and I are Catholic and were christened
> at birth we are not, you know, practising, but we have a
> strong connection with the church [reason deleted], so
> in an odd way I never expected to have that connection
> with the church again, but my goodness, if you've got
> that situation you are thrown back into it.... I applied for
> Lauriston and didn't get a place and got a place at my third
> choice which was Orchard, and I appealed against that and
> lost which I knew I would.... So, I then literally rang Saint
> Elizabeth's and said have you got any places and that this is
> my connection with the church. I didn't lie in the slightest.
> I never misrepresented anything, because to be honest if you
> have to provide a baptism certificate I couldn't because she
> wasn't baptised, but I think they had a place that somebody
> hadn't taken so I was really lucky. She was really lucky. So she
> went to that school, and that school has been interesting....'
> (White British, female, Victoria Park)

While in Victoria Park most of the focus on faith schools was on
primary schools by a white professional intelligentsia unable or
unwilling to consider private education or insufficiently mixed state
schools, elsewhere it marked a way of avoiding the 'road to failure' for
Black Caribbean and Black African Christian parents who felt their
children were disadvantaged and wanted to try to avoid exposing them
to what they saw as a dominance of 'street culture' in the mainstream
comprehensives.

One Black Caribbean female respondent moved to the borders of
Newham, Waltham Forest and Redbridge to maximise, as she hoped,
her chances of getting her daughter into one of the better schools but
failed in both of her first two choices (in Newham and Waltham Forest)
and ended up sending her to a Roman Catholic school in Havering.
This created quite a difficult situation for a black girl brought up in a

highly multi-ethnic area who found herself being schooled in one of London's few predominantly white boroughs. This respondent wanted a school which would 'push' her daughter, but also faced the problem that she wasn't really a Catholic so managed to squeeze her in under the rule that such schools needed to take a quota of non-faith pupils:

> '... they *seemed* to be a bit more disciplined. And they seemed to be a bit more ... you know they seemed to push them a bit more. Not all faith schools were like that but the ones I looked at seemed to be. We did look at a school – Saint Angela's [Ursuline Convent school – all-girls in Newham] – but you had to be Catholic, otherwise you couldn't go. So ... I think actually filled the form in for that one but it just wasn't worth it, I mean they had six or seven girls for every place.'

She articulated a real tension about wanting to keep her daughter away from a peer group and a series of schools in Newham in which she felt she would not 'be stretched' and, on the other hand, fretted about what she was doing taking a young black woman out of her local environment and exposing her to the 'whitelands' of working-class outer East London. This dilemma was one articulated by a number of parents although, unlike this respondent, many were well embedded in the life of their church.

Faith and cash were therefore the main resources deployed by parents to maintain their relative social privilege, to avoid them becoming submerged in an ethnic or class 'other' or to articulate their desire for their children to be part of an upward social trajectory. In the case of most non-white parents, this was seen as part of a generational struggle to improve themselves in which education played a crucial role.

## Catchment areas and balancing of supply and demand

The *third* element to the choice/constraint relation was the 'taken for granted' assumption that most 'choices' were unavailable for the simple reason that access to any school to which a parent might want to send their child was determined by where they lived. The nearer the school, the more likely you were to get in.

> ['Do you feel you have plenty of choice of school, that you are able to choose the school which is most appropriate for your daughter?']

'Not really. I'm quite happy with the school that she goes to because I think, all-in-all, schools in Redbridge are pretty good anyway but you do still get the feeling that if I wanted her to go to a school that was further away, and she didn't have any siblings in that school then there wasn't a hope in hell of her getting in there. So it was pretty pointless putting it down really as a choice.' (White British, female, Barkingside)

Nevertheless, as some respondents understood, catchment areas were not always what they seemed and there was a crucial difference between what you could apply for and what you might actually get. This third set of constraints therefore revolves around the role of catchment areas as a geographical rationing mechanism to balance the supply and demand for school places, particularly at 'good' schools. There was a general view that most parents had very little real choice and that the reality was that unless they were lucky in their first choice or managed to get a place at a faith school most children were allocated to their nearest school or a school with places left, and there was no guarantee that living in the catchment area would offer a place unless they were very near to the school gates.

'I don't think there is any choice, if they're in the catchment for the school, then for 90% of parents that's where their child's gotta go. I know parents try, occasionally they do, they plump for a school that's not, that they really don't stand a chance of getting into, but it's either one or the other.' (White British, female, Barkingside)

'I think the idea of "selection" of schools is a bit of a myth really because certainly in Newham you are linked to a school because of where you live. The choice the government promotes is really a bit of a myth and actually it's so difficult to get your children into a school other than your local one. It just depends, you know, how popular that school is.' (White British, male, Newham)

'I think you just get stuck with the catchment … there was no other choice. I mean you get the form from the borough and it says, right you've got a place at your catchment – that's it. The only choice you've got. OK you've got the grammar schools here but you've got to pay for extra tuition to get them in there, or you've got the faith schools. I only think I would have done differently if we'd had the money and paid private.' (White British, female, Barkingside)

The next two respondents talk explicitly about moving into a catchment area, but as others have noted, this is an elastic concept that changes year by year depending on demand, and you could get it disastrously wrong. In the case of the popular Seven Kings School or Lauriston Primary in Victoria Park, whether you get a place can depend on how far your front door is from the designated entrance at the school. It can come to literally a matter of metres and the consequences of failure can be traumatic and dramatic for parents and their children.

> 'You are not really given much choice it's all to do with catchment areas and the only school offered was Loxford, they give you the chance to list six schools but really you know that Loxford is realistically the only one they will offer you and I didn't really want my eldest to go there, so the only other option was Park School Girls, it's a [private] girls school and it's a small school, there are 13 children in each class and I was happy with it.' (Pakistani, female, Central Redbridge)

The rules of the game are increasingly clear: not giving a first choice for which you have a realistic chance of success can be highly problematic. If a parent fails to get their first choice, there is a danger that they may not get any of the schools on their list of preferences or at best one of the ones towards the bottom.[9] The dilemma is then whether a parent puts down a highly rated school as first choice where there is only a slim chance of getting in, or whether they opt for a less good school further down the hierarchy which they may stand a better chance of getting in. It requires a calculated assessment of risk in which an overambitious choice can result in an allocation to a much lower ranked school. One parent who felt that the choice system had effectively denied her son the chance of applying for a selective grammar school put it as follows:

> 'The school managed to take away some of the choice – when ... not that I would put my children through it, but the option of having them take the 11 plus was taken away from me. The school, the headteacher there had said that if you want your child to come to my school, then they cannot sit their 11 plus because if they sit the 11 plus, that

means that your choice is for your child to go to a grammar school. And if [name suppressed] is not your first choice, then we don't want your child to be in it. And I think that was quite.... I don't know, I mean I kind of agree with him, but for the children who maybe had a chance of passing their 11 plus, it took away that choice for them.' (White British, female, Barkingside)

One response of parents faced by limited choice and the constraints of catchment area is to play the system. Gaming works both ways: we came across a number of instances of parents playing the system to get their child into the school of choice. Some parents are prepared to do this while others are highly critical of what they perceive as selfish and anti-social behaviour:

'People do what they can to get the best education that they can for their child. Now the ways and means that you do it, which might mean paying for it, which might mean lying and saying that you've bought a place in the catchment area of a good school, saying that the child lives with grandma when in fact they don't! [laughs] But people use whatever means they can to get their child into the best school.' (White British, female, Redbridge)

One case was particularly notable in respect of the lengths to which the parents were prepared to go to get their child into their preferred school, which involved considerable deployment of resources of time, money and ingenuity. When asked how he had got his son into Seven Kings, one Asian parent replied:

'We did actually [laughing] have to rent a flat out for a whole year, but it was cheaper in the long run than actually sending him to a private school for the long term. It's making a sacrifice – a whole year of rent is like paying a second mortgage but we thought that was better than sending him private which was £14,000 a year, so in the long term it suited us, he is in the school where I wanted him to be. Unfortunately it is a little bit underhand but we had to do it.'

['Can I ask who rented our flat from?']

'My next door neighbour actually, she bought one in the catchment specifically for the same purpose, so that when her daughter grows up she can send her to Seven Kings School so [laugh] She is ... married to an English guy, her son goes to Seven Kings School ... but she actually had to do the same, buy a flat, her brother had a flat in the area so she used that address and paid the council tax on it for a year, but now she has actually bought a place in that area specifically for that purpose.' (Pakistani, male, Central Redbridge)

This last respondent, who is ruthlessly focused and realistic, indicates precisely how difficult it can be to negotiate what is meant by a catchment area. We have focused mainly here on how parents worked to get their children into, if not a school of choice, than at least an acceptable one. In the final part we look at the lengths to which they go to *avoid* schools that are *perceived* as failing although, as we have suggested, their results may be not much worse than more popular schools.

## Social reproduction and social avoidance

Some respondents also highlighted a more general set of issues regarding the operation of the preference and allocation system within local authorities, namely the way in which a hierarchy of choices based on the reputation of schools operated to produce a situation where places at the most popular schools quickly fill up, or are restricted on the basis of catchment areas. Then parents have to choose between the less popular schools until, at the bottom of the preference hierarchy, there are one or more schools which relatively few parents want their children to go to. These schools will be the ones which few parents put on their list of choices. Consequently, as they have a lower ratio of applications to places or even a surplus of places, they will inevitably be used by the local authority to balance their books between supply and demand for places.

'I think you're going into the background of the people who live in the surrounding area are, I mean in Hainault there are lots of white working-class people who live around there and who are just not very concerned in their children's education, or in the discipline. There is also the fact that the school doesn't really help themselves within the structure of the school itself, so put the two together and it gives a disaster, really, for everybody concerned.... Then parents who move into the area and the school is full; in Seven Kings, even though they're in catchment for instance, they will have to go to a school where there are places, either Hainault – with no other places, they will invariably end up in Hainault! ... a lot of those families are happy to send their children to Hainault, they don't care, but as long as their child goes to a school, they don't ... but the 40% of parents that maybe are better-off and can afford to, will move out. They do want something better for their children. And I also find that in Year 6 – I teach in Year 6 – we do tend to lose, unfortunately, the nicer families of the kids that are succeeding, and their parents take them out during Year 6 because they don't want them to go on to Hainault.' (White British, female, Barkingside)

Our research was undertaken towards the end of a huge price-bubble in the London housing market (Hamnett, 2009) in which respondents had found themselves pushed to the outer edges of traditional middle-class housing markets or into what were previously council estates (such as Hainault). Often the former working-class tenants had bought cheaply, using the 1981 'right to buy' legislation and then sold, thus creating a deposit for their own leap onto the housing ladder elsewhere. Many of the new residents often viewed their children going to Hainault schools with horror.

Given the highly charged nature of educational attainment for many of those living in Redbridge, it was perhaps unsurprising that Hainault Forest was a school they would seek to avoid at all costs:

'If you have a situation which the government proposed, where everybody can choose their school, I mean what's going to happen to schools like Seven Kings? You know that we are going to be able to select the best students, everybody will get A★. And then, you know, it will sort of filter down, and Valentines will get the next best lot, and Oaks Park will get the next best lot, and then children who end up in Hainault have no chance of going up on the social ladder.' (White British, female, Barkingside)

'... what I want for my girls – I want the best education there is. But the catchment's secondary school is Hainault

Forest, and they are not going there. Over my dead body will they go there! I'll teach them at home…. There's bullying, there's drugs … they were on special measures for a while, I believe they've come off it now. They're changing their name but it's like anything, you know – a change of name isn't, I know they wanna get away from the image of Hainault High, but it was a bad school when I was at school.' (White British, female, Barkingside)

Such was the problem of Hainault in the next respondent's mind that she and her partner scraped together sufficient money to send her daughter to a private school until she was eligible to get into the sixth form college:

'The local comprehensive in Hainault is Hainault High School, and I'm sure you've heard from a lot of people about the problems that go on at Hainault High School. Behavioural. Academic expectation. My daughter went there for two years, and at the end of two years she was still doing colouring in for homework. Colouring in and sticking. So when my son passed his 11 plus, we decided that we could afford to pay for her to go to a private school for three years until she went to sixth form. So we put her into Ursuline which was a private, all-girls Catholic. Your own ethics go out of the window when it comes to your children.' (White British, female, Barkingside)

It is interesting that some of the strongest avoidance narratives came from Redbridge, where the creation of a successful infrastructure of selective and non-selective schools had created some of the strongest perceptions of failure and unacceptability. The arguments for a 'rising tide' in which good provision lifts the less good, would not appear to be working in Redbridge, where it has created perceptions of failure and polarisation.

## Conclusions

We have shown in this chapter that there are marked differences both between boroughs and between schools in East London in terms of attainment. This is reflected in terms of reputation as well as the ratio of applications to places, which vary markedly from the most popular to the least popular schools. Many parents felt that if it was not possible or desirable to go private or to get access to a faith school, the limits of choice were much reduced and, in practice, some parents felt that they had little effective choice. Unless a child already had siblings at a favoured school, local authorities would generally tend to allocate them on the basis of place of residence and catchment area. For those fortunate enough to live in a favoured catchment area and sufficiently close to the school, that was no problem, but those who did not were often forced to make difficult decisions based on the calculation of risk. Some parents also thought that the operation of the system tended to produce a set of schools ranked in terms of desirability where the least-favoured and generally lower-achieving schools tended to get pupils whose parents had least choice or were less bothered about exercising choice. Thus the intake of the least-favoured schools was seen to be partly self-reproducing on the basis of social class, ethnicity, school behaviour and reputation. Once a reputation has been generated it can persist for many years, even if the real situation has changed – as witnessed by some of the views expressed above about Hainault High School.

The responses of many of the parents interviewed suggested that they believed the degree of choice they had in choosing schools for their children within the state sector was extremely limited, by the competition for the best schools and reliance on catchment areas as a rationing device within local authorities. Many felt that the reality was that there was no choice, as you had to take what you were offered. This raises some pertinent questions about the feasibility of the former New Labour government's stress on parental choice as a way to drive up school quality. While in theory it might have seemed attractive, the demand for places at schools with good reputations and performance far exceeds the number of places available and many parents and their children are disappointed and are forced to accept places in their local catchment area irrespective of quality. The ideology of parental choice thus seems rather threadbare in practice. Schools perceived as good are 'positional goods' and access to them is inevitably limited, and a stress on choice, it might be argued, is in danger of creating hard-to-shift perceptions of failing schools.

Perhaps the main lesson we can learn is that success has its dangers. In Redbridge, public policy is creating a divided and polarised system in a borough admired for its diverse and successful schools. The danger is that in the long term a policy that was designed to raise standards for all will drive them down for those who fail to get into the most popular schools. How government and policy makers should best deal with this is difficult to judge. In large part, the school strategy of New Labour was to focus on league tables and performance indicators in an attempt to drive up quality and to put pressure on so-called 'failing schools' to improve performance. But in a situation where 'distance to school' is the key rationing mechanism for allocating places to the most popular schools, the reality of school choice often means that unless parents live close to a popular school, they must accept a place at their local school that may be less popular. Thus the social composition of school catchment areas is reflected in their attainment and class-based 'circuits of schooling', and these circuits become perpetuated as residentially based cycles of (dis)advantage.

## Notes

[1] This excludes the City of London, where the figures are miniscule and there is no state secondary schooling.

[2] Alastair Campbell was former Prime Minister Tony Blair's Director of Communication (and enforcer) in his first two administrations. His partner, Fiona Millar, has been a forthright champion of non-selective educational provision.

[3] We are aware, and have been made further aware by the comments of colleagues, of the danger of using the term *good* in relation to schools, even when safely escorted by 'scare' quotes. However, we are reporting the comments of respondents who made these distinctions with varying degrees of self-awareness. We do not wish any of our findings to imply that popular schools are necessarily good schools or vice versa. It is probably fair to say that the more popular schools get better results at the Key Stages and the least popular schools do worst; for those in the middle the equation is much less clear: some schools with a high proportion of middle-class children are probably 'coasting', as one of us has implied elsewhere in relation to the notion of 'value added' (Webber and Butler, 2007).

[4] There is an important methodological point that needs to be noted here. While the ratio of applications to places is a useful measure of popularity, it is a rather crude one in that parents are allowed to express up to six preferences of school in rank order and the applications/places ratio does not tell us how many of the applications were top-ranked preferences and how many were at the bottom of the list. Thus, two schools with an equal number of places may each receive 500 applications, but for one all applications were ranked first, while for the other most of them were ranked sixth. Both would have an equal applications/places ratio but the first school would be far more popular. This is a highly unlikely scenario but it means that our use

of the terms 'popular' and 'unpopular' does not necessarily reflect the actual structure of school preferences. The only borough to publish figures on ranked preferences is Havering, which we consider below. While there is a correlation between the applications/places ratio and the percentage of first preferences, it is not a perfect one.

[5] Similar tables to those produced for Redbridge are available – see Hamnett and Butler (forthcoming).

[6] A second methodological note is also needed here as the applications/places ratio of popularity and the percentage of first and second preferences do not produce exactly the same ranking. This is particularly the case where the two Catholic schools are concerned as they have a very high percentage of first preferences but rank much lower in terms of the applications/places ratio as they only accept Catholics, and applicants from other faiths are not permitted, which depresses the ratio. A correlation analysis of percentage first preference and applications/places ratio gave a correlation of 0.47 and, when Catholic schools were excluded, a value of 0.59. Proximity to school is thus an important factor for allocating places only to the more popular comprehensive and foundation schools. Faith schools allocate places first and foremost to those of the designated faith, and whether the family are regarded as 'good Catholics' is more important than distance to these schools. The application criteria for such schools are often highly specific in terms of faith requirements and regularity of church attendance. An additional note concerns the accuracy of the applications/places ratio when single-sex schools are included, as theoretically these are likely to attract less applicants than an equivalent co-educational school as only girls or boys can apply. This may be offset, however, by the attraction of single-sex education to some parents.

[7] For a more detailed borough-by-borough discussion, see Hamnett and Butler (forthcoming).

[8] Although the Jewish faith school, King Solomon, had a low GCSE score.

[9] Formally, schools in London allocate places without knowledge of where parents have placed them on their list of preferences but this certainly was not the experience of the vast majority of parents we interviewed. It may be that they had made their selections before the implementation of the changes to the admissions system in London in 2006 and that the situation will now change; however, we do not believe most parents will see it this way.

# SEVEN

# Reputation and working the system

'I think you're going into the background of ... the people who live in the surrounding area are, I mean in Hainault there are lots of white working-class people who live around there and who are just not very concerned in their children's education, or in the discipline. There is also the fact that the school doesn't really help themselves within the structure of the school itself, so put the two together and it gives a disaster, really, for everybody concerned. And I think definitely plenty of parents would like to have a school like Seven Kings because they see it, you know, as the beacon of all schools. But I don't know to what lengths they'd be prepared to send their children there. And there is very much the sense – again from the parents who live around the Hainault area – that they do despair of having to send their children to Kingswood, because of the nature of the intake of the schools.' (White British, female, Barkingside)

## Introduction

In the previous two chapters we developed our focus on how education has been the means of realising parental aspiration for the respondents' children's future. We have done so largely through an analysis of published statistics, our dataset from the PLASC and our own survey and interview data. Aggregate quantitative data are invaluable as a source of information but they do not give us the 'thinking' behind the way in which individuals are making choices (or not) about schooling and where to live. Our analysis so far confirms what may be blindingly obvious to most people – that schools with pupils from advantaged backgrounds do well and vice versa – but our combination of PLASC with Mosaic has enabled us to attach some numbers to these findings rather than relying solely on the kind of qualitative data which typifies this kind of research.[1]

Nevertheless, without reference to the 'voices' of those concerned in the process if we just look at the 'facts' we understand little of the reasoning behind them. In this chapter, therefore, we listen to the respondents both through the boxes they ticked in the 300 face-to-face survey responses we carried out and, more tellingly, from the transcripts of the 100 follow-up in-depth semi-structured interviews undertaken across the five study areas. These interviews provide a rich insight into why education is so important, why people hold the perceptions they do about particular schools often in the face of 'the figures' and, most importantly, why they do (or do not) act on those feelings. It also shows that, while there are consistent differences between different social class and ethnic groups living in different parts of London, there is also a huge range of variation in behaviour which can only be explained by the kinds of values that people hold about the society they live in, how they want to live their lives and what they want for their children in terms of ethical choices. This chapter therefore builds on the material presented in Chapters Five and Six but, in particular, refers back to the respondent interviews in Chapters Three and Four about their choices about where to live, the role that education played in that and how this was intended to realise their more general sense of aspiration for themselves and their children.

Our focus in this chapter is therefore less on the general notion of aspiration and the respondents' articulation of it and rather more on a number of key concerns about the ways in which they have set out to achieve that – particularly through choices about schooling for their children. For some this has meant building on their existing privilege (although they would probably never express it like this) whereas for others, a majority of the respondents, it has meant planning their children's education in order to get them onto the lower rungs at least of the occupational ladders that signify economic security and social belonging. We therefore look at what it was that they valued and wanted out of the schooling system and then – crudely – how they set about achieving this; what they saw as the choices open to them and how they made those choices (or equally important, did not). We identify the strategies they pursued, or considered pursuing, in the light of their analysis of the kinds of schools that were open to them and what they thought of those schools. What emerges generally reinforces the analysis we undertook in Chapters Five and Six but also shows how *perceptions* matter and how critical the whole issue of catchment areas is. In terms of choosing a suitable secondary school for children, league tables and Ofsted reports were important but not as important as the *reputation* of the school and what parents thought their child would get from the school (see Table 7.1). Accordingly, they listened most to other parents and especially the views of friends and neighbours about particular schools. Official sources of information (LEA publicity handouts, websites and teachers' views) were generally less important than the views of other parents or friends. These, then, were particularistic rather than universalistic grounds for making educational choices. In all areas, parents indicated a strong commitment to their child's schooling, with 80% always attending parents' evenings.

Approximately 30% of survey respondents had attempted, but failed, to get their child into another school but, despite this, levels of satisfaction with schooling were – perhaps surprisingly – high; approximately 70% of respondents were satisfied with their child's primary school education (measured on a five-point scale from 'very poor' to 'excellent') with about 15% 'don't knows' and 15% feeling it was 'poor' and 'very poor'. At secondary level, this fell to about half being satisfied, with about a quarter dissatisfied and a similar proportion of 'don't knows'.

However, at neither primary nor secondary level were there massive levels of dissatisfaction; this finding correlated with the very small numbers who had actually moved because of dissatisfaction with their child's schooling. Nearly 40% felt standards in primary and secondary schools were improving. We need to be cautious here as nearly a third felt that they 'didn't know', which in itself is interesting. Only about 10% thought standards were getting worse. Overall, our survey data suggest that while there is a massive concern about education and doing the best for one's child, most parents were satisfied with the education their children were getting, felt that it was improving and were highly supportive, both of their child within the school and of

**Table 7.1: Sources of information about school choice**

|  | Yes | No |
|---|---|---|
| League tables | 49 | 51 |
| Ofsted reports | 40 | 60 |
| Other parents | 57 | 43 |
| Friends or neighbours | 68 | 32 |
| Open days | 51 | 49 |
| Visits | 50 | 50 |
| Websites | 23 | 77 |
| Material from the LEA | 34 | 66 |
| Teachers | 34 | 66 |

*Note: n* = 271.

the school itself. This apparent satisfaction with schooling (although not the lack of real choice) was one of the more surprising findings of the survey and was largely confirmed by the subsequent in-depth interviews. This perhaps is explained by the fact that, as we have seen, many respondents had moved or otherwise manoeuvred to optimise their position in the education market and had found ways around problems – such as the lack of real choice – and arrived at outcomes with which they could live. What is abundantly clear, however, is that there were very low levels of non-involvement among our generally middle-class and aspirational sample of respondents.

There were also significant differences between respondents in Victoria Park and those in the other areas. Many of those in Victoria Park were successfully established in their careers and either able to afford private education for their children or were sufficiently self-confident in their ability to manage poor provision, to take a relatively relaxed view of current obsessions with performance and standards. They felt, for the most part, that they could afford to take a longer view, while also assuming that their children would 'do alright'. Elsewhere, we found that social aspirants from BME populations were keen to distance themselves from their origins both in terms of social class and social space in order to seek a better and more distinctive life for themselves and their children – for them there was all to play for and the dangers of slipping back were all too apparent. At the same time, there was a group of white middle-class lower professionals who were committed to living in an area whose mix and diversity they valued and to which they had a commitment to 'making it work'. They were generally happy for their children to attend local schools and, although they actively avoided the worst schools, were broadly satisfied with the quality and improvements in the education they were receiving. Many of these middle-class parents were characterised by a notably quiet and unassuming confidence that their children would perform to their desired levels academically in the local state school as well as valuing other aspects of the school experience. References to a 'rounded' education were commonplace, with an intrinsic element of this being at a school whose roll reflected the ethnic and social diversity of its constituent neighbourhoods.[2] For many, becoming a parent meant negotiating the city in a new way. It meant Ofsteds and catchments, childcare and after-school. The schools conundrum and its consequences for residential preferences cannot be overstated. It also becomes more troubling as children make the transition from primary to secondary school since the majority of parents attached less importance to the primary stages of education, seeing them as equipping children 'only' with the 'basics' in numbers and language while setting children off on the correct path towards becoming 'rounded', responsible and caring adults. Unsurprisingly, it was parents whose eldest children were about to enter primary or secondary education who exhibited most anxiety and expressed the greatest desire to suburbanise or move out of the London metropolis altogether.

Many of the BME parents whom we interviewed were particularly concerned about education and were determined to distance their children from what they saw as the 'contaminating' effect of low-performing (usually expressed as 'disruptive') children who, they were convinced, would 'drag them down' or worse. For black parents, who could often claim membership of a Christian religion, the attraction of the 'discipline' of faith schools was an especially strong pull. Asian parents tended to stress more the pull of the high-performing schools in Redbridge (selective and non-selective) and the informal (and sometimes what seems almost taunting) advice of other Asian parents who already had children in those schools. For many in Victoria Park, the desirability of the area and its housing as somewhere to live (and its proximity to the centre) had to be compensated for by paying for private schooling or a move out of London at the time of the secondary transition. For others in this area who could not afford housing near to the desired primary school or the fees of independent schooling and were not prepared to move out of London, this was a permanent dilemma in which they invested considerable time and emotional energy. They tended to eschew many of the other primary schools, as we have seen, on the grounds that they were insufficiently diverse – either too dominated by Asians or too mono-ethnically white with a working-class ethos which was often interpreted as bordering on racist. Nevertheless, many of these parents expressed reservations about the nature of the education offered by faith schools, which they saw as over-disciplined; they resented the intrusion of religion into what they saw as an essentially secular activity. What perhaps is most striking is that – with the exception of the established gentry of Victoria Park and possibly the white lower professionals in Newham – many of the respondents were not sufficiently established on their own trajectory of upward social mobility to do other than to focus single-mindedly on securing their children's futures, and this gave rise to a tightly focused attention to what might be seen as a narrow set of measures of educational attainment.

How then do these aspirations – ranging from the narrowly and occupationally focused to the broader ones about the benefits of a well-rounded education – play out when it comes to choosing a school for one's child? Not surprisingly, they vary between the strategic and focused to the passive and accepting of what is offered; there is often a lack of fit between what people would like and what they settle for. Such is the pressure 'to do the best for one's child' that many parents admit to a feeling that they have somehow failed as a parent if they don't express a desire for their child to go to the best school, despite knowing that it is either unachievable or probably wouldn't suit her/ him. Having tried and failed, they sometimes appeared quietly relieved to have had the decision taken out of their hands by being offered what they often suspected they were probably going to get in the first place. Nevertheless, the experience of having gone through the choice process and having failed leaves a sense of failure or frustration in most parents. In the next section we look at the different expectations of what respondents said they would like to see in a school.

## What do you value in a school?

For many respondents, what mattered most was the process of education – what Basil Bernstein (1975) called 'the normative order' of the school – which is often well expressed in the Ofsted reports which describe how the pupils behave, how they use the space, as well as how the teachers approach the delivery of the curriculum. Indeed, with the standardisation of a national curriculum, the manner of its delivery becomes a major distinguishing feature between schools. In much of East London, however, there is also a realisation that schools can either reflect or challenge the 'street culture' and this is particularly strong among those respondents who feel that they themselves have only recently begun to move away from the feeling that they were permanently moored at the bottom of British society. For them the values of the school and often those of the headteacher become critical; reference to 'discipline' is a recurring theme in our interview transcripts:

> '... the culture of a school, that is the more important than the studies itself. I would prefer to send them to a Catholic school than a school where the culture is no good, even if it performs well in results. I think the most important thing is to get them away from the street culture. I don't worry about whether they perform extremely well or not.' (Pakistani, male, Central Redbridge)

We have already noted that, for many of the respondents, their focus is on secondary schools because that is where success or failure becomes apparent, and they regard primary schools as simply preparatory. However, as one respondent indicates, these values emerge at primary school and can often carry over into how the young people subsequently conduct themselves at secondary school – this reinforces and contextualises the findings outlined in Chapter Five about 'school composition' effects, which are, mistakenly perhaps, elided with social class background:

> 'I wanted them to do well academically but I also wanted them to come out with a caring attitude and more, I suppose, manners. I'm not quite sure if you'd say manners but more, just nicer people. Nicer, you know, they teach them to be very caring towards each other, very caring towards the community and to, you know, it was just a nice way they taught the children. And I've noticed when my older one's gone to the secondary school he's so different in his attitude, you know. Because he's had it at home and school he's got kind of a different attitude.' (White British, female, Barkingside)

One of the options taken up by some respondents, unable or unwilling to pay for an elite private education and ineligible or ideologically opposed to faith schools, was to seek out what might be seen as a state equivalent to private education. The European School at Ingatestone – half an hour down the main line railway in Essex from Stratford – combined high academic standards with good sporting and cultural facilities:

> ['Can you tell me a bit about how your eldest came about going to Ingatestone?']

> '... we had a look at all the schools locally, and in neighbouring boroughs,... we wanted a school that had high academic achievement and expectations of their pupils and had the same for sport. So it was rounded, I didn't want one that was just academic, but he is very sporty, he swims for the borough, and, you know, he likes to play cricket and rugby and that kind of thing, we wanted one that did very traditional sports as well, across the fields kind of thing, rather than just on a piece of tarmac to be honest, and they do. The Anglo–European did that, and it also had the exchange visits, so it does a lot of trips to Europe, you know.

It just seemed more rounded, the children who we met seemed, you know, mature, sensible, what we wanted really.'

It is the non-academic issue of discipline, not results as such, that was clearly the motivating factor for choosing Ingatestone, as emerges later in the interview:

['Were you ever close to sending your children to one of the local secondary schools?']

'Well, I was a bit. My husband wasn't, he's a teacher. I went round, I did go round, and I must say that his contemporaries – his junior school friends who did go there [Forest Gate, the local comprehensive], probably half the class went there, [they] are doing very well actually, academically they are doing very well, some of them have passed a couple of GCSEs and they're only Year 9, and they sat them in Year 8.... I think we were concerned about behaviour ... as I say, my husband is a teacher, we know people who work in the borough, and in neighbouring boroughs, and we felt that they didn't have a handle on behaviour. Even some minor things, they just didn't deal with them. They had more serious things to deal with. So, back-chatting to teachers, that kind of thing which I don't think is acceptable, wouldn't be picked up, and so ... but it is at Anglo-European!' (White British, female, Newham)

Outside the faith and private sectors, there are few alternatives such as the European School, which scores high on most liberal agendas – except of course that it is not a local school. It would be highly misleading to suggest that there were no respondents who both 'talked the talk and walked the walk' by sending their children to school locally. One respondent and his wife had lived in Victoria Park for a long time:

'I think we are saddled with the curse of this word "delivery", which is used all the time, it wasn't used earlier in my working life. But, somehow the assumption was that the school is a commodity and the family is the consumer of the commodity. Well, we've never – as far as I'm aware – construed our relationship between ourselves and the school as one where ... OK? We see ourselves as *co-creators* of the educational experience with the school. The thing is, we certainly did expect the school to do certain things – keep our children safe, you know, keep them stretched and so-on-and-so-forth – but … if … nothing did really go wrong at all. But our first assumption would be that if things were not right we would have a conversation, and it would be up to us to contribute to that as much as the school.' (White British, male, Victoria Park)

This feeling that the state can deliver what people are looking for without creating an often non-existent European heritage and putting the child on a 45-minute commute, or paying out many thousands of pounds in fees or calling on a long-abandoned religious background, is described at some length with passion by this (single parent) respondent in Newham, who actively chose a local school despite it not having a very positive Ofsted report:

['What criteria did you use to distinguish between schools? How did you come to your final choice of Galleons?']

'… I was looking at whether the building was very imposing, whether they looked daunting, what the people outside were treated like and what the children were behaving like and how the school would meet … I knew from an earlier age, I suppose every other parent feels the same, but I knew [my son] had a lot of gifts, he was able to talk and communicate really well. His knowledge was quite … because I'm at home I'm doing a lot with him and I knew he had potential so I was definitely looking for a school that would focus on it, encourage it, and bring it out. From the schools I was seeing, none of them were really catching me, they were just general run-of-the-mill schools and they weren't offering anything special.'

'When I saw Galleons, number one it was a new school so the layout was beautiful. The original Ofsted report – because it was new, this was back in 2002, so it had only just opened for two years – it wasn't really performing fantastically because obviously it had taken children from all the other schools … but, from their perspective, and from what they were portraying, it was an arts-based school so they planned to teach in a very different way from all the other schools I had saw. They all perform musically; they have lessons from

Year 1 twice a week. If they were doing shapes they would do it in music and art. It was just so different and I thought that if [my son] is in any way artistically minded, this is the place to bring it out. Also, academically, I think that if children are able to develop in their own way, they would be able to bring out the academic side so I thought, OK, they will encourage the child's thinking. When I also stood outside the school the children were so well behaved. There wasn't any fighting or swearing – only between parents I would say! And the neighbourhood itself is not a brilliant neighbourhood, but it was a very appealing feeling I got from the place. The teachers were just *so* nice, they were warm and welcoming. Obviously I looked at the nursery first and it was a really big nursery, all the children looked happy there. And all my sisters were saying, "are you sure it's the right one? They aren't getting the best grades", now, they are sixth for their grades, they are beating all the Catholic schools and everything, and I said, I knew I chose the right school, and the things they are doing in his school – my friend, she pays for private school, he doesn't seem to do half as much [as my own child] and they are paying for it!' (Mixed Race, female, Newham)

These accounts of values and outcomes seem, at first sight, somewhat at odds with the material presented in the previous chapter in which the emphasis was on constrained choice. Most, but not all, the respondents were generally able to make choices with which they were comfortable, even if it wasn't their first or preferred choice. Table 7.2 indicates that finding a particular school was important to the majority of respondents – particularly so in Redbridge where one might argue that the large number of good schools should make admission to a particular school less problematic. This was not so, quite the reverse in fact, because of the rhetoric of school choice in Redbridge that served to polarise outcomes between very popular schools (notably Seven Kings) and 'unacceptable' ones (notably Hainault), as we have seen (see Table 7.3). This is clearly shown in the 2009 DCSF data for preferences and offers for East London boroughs. London boroughs took 8 of the 10 bottom LEAs for success in first preference, and 17 of the bottom 20. Redbridge was the lowest of all London boroughs.

Just under one third of all respondents had tried to get their child into another school; in this case the proportion so doing was higher in Victoria Park, Newham and Leytonstone, as indicated in Table 7.4. Only in Hackney was this more likely to be outside the borough than

**Table 7.2: School preference (%)**

|  | First prefer-ence | Second prefer-ence | Third prefer-ence | One of top 3 (%) | Any prefer-ence | Rank in LEAs from bottom |
|---|---|---|---|---|---|---|
| Redbridge | 56.6 | 18 | 7.4 | 82 | 91.4 | 7th |
| Hackney | 61.7 | 12.6 | 8 | 82.3 | 89 | 14th |
| Barking & Dagenham | 66.9 | 13.6 | 5 | 85.5 | 90.6 | 21st |
| Tower Hamlets | 72.1 | 12.6 | 4.9 | 89.7 | 92.5 | 36th |
| Havering | 77 | 12.8 | 4.1 | 93.9 | 100 | 44th |
| Waltham Forest | 78.7 | 10.7 | 4 | 93.3 | 96.4 | 51st |
| Newham | 79.8 | 9.7 | 3.9 | 93.4 | 95.5 | 54th |
| England | 83.2 | 8.4 | 3.1 | 94.6 | 96.2 | |

*Source:* DCSF (2010)

**Table 7.3: Choices: how important was a specific school?**

|  | Extremely important (%) | Important, but by no means crucial (%) |
|---|---|---|
| Victoria Park | 61 | 36 |
| Newham | 54 | 39 |
| Leytonstone | 54 | 4 |
| Central Redbridge | 63 | 33 |
| Barkingside | 67 | 30 |
| Total (*n* = 281) | 176 | 105 |
| % | 60 | 36 |

**Table 7.4: Did you try to get your child into another school?**

|  | Yes (%) | No (%) | Not sure/don't know (%) | Total |
|---|---|---|---|---|
| Victoria Park | 39 | 60 | 12 | 67 |
| Newham | 26 | 74 | 0 | 57 |
| Leytonstone | 49 | 51 | 0 | 43 |
| Central Redbridge | 26 | 72 | 2 | 50 |
| Barkingside | 21 | 79 | 0 | 52 |
| Total (*n* = 269) | 86 | 181 | 2 | 269 |
| % | 32 | 67 | 1 | 100.0 |

within (Table 7.5), which fits with our figures about the high numbers of children being educated outside the borough in Hackney.

As indicated in Chapter Six, there has recently been a tightening up in respect of school choice and the opportunities to educate your

**Table 7.5: Where was your preferred school?**

|  | In borough (%) | Outside borough (%) | State school elsewhere (%) | Total |
|---|---|---|---|---|
| Victoria Park | 35 | 62 | 3 | 37 |
| Newham | 60 | 40 | 0 | 38 |
| Leytonstone | 76 | 24 | 0 | 25 |
| Central Redbridge | 82 | 18 | 0 | 28 |
| Barkingside | 76 | 24 | 0 | 21, |
| Total | 93 | 54 | 1 | 149 |
| % | 62 | 36 | 2 | 100.0 |

child out of borough or even out of catchment area are becoming increasingly constrained. This has been particularly the case since the unified secondary school selection process operated by all London boroughs was introduced in 2006. Most of the respondents were talking about the previous situation when their chances of circumventing narrowly drawn catchment areas and recruitment procedures were relatively easier to achieve, as we show in the next section – although the figures quoted about those who tried and failed should also be noted. Additionally, many parents will be able to benefit for some years to come from the 'sibling rule' that gives them priority access if they already have an elder child in the school.

## Strategising school choice

For many respondents, there was a clear trade-off between deciding where to live and where to educate their children. For the upper and upper middle classes, this has never been a consideration given the parallel circuit of private (that is, fee-paying) schools in Britain. However, it is not simply a matter of getting your chequebook out – many of these schools are popular and have entrance exams for which 'preparatory schools' coach children assiduously. Charting a route through high-quality private education, particularly in an area of high demand such as London, requires some planning.

> 'The other thing is that if you get in early on the private route then it's quite easy to just go straight through because just getting money out of your wallet isn't enough, you have to make sure that you register early and so forth because so many of the good private schools are over-subscribed so basically my three children were registered very early

at Saint Paul's Cathedral School to ensure that, you know, they got a place. They were, ah, very carefully tutored for the little entrance test that they had so as to make sure there weren't any hiccups there. And then looking ahead to secondary education, the children have been registered very early at their senior schools so there's no question of them not having a place when they reach the end of Year 8.' (White British, male, Victoria Park)

Investment in a good preparatory school can have other benefits – notably for getting children through the so-called '11 plus' to win a competitive place at one of the remaining selective 'grammar schools'. Unlike the state sector, where schools are prohibited from 'teaching to the test' (or at least to that test), such schools had a ready market preparing children for Redbridge's two selective grammar schools.

'... I have put her in a prep school yes, which has a good success doing the 11 plus. Because I didn't do it I missed out on the opportunity and I feel that my parents didn't have ... you know, the situation was then different and now that I have the opportunity I would like to give her that. Because I do think it makes a difference, it's so competitive out there and it depends on ... I would at least like her to have that opportunity rather than not have it. But whether, you know, who knows what the future holds, but at least she's got the chance to do it.' (Indian, female, Barkingside)

However, for those wanting to get their children into well-regarded comprehensive schools, such as Seven Kings, it increasingly comes down to geography, as indicated in Chapter Six. One respondent was prepared to try any trick in the book to avoid his allocated secondary school – Mayfield. His wife went out to work full time to afford a private education for their youngest and they rented a flat in the Seven Kings catchment for their son, a flat rented from a neighbour who bought the flat to get her own daughter in 'down the line' but in the meantime was able to realise the value of the property by renting it out to other parents with similar concerns, as we saw in Chapter Six.

The other asset that parents were able to deploy was religion, discussed in Chapter Six in more detail, although it is worth noting once more that this was particularly available to Black African and Black Caribbean respondents who were regular church attenders.

## Catchment areas

As we saw in Chapter Six, where there was oversupply, rationing was achieved by using a 'distance to school measure' even within specified catchment areas where they existed, as they did in Redbridge. By the same token, where schools failed to recruit up to their target, then children were allocated to them from across the borough. Redbridge, as we showed, publishes maps of the catchment area for each school, although what actually matters is how far you live from school and how many people are applying in any particular year. This might seem a fair way of rationing places in a situation of excess demand over supply; however, it can sometimes seem very unfair when children living far from the school are given priority. The following respondent, who lives in Central Redbridge, thought she was well set up for a popular primary for her daughter only to discover that she had been trumped by other children who lived out of catchment but who had siblings already at the school:

['Thinking about schools for [your daughter], what are your considerations and what thought processes as far as possible schooling options are concerned?']

'Well, it's funny actually because I have been thinking more about this. And my mum and I have been considering it and we're of mixed opinions at the moment. We're both quite socialist in our views of life, so we would like her to be schooled in a normal state-funded school. One of the best schools in the whole borough is Christchurch, which is just down the road, and I've looked at the Ofsted report and it is very good, high educational attainment, good grades on sort of all levels really. It's heavily oversubscribed and they regularly change the … the catchment area. There's a little girl that lived across the road and the year that she needed to apply, they moved the boundary down to Brisbane Road – it's normally at her road, that road, we're in it, and they moved it there. So even though it is literally a four-minute walk, she didn't qualify, so she didn't get in because it is so over-subscribed. And I have to say a symptom of that is that a lot of the people that live on this estate, the houses are big, and they have big families – four, five, six kids. So once you've got one child in there, you get all of them in there. So that's a third thing really, that's a really good school, and that she wouldn't actually get in there.' (White British, female, Central Redbridge)

Another respondent had been a beneficiary of the distance-to-school rule, getting her child into a popular school that was actually across the border from Redbridge in Essex:

['Right. So, did you move into Chigwell catchment by moving here or …']

'Not really, because West Hatch is oversubscribed every year, they take on 180 pupils a year and over 500 apply every year, so it is quite competitive to get into. But their criteria is siblings first, and then distance from the school on an increasing circle. So it's not actually, because it comes under Essex Council, we actually come under London Borough of Redbridge here – we're literally about eight houses away from the boundary for Essex – but we still get into West Hatch because of the nearness of the school and obviously the siblings now.'

['Now … can you tell me about, how did you get your eldest child into West Hatch then? Can you tell me about the criteria you had to meet and so on?']

'Yes, well I just applied, I phoned up and asked if I could apply, but it was mid-year, it was in February, and they straight away said to me, we don't take people mid-year. So I sort of persisted as well, you know, you must have some sort of policy in place for people that have moved to the area, surely, you know, if they had moved from Wales for example, you know, so in the end they said OK, we can send you an application form but you probably won't stand a chance. So I sent it out and they sent a letter back saying no, you haven't been successful but you can appeal. So I thought OK, I'll appeal then. And I got her in under the appeal process … well, I just went on and on, but what it was for me, the thing at the time was, my daughter was getting the two buses – we'd moved here by now – and she was getting the two buses to school and home again. And honestly, it was terrible. And you know what buses are like, all the school kids and that, and she's not really used to being on public transport until we moved here – she used to walk to school. And on this day, the bus driver – there must have been trouble on the bus and he stopped the bus and refused to drive it, and threw the children off. And she phoned me up crying, she was in Hainault, come and get me. I'm heavily pregnant with my last child at the time, and it was just such a nightmare, and it was all in the paper that week, the local paper, so I attached all that to it saying public transport's not for her, she doesn't feel safe, I can't be there to pick her up because I've got a baby now, I can't drive. And also it said if they have any special qualities – well she's good at piano and she was good at swimming, she used to swim for Redbridge council. So, and they love all that up there because Sally Gunnell went to that school, so it's a very sporty school and I think they want another Sally Gunnell! So I think that sort of swayed it really. And then she had to write her own part as well, by herself, why she wanted to go there. They've got a swimming pool there so she put some swimming things, so I don't really know at the end of the day what it was that clinched it for us, but … I think overall they read it and thought oh….' (White British, female, Barkingside)

This is quite a typical narrative – 'I was lucky' (Mattinson, 2010); although the respondent knew that she didn't have a strong case, she nevertheless pursued all avenues open to her and got her daughter in. She was thus able to give an account that implied that nothing untoward or unjust in relation to others was done although in practice somebody else's child probably was denied a place. Another quite common approach to school choice is to make a virtue out of marital or relationship breakdowns in which the estranged parents live in different boroughs or different parts of the same borough. With some imagination and manipulation of procedures, they can then opt to send their child to school in whichever catchment area they favour:

['So was it just luck that the school you liked was opposite your son's father?']

'… he, well, he was living in private rented accommodation anyway, so I was living a little bit further so he could choose when he wanted to move, so it wasn't really – for him it didn't matter as much where he lived, so that may have affected as well that he made his choice around the school. Yes, and it just happened to be important to registration and all that stuff. And also … yes, he was also, my son was going to nursery that had taken him as well. One more factor was they increased the numbers of the kids they are taking from 30 to 60 that year, so one extra class. It was a bit of luck as well as tricks, but it was also a lot of work anyway – although it's a bit far, at the other end, it's in this borough and all council tax has to be paid in this borough anyway, but … it was lucky, and if his father did not live there he would not be able to get in maybe. But I tried.' (Indian, female, Leyton)

For each story, however, with its serendipitous upside, there are situations in which even the most articulate middle-class parents experience the rejection of not getting what they felt was their deserved choice. The following respondent recounts how she felt about – and then dealt with – the rejection of her child for Lauriston, the favoured primary school in Victoria Park:

'I can practically spit into the playground. You know, it's 194 metres away which they tell you when you haven't got a place and to not be able to go to that school is very destabilising. It's very distressing – you feel a sense of ownership of your local school, almost irrespective of whether you take up a place; it's there, it's yours. And if someone tells you can't come and the door is slammed in your face, particularly when your child is at the nursery – even though we know that doesn't entitle you to a place at the school – that's really hard to cope with. And you start to feel that this whole "isn't it a lovely community in Victoria Park?" is a massive big fake and all it is is a collection of sharp-elbowed people who are all out for themselves and you are falling by the wayside, and you wonder whether you should have done what other people do which is to buy a flat in those bloody flats across from the school and move into that and pretend to be there, or should you have pretended to divorce like some people do, you know, should you pull some trick, no, because you couldn't live with yourself. What would you tell your children? How do you explain that you've fiddled this to get them into the school – it's appalling. And also, not that this is my motivation, but everyone knows people do things like that. You know, do you want to be that person in the community? No. Do you know what, I'd rather pay than do that. I just think it is so dishonest and then to, sort of, maintain your credentials as this lovely *Guardian*-reading lefty person when you've bloody pulled off a trick to abuse the system....'

This respondent's account of a foiled middle-class sense of entitlement is interesting in terms of what she did next, having been rejected by what she considered her 'local school', she then promptly refused to consider what the LEA considered her local school, mainly on the grounds of it being too working class:

['How seriously did you consider sending your children to another local state school?']

'The only other one would have been Orchard. I did know the school, and I think Orchard is actually really trying, and it has really improved an awful lot. But I honestly felt – and I read an Ofsted report that pulled this out – it didn't, it wasn't very good at helping and supporting kids who didn't have any special needs. I think they just sort of say, thank god for them, they're alright, and spend a lot of time nurturing a lot of kids that need a lot of help and there *really are* a lot of children there who need lots of support. But I thought I'm not sure that's going to serve my child. Because Orchard is the flip side of Lauriston – it's a mirror image, it's you know, all the middle-class people get sucked into Lauriston and that leaves Orchard similarly skewed. And also it does look towards Hampton Park Estate, it's very ethnically mixed with lots of children on free school meals. I think once you get a proportion of middle-class kids that go there – a critical mass – then this area has to support more than one decent school, and at the moment Saint Elizabeth has become the kind of alternative school of choice that people are now talking about, but a lot of people are locked out of it because they are not Catholic or church-going in some way. And whether Orchard will become the target for those people as it should ... it's mad.'

['What do you put that down to?']

'I think there is a certain chipperness about, you know, you middle-class people, half of you want to go to Lauriston anyway. They just don't see it as their job to reach out to those people. And I think actually, I understand that it is right to care for the groups that they have always catered for ... but I think they should aim to have a school that reflects their area and they don't. And the school would involve a balance – a range of socioeconomic backgrounds – but they [Orchard] almost perversely don't want that.' (White British, female, Victoria Park)

What is interesting here is, who is rejecting whom? Orchard was rejected because it would not conform to her expectations of what she needed for her child ("it didn't, it wasn't very good at helping and supporting kids who didn't have any special needs") and it would not welcome her with open arms. It was rejected because it was a working-class school. Her response was to 'dust off' her (and her partner's) Catholic credentials and get her daughter into a local faith primary school. The important point to stress here is the class-specific nature of the education she was prepared to consider for her daughter – 'when push comes to shove', a Catholic predominantly white middle-class school trumps a secular working-class one.

As Table 7.1 indicated, one of the findings of our survey was that parents rely most heavily on friends and other parents for their information about particular schools before making choices – above league tables, Ofsted reports and other official sources of information. This works both ways, as the following excerpt shows. Hainault (the demonised school introduced in the previous chapter) is, in some people's book, an improving school, but not according to the parental grapevine – a number of the respondents went there as pupils and, on the basis that leopards never change their spots, were determined that their children would not follow them – "over my dead body" was said by more than one respondent!

'... it's all very well seeing somebody with a piece of paper and Ofsted, but until you actually speak to a parent whose child goes there, I don't really think you're gonna get the full picture. So, and obviously I can remember what the school was like ... that was quite a while ago! [laughs] But I can remember what it was like. I mean the secondary school was more of a problem.'

['What are your intentions as far as secondary schooling's concerned?']

'They're not going to Hainault High! Over my dead body! ... a lot of the children at my son's school, they live at the other end towards New North Road end of Hainault ... some didn't mind if they actually went to Hainault High and I think the reputation might be worse than the actual – I didn't visit the school, I don't actually know the school, so I can't really say, but I know it's got a very bad reputation that kind of gets round. *You can't really get rid of a reputation once you've got one!*' (White British, female, Barkingside)

In Chapter Six we concluded that each borough has at least a couple of schools like Hainault, where there are significantly fewer applicants than places; in such schools, applicants are often those who were rejected elsewhere and are directed there by the LEA who use them to balance applicants with places available. We take Hainault as an exemplar because it is an unpopular school in a borough with high achieving and popular schools. This adds to the perception of the marginality of Hainault – not because it is necessarily a bad school but because it is not the school that parents wanted to get their children into and because of what it used to be. It is also importantly, as we showed in Chapter Six, a school where parents are not actively *choosing* to send their children and for that reason alone it is condemned. In many respects, Hainault is improving and its results are not that much worse than other schools deemed acceptable elsewhere, but it carries its history with it – of being the school for a working-class housing estate where little attention was paid to education:

'I think you're going into the background of ... the people who live in the surrounding area are, I mean in Hainault there are lots of white working-class people who live around there and who are just not very concerned in their children's education, or in the discipline. There is also the fact that the school doesn't really help themselves within the structure of the school itself, so put the two together and it gives a disaster, really, for everybody concerned.'

['So there's a lot of children in limbo. I was told the other day that quite a few children who live in Ilford area come to school up here to Hainault Forest because it has places.']

'Yes, they sort of move into the area and the school is full; in Seven Kings, even though they're in catchment for instance, they will have to go to a school where there is places, either Hainault – with no other places, they will invariably end up in Hainault!' (White British, female, Barkingside)

What often happens is that people move to Barkingside because they cannot afford the housing in the south of the borough and then 'hope for the best', but when they find that they have been allocated to Hainault, they panic. In some cases, they even rent out their house, rent one for themselves in the catchment of a popular school and so displace somebody else's child, adding to the further 'moral panic' about admissions. The record is rather different; at the time of our interviews Hainault was indeed coming out of 'special measures' but has been recognised in a subsequent (2008) Ofsted inspection as being 'satisfactory'. The following excerpt is the inspection team's summary of the school:

The school is smaller than average with a small sixth form. It has been designated as a Specialist Business and Enterprise College. Almost 60% of students come from minority ethnic backgrounds and half have English as an additional language, both figures well above average. Large numbers of students either join or leave the school at other than the usual times. The proportion of students identified with learning difficulties is average. Over a third of these have moderate learning difficulties, just under a third have behavioural, emotional and social difficulties, about 12% have speech and language difficulties and 5% have severe learning difficulties. At the time of the previous inspection the school was removed from special measures. The school has gained the 'Healthy Schools Award' and 'Sportsmark'. (Ofsted, 2008)

While Hainault has clearly had a problematic past – including its recent past – it is hard to square some of the respondent accounts with its current performance; in particular it is clearly no longer a white working-class school with the kind of demographic referred to above. It therefore carries a reputation from a quite long distant past before it today.

There is an ethnic narrative in these accounts; in respondent accounts Hainault is seen as the bastion of the white working class – itself now a popular cause for concern among aspirational parents of any ethnicity. In contrast the Catholic faith school Canon Palmer is often referred to in terms of its predominantly black enrolment. Both schools are generally held to be 'improving' by most professionals but nevertheless illustrate that school reputations are at the same time fragile and long-standing and subject to 'classed' and ethnicised narratives.

'I'll say, why you moving? And they'll say, oh, no, reason, no reason, just fancied a change! They are moving into the Hainault area to try to get into Trinity but if they don't get in they have to go to Hainault High! But I don't particularly like Hainault people. I mean, I find them very racist actually. You can guarantee that if you meet someone from Hainault, I just find them very racist people, they are real, sort of, not people I like very much! [laughing] I'm not going to go into detail ... very much Basildon sort of people, you know? You can tell the people from there, they're all over-made-up, people whose kids are totally obnoxious, they have no manners, really rude and run about eating sweets all day long. They are horrible children and I'm quite happy for them to go off to another school. I would much rather my children go to Canon Palmer where the kids are not so rude. I'm sorry, the reason their school is rubbish [Hainault] is because their kids go to it! You know, that's all it is.

It's their attitude [that's at fault]. I don't have any sympathy; I just find it amusing that they all end up in Hainault High when they've desperately tried to get into Trinity. Because Canon Palmer is doing quite well now ... they always ask me what schools I think are best and I just say Canon Palmer and you can see the look of horror on their faces as they think, oh, my kids have to mix with non-white children down there so we would never send them down there when, actually, it's got a pretty good reputation now. I think it's quite funny really, I know I shouldn't.' (White British, female, Barkingside)

## Going private: running the gamut of attitudes

Attitudes towards private education range from those of unthinking acceptability through instrumental engagement to principled objection. The former fall into two main groups: those who come from a family background in which private schooling was taken for granted and those who 'would if they could'; among the latter, views range from those who are opposed to the purchase of privilege and/or those who believe that you should educate your children where you live. The first position is articulated by this white, male respondent:

> 'I'll tell you what is the salient point here; [reference here to a close friend/relative] he decided to send his two children into the state sector, he lived in [up North] and he sent them to the local secondary modern school as it then was, and those children were failed educationally. [He] was an extremely bright man, he was [senior professional position] so he had a very responsible job. He had a degree from [Oxbridge], the home was filled with books, his wife was a [...] teacher, so what you might think of is this brilliant, intellectually nourishing environment for children to grow up in, but those children never got their A-levels and they had to then to do some further education to get some A-levels, and they struggled to get started on the ... in the working world, and only now have they really got themselves established. One of them is working as a teacher [... details suppressed] and the other is working in [a lowly public sector professional job in London]. And I just think, my goodness, if [he] hadn't had this ideological thing about sending the children to state school no matter what, and if – as he could well afford – [he had] sent those children to a good private school, those children would have, just, attained so much in their working lives. And so in many ways I felt that I was determined that I wasn't going to make the same mistake ... I'm not going to sacrifice my children's educational attainment just to make an ideological point.' (White British, male, Victoria Park)

A fellow Victoria Park resident sees it slightly differently, and nuances the case rather more subtly but basically takes the same view:

> 'Well, two of them went to school in the Barbican, that's City of London School for Girls which is a private school, and before that prep schools....'

> ['Did you ever contemplate sending them to a local school?']

'If there had been a good local school then, of course, we would have sent them there, you know, because it's not cheap having children go to private schools. But, you know, given that we could afford it we didn't. Lauriston, I think, has a reasonably good reputation. Actually ... [refers to somebody who teaches there]. It's not that it's terrible but secondary schools I think really round here I don't think secondary schools round here have a decent reputation at all. And I think some of them are pretty hellish, frankly ...

I can't think of anyone who's actually said that they wouldn't move to Hackney because of the education but I think if you move here then I think you've got to accept that if you want your children to, you know, go to a decent university or wherever, if you move to Hackney you're not going to go through the state system and achieve that easily. I mean if they are exceptionally bright then maybe they will but if they're just averagely able the state schools around here are not going to get them a decent university, I don't think.' (Indian, male, Victoria Park)

Private schooling, however, was not always the panacea that some believe it to be, as the following respondents showed:

'... we were both Labour Party supporters so we both probably would have preferred it if he had been able to be educated in a state school but because, as I explained to you, we were here for job reasons rather than educational reasons the schooling available to us in Tower Hamlets when we first moved here and when we first had our son was not of a very high standard, and so we took the view that we would have to educate him privately. Now, I understand from the results over the last couple of years they have improved a lot but we moved him out of his last school at the end of the summer term and we did offer him the option of going to a state school locally and he wasn't having any of it, so it didn't appeal to him....'

['So have you been happy with your selection of private schools?']

'Well it's been a bit of a disaster actually [laughs]. When I say we moved him out of [...] at the end of last term, we

moved him just before he was pushed. So had we not taken him out he would have been expelled. It was a question of him not liking the level of discipline at the school … he generally was unhappy, the school he's at now, it's for children who basically haven't survived in the mainstream private sphere, so this was kind of a "last chance saloon". So, no, we haven't done very well on choice up till now.'
(White British, female, Victoria Park)

However, for many of the respondents, private schooling represented the promised land and the following respondent was not the only one who called in family resources to educate her children privately, as a way of avoiding Loxford, Redbridge's other unpopular school:

'I was lucky because my mum could help, but it was a bit unfair … there is a difference between the haves and the have-nots and it was only because my mum was helping that my children ended up at private school. Had Loxford had a better education then I think they would have ended up going there and I do feel that we are paying all this money, it is difficult for my mum, but ultimately it is done now … and there are times when I feel very happy that they are there because the kinds of people that they are with, they're similar … many of the children's parents there are professionals.

A lot of the girls who go there don't come from this area so they are travelling in from outside areas and I'd say that maybe some people's perceptions are that at a private school you are guaranteed that your kids will do well and that they will be mixing with good girls, you know, but I don't necessarily agree with that … but it could be that. It could be that because people are paying for something they think they are getting the best, I can't really think of any other [reasons]. And there aren't many all girls secondary schools in Redbridge anyway and it's an important thing for Asian people with girls that they are in with other girls only.' (Pakistani, female, Central Redbridge)

## Social and ethnic segregation in schools

Social and ethnic mixing is at the heart of most urban policy, something that many pay lip service to and also something that many do their best to avoid; this respondent is a notable, and, it has to be said, rare, exception:

> '... One thing we did talk about when the children were small was that we wanted them to grow up in a very mixed area. We both [wife and I] grew up in monochrome areas. I can remember seeing a black person for the first time, you know, I can remember where in the street it was and so on, it was *so* unusual. But we are not just talking about ethnicity. It's about the breadth of human experience that they were going to encounter as well.... I think it was on the agenda for us to bring our kids up in a very mixed area, and we would say that is one of the great things about being in Tower Hamlets, but again, of course, it is not a simple issue. And I do sympathise with parents whose child is practically the only child who speaks English at home, or in the entire school or something like that. So, we are talking *mix* here....'
> (White British, male, Victoria Park)

The issue of segregation is an important one. In Chapter Six we quoted sources showing there is more ethnic mixing in London schools than elsewhere and also how in some parts, notably Tower Hamlets, some schools were almost exclusively Asian. At the same time, we have argued that how well students do can largely be explained by the social composition of the school. By this we mean that social background is more important than that of ethnicity and can affect individual performance. This chimes with many parents' 'gut feeling' that what matters is the social mix in the school, which can either benefit their child or 'drag them down'. Thus, not surprisingly, the issue of mix weighs heavily on respondents' minds when thinking about their children's education – mix meant both social and ethnic and the two usually became hopelessly confused. The nature of social and ethnic mixing changes as we move out from the Victoria Park study area where it is between white middle class, Asian and white (non-)working class:

> 'Secondary schools in Tower Hamlets are not brilliant, and there is a lot of segregation, partly by ... well, it goes basically along religious lines ... and gender. There are a

few mixed schools with mixed boys and girls and mixed racial backgrounds. This is an incredibly mixed area but we get this thing where the church schools take all of the white and Afro-Caribbean background kids and the state school system seem to get all that's left. So you get secondary schools that are 99% Bengali.

You either get all Bengali or you get all white and black and that's not how it should be, it should be a mixture of all three.... Nobody is unhappy with the schools we just don't want to be the first one – I don't want to be the first white, middle-class parent in my area to send my boy to a 99% Bengali high school. If it was going to be a true reflection of the borough then I would send them.

From what I've observed my kids are the only kids in the square who go to a state school. All the others go to mostly public schools. Some go to state primaries but they don't go to state secondaries.' (White British, female, Victoria Park)

An idealised conception of a 'nice' school is given by the next respondent, who also lives in the Victoria Park area:

['What do you think of education as a whole in the borough?']

'I think one problem in this borough is maybe I think our school [Catholic] is really nice because it is a really mixed, culturally ... they have children from absolutely everywhere except that there are no Asian kids which is really bizarre. But the ideal school of what I see is a nice, calm school where they have a bit of discipline and where they actually do learn something at the end of the day and there is a big mixture of people, people of all backgrounds. And that is what it is, it's a really lovely school. But I think probably one of the problems in this area is that it is so polarised. You get schools where all the kids are Asian and you have one white kid in the class or you go a bit further east of here and it's all white kids and like [school] for example which is just down the road from here, that's almost all white and it just seems so extreme that you can go half a mile and you can have a completely different but extreme mixture of kids and I think that's a pity. In an ideal world it would be mixed....

... there's one school that's too far from us but called, Bangabandhu, and the white parents were saying that it has got a good reputation but it would be the only white child in the school, which isn't ideal really. There's nothing wrong with it but it's not ideal. So, and I know that [...] down the road who goes to Bonner has said that in the holidays he's the only child left in the class really, there's three of them in the class and I don't know what festivals but Eid, yes I think it was Eid when there was only three kids left in the class which is a shame.'

['Would it put you off if a school was dominated by a particular ethnic group?']

'Yes, if there wasn't a mix, yes. I mean there's a school just around the corner from here, it's a Catholic school and it's interesting just how divided the community is around here – Cardinal Pole and that's all, there it's completely black Afro-Caribbean and so few white kids there as well. And again fine but I wouldn't want to be, it's not ideal to be the only white kid in the class.' (White British, female, Victoria Park)

We referred in Chapter Six to the Black Caribbean respondent, who moved from Newham to Leyton to give her a better choice of school for her daughter only to send her to a faith school in Havering (London's whitest borough):

'It's so white in Havering. And I haven't ... because she grew up in Newham and went to school in Newham, very very mixed, and she then had the complete reverse to go to Havering. Being in school it's alright most of the time....

It's in Upminster. And they haven't got any ... all the teachers are white, all the teachers are white. And, um, there was one temporary teacher from South Africa when she was in Year 7 and since then there has been no one. And, you know, people still have very interesting ideas about, about difference ... and ... and then the other thing I didn't consider was the journey ... I considered the amount of time it took, but I didn't consider the kind of....'

['The toll it would take on your daughter?']

'Yeah, because they get off at West Ham and there is black people and Asian people but when you get off at the other end no one looks like you ... and people *still* shout things in the street. And they do say things ... and they do get treated differently at the bus stop and they do, you know....'

['What's the ethnic mix like at [her school] though?']

[The respondent goes to the mantelpiece and gets a collective photograph showing every pupil at her daughter's school – it is nearly all white] (Black Caribbean, female, Leyton)

The following respondent, who also has a black daughter, tells an interesting story about ethnic mix in Redbridge, where the grammar school to which her daughter goes is largely populated by white and Asian children:

'I do think the performance does have a lot to do with it, but I think that they see the influence of the school in the borough they're actually living in, and the ... the group of children that the daughter would actually mix with, and I think because they want them to do well, they felt that they'd be pulled back or kept back because of people they'd probably mix with, you know. And I'm sure that's what most of them think. I wasn't sure – at first when my daughter started school in Woodford, she mixed for a year or two with quite a number of white girls, you know, and ... but I wasn't unduly worried about it 'cos ... it seemed that after the two years, she began to mix more with her own blacks and Asians – in the end that's who she actually went around with. But initially, she definitely mixed with more white people – she used to have sleepovers, go to their house – they actually came down here too so I was quite surprised as at first I thought they wouldn't, but there were a few of them that had actually lived in East London before and had moved out. But I still wasn't sure if they were uneasy about their daughter coming to our house, but they were ok and as I say they came here a few times.' (Black Caribbean, female, Leyton)

Canon Palmer, a Catholic faith school in Redbridge, was perceived by white respondents as having a largely black enrolment, and this appeared to be equated with poor behaviour and poor attainment although the latter was increasingly not the case. Its current enrolment is 30% black, 24% Asian and 46% white (see Table 7.6).

'I think it was just predominantly black, well, I wouldn't say it was predominantly black, there are a large number of black children, and the reputation of the black children has just gone downhill. Whether this was the same when we went to school, I don't know, their behaviour is just diabolical and I didn't want that for my child.' (White British, female, Barkingside)

It is worth noting that in its most recent Ofsted inspection (in 2007) the school was rated overall as 'outstanding' and it was also noted that

**Table 7.6: Ethnic composition of faith secondary schools, East London, 2007**

| School name | Borough | Total pupils | Black | Asian | White |
|---|---|---|---|---|---|
| All Saints RC | Barking | 1,089 | 27.7 | 3.3 | 69.0 |
| Yesodey Hatorah Girls | Hackney | 235 | 0.0 | 0.0 | 100.0 |
| Our Lady's Convent RC | Hackney | 738 | 50.5 | 7.1 | 42.4 |
| Cardinal Pole RC | Hackney | 999 | 60.5 | 2.6 | 36.9 |
| The Campion RC | Havering | 995 | 3.4 | 0.3 | 96.3 |
| Sacred Heart Girls' | Havering | 807 | 8.2 | 1.2 | 90.6 |
| St Edward's C of E | Havering | 1,255 | 17.1 | 2.3 | 80.6 |
| St Bonaventure's RC | Newham | 1,285 | 47.6 | 13.6 | 38.8 |
| St Angela's Ursuline RC | Newham | 1,322 | 55.8 | 19.4 | 24.7 |
| King Solomon | Redbridge | 908 | 0.0 | 0.0 | 100.0 |
| Trinity Catholic | Redbridge | 1,687 | 9.3 | 3.1 | 87.6 |
| Canon Palmer RC | Redbridge | 1,281 | 30.1 | 24.3 | 45.7 |
| Ilford Ursuline RC | Redbridge | 607 | 29.2 | 27.5 | 43.3 |
| Raine's Foundation | Tower Hamlets | 867 | 29.3 | 8.9 | 61.8 |
| Bishop Challoner RC Boys | Tower Hamlets | 527 | 34.9 | 9.5 | 55.6 |
| Bishop Challoner RC Girls | Tower Hamlets | 965 | 38.4 | 9.6 | 51.9 |
| Sir John Cass C of E | Tower Hamlets | 1,234 | 18.4 | 68.1 | 13.5 |
| The Holy Family RC | Waltham Forest | 1,043 | 41.0 | 7.8 | 51.2 |

*Source:* Calculated by authors from PLASC data

30% of its pupils spoke English as an additional language. On most counts, this is clearly a strongly performing school.

## School ethos and management

Underlying the concern about education is one about social and ethnic mix and whom one's child will be mixing with. This concern can be amplified or assuaged by the way in which schools are perceived to be managed. Critical to this perception is the question of discipline – successful schools have headteachers who are seen to offer a traditionally clear leadership. We have argued that the main factors affecting school performance are the social composition of the school in terms of the home background of the pupils. Pupils from better-off home backgrounds achieve better and schools with good attainment tend to have high concentrations of such pupils. Such schools are, by and large, popular schools, and what makes them such is the appeal they have to parents worried about the social relations within the school. Appeals to discipline do not, in themselves, we would argue, lead to high standards but they do help make a school popular and so increase the 'quality' of its intake.[3] This comes across again and again in relation to Seven Kings, whose head (Sir Alan Steer) is strongly identified with maintaining a well-disciplined school ethos – which also happens to be a meritocratic, egalitarian and localist one:

> '... Behaviour is definitely – it's the key. I mean our head is the leader of the leading group on discipline and, ... for him the discipline is the key to everything, it's the key to achievement.'

> 'Well, I think it has a very, very strong head who's been there for about 15 years, and he's really wanted to ... to change things, and didn't accept that kids were a product of their background. For him, it was very much, you know, the school could do a lot for the children, and he went about linking achievement to behaviour and also the dissemination of his thought throughout the entire staff. So we have a programme of everybody in the school doing the same thing, in terms of everyone following exactly the same pattern in terms of lessons, so children will line up outside the classroom, they will enter in an orderly manner. Then the uniform's got to be adhered to at all times, and you see members of staff pulling up kids to show and comment, and

it may sound silly but often, you know, if children haven't got on the right uniform, it's still not sort of bending the rules to the extreme, but if they bend the rules to, with the uniform, they're going to bend it elsewhere. And the head is also very ... didactic in terms of how you should teach the lessons – the lesson should be, you know, how much should they be given at the beginning of the lesson and, you know, you should have the three-part lessons and with a re-cap at the end of the lesson, and that's everybody should do it. I'm not saying that everybody does but this is the way that it should be done. There is also a disciplinary process, which is very, very ... very gradual, you know. It's, such and such a thing happened, then this will happen, so if you don't do your homework the teacher will give you a detention, then it carries on to the head of department. If there is, sort of, minor offences, disciplinary offences, the head of year is there to deal with it. And the head of year has quite a load of time relief in his or her timetable to deal with such issues.' (White British, female, Barkingside)

Compare this with a respondent talking about Hainault, which she knew quite well:

'... Even working in class, the children can't be bothered and they're not interested in learning. They'd rather talk, put their make-up on, on the phone ... and no matter how many times a teacher would ask them to put it away, it's just ignored. And it's just this attitude that they have, you know. And I feel sorry because there are some really lovely children in the school that want to get on and it's so hard because the structure is changing now. Instead of having a top set – last year we had a top, middle and a bottom – but now it seems to be, there are only a couple of subjects that still do it, but then they're just in mixed ability in all the classes. And when you've got this element of disruption, the ones that want to work, they can't. It's very, very difficult.' (White British, female, Barkingside)

## Conclusions

In this chapter the respondents spoke about some of the key concerns driving their views about education. We talked about two groups pushing past each other in and out of the city; those going in were well established and quite prepared (for the most part) to take on its historically poor education system designed in a previous age to fail a working class. Those going out had to grasp out of necessity every opportunity offered by an education system that was unevenly and thinly spread across East London. For them, there was no alternative and they embraced the New Labour reform agenda, based, as it was, around a narrowly conceived curriculum but in the context where educational achievement was possible and the only route out of inner East London. Both groups therefore strategised and manoeuvred around these new markets in housing, education and ultimately aspiration. The inbound whites were reasonably confident in their ability to manage whatever the inner city could throw at them while celebrating its diverse social environments and congratulating themselves for so doing. The outbound minorities were fleeing an inner city rapidly becoming a new zone of transition and enthusiastically dis/re-placing a white lower middle and white working class of clerks and taxi drivers from Redbridge for whom the new promised land was Essex. For neither group was it going to be easy, and both had to make compromises, suffer defeats and then regroup and redefine the problem. So bright, Oxbridge-educated journalists unused to finding their view of the world contradicted by reality had to re-engineer their secular lives to embrace a rejected Catholicism rather than engage a distastefully racist white working class. For them, as ever, the optimal solution was a 'Goldilocks' one – of getting the social and ethnic mix just right, which meant leaving them and their friends in control. For the outbound minorities, they were largely entering a *terra incognita* in that while they would be joining their fellow Asians who had also made the trek from Newham, they were also clambering up the class ladder with little knowledge of where the snakes were located. All they knew was that there were snakes and the danger of falling back was ever present.

## Notes

[1] This is not in any way meant to demean this rich strand of research that has had a recent and very welcome resurgence in the sociology of education with the work of (among others) Stephen Ball (2002), Diane Reay (2005), Stephen Ball and Carol Vincent (1998) and Sally Power et al (2003). The PLASC analysis with Mosaic simply uses a different source of data that looks at all children and therefore overcomes precisely the objections to both survey and in-depth interviewing raised by Savage and Burrows (2007, 2009).

[2] See Diane Reay's interesting comments on this phenomenon, which she broadly argues is an attempt to have it both ways (Reay et al, 2007).

[3] What the data do not show is how this might operate within a school (for example, by set or class group that are often divided by social background; see Webber and Butler, 2007); PLASC only collects data at school level.

# EIGHT

# Conclusions: achieving aspiration?

'What I wanted was get them educated first, good education, good living standards, get some A-levels. I didn't want my children to be a drug dealer. That was my major objective which I achieved.' (Ugandan Indian, male, Barkingside)

## Introduction: the transformation of East London

We have argued in this book that East London has undergone a series of dramatic and far-reaching economic and social transformations over the last 40 years. First, its traditional economic base rooted in the docks and associated manufacturing has largely disappeared to be replaced by a new, service-based, economy. Second, and as a direct consequence of these changes, its occupational class structure has also been transformed. As the previous jobs in manufacturing and the docks have disappeared, so has much of its traditional working class – through retirement, economic inactivity, outmigration and death. They have been replaced in part by a large new white-collar lower middle class, working in non-manual employment often in the burgeoning financial services sector. This is not to say, of course, that the traditional working class has disappeared, but it has shrunk and been transformed. Third, London's ethnic mix has changed over the last 20–30 years, and this change has been particularly dramatic over the last 15 years. London has gone from being an overwhelmingly white, mono-ethnic city in the 1960s and 1970s to one in which minority ethnic groups comprised a third of the population in 2001, and this could grow to over 40% by the 2011 Census. As they have expanded in number, they have also expanded geographically, moving out into what were previously largely white suburban areas. At the same time, the white population is also declining and the traditional East End collectivist white working-class culture has been in rapid decline. The new East London that is in the process of emergence is a firmly multi-ethnic one.

Unlike some of the negative urban social changes which have been so tellingly analysed elsewhere by writers such as W. Julius Wilson in his book *When work disappears* (1996), which analyses the problems which beset black inner-city neighbourhoods when the economic base collapses, or Loic Wacquant's work on advanced, urban marginality (2008), or Roger Waldinger's (1996) *Still the promised city*, which examined how African Americans have lost out to immigrants in the New York labour market, our account of what is happening in East London is rather more optimistic – largely because our focus has been different, although the processes of change are not without their problems. Essentially, we argue that we are seeing the growth of a new minority ethnic middle class, with strong educational and residential aspirations, who are managing to move out of the inner-city areas where they or their parents, or grandparents, settled, and into the suburbs and better housing. Some are unemployed, some are economically inactive, but some are managing to move upwards and outwards. We do not for a moment deny the growth of 'urban marginality' – indeed, we have argued those in such positions constitute one of the largest social groups in contemporary London and this group is disproportionately located in East London.

Nevertheless, the way in which some of the well-established minorities have appeared to prosper in East London's transition from a Fordist industrial city to a neoliberal post-industrial one is a crucially important story and one we have attempted to tell. There is no doubt that in some parts of London there are major problems in terms of low educational attainment, high rates of unemployment and economic inactivity, benefit dependency, crime and poor housing, but some groups are managing to transcend disadvantaged backgrounds.

These changes have taken place in the context of a rapidly changing housing market in which the long-term postwar growth of home ownership has slowed in recent years, to be replaced by the growth of private renting. The decline of council housing has been parallelled by the growth of other forms of social housing, notably housing associations (or registered social landlords). What is particularly significant is that the net growth of home ownership appears to be almost wholly confined to minority ethnic groups in East London. These changes have not been confined to East London but they have been very marked there and the respondents were clearly aware of the nature of the ethnic changes which had taken place and were taking place, although their reactions to them varied considerably, with some evidence of 'white flight' to the outer suburbs and beyond into the county of Essex. Many of the respondents shared the view that some parts of the area were now much more transient, with common perceptions of social and environmental decline as a result of population and density increases associated in part with the growth of 'buy to let'.

Although most minority ethnic groups have long been at the bottom of the occupational and income pile, this is now beginning to change. This group is (or probably more accurately, these groups are) now aspiring to professional and managerial jobs, both for themselves and especially for their children. Educational aspiration, both for children to do well at school and to go on to high-quality university education, was widespread among the minority ethnic households we interviewed; they saw education as the key to subsequent occupational success and upward social and economic mobility. In this respect, they have joined the white professional classes in recognising the key role education plays in successful social reproduction. There is also an awareness of the costs of failure and a desire on the part of many minority ethnic groups to keep their children away from what are seen as the pervasive dangers of 'street culture' and the risk of 'falling back' that is implied in all of this. In other words, a group that has for so long been regarded as the 'social other' is now itself becoming concerned with the danger of 'social contagion' which has long been at the heart of the white middle-class obsession with education and social reproduction (Power et al, 2003).

We have argued from the evidence of our interviews in East London that many respondents, particularly those from minority ethnic backgrounds, have been able, over the last 15–20 years, not merely to articulate but begin to realise a longstanding set of aspirations for the future. Key to these has been a sense of self-confidence that has enabled some of them for the first time in the years since first settlement to move out of the inner city to suburban boroughs of outer London. Not only are these areas equated with success, their semi-detached housing with off-road parking are more representative of achievement than the long lines of inner-city terraced housing, much of which was in multiple occupation when they first arrived, but they also have some of the best-attaining schools in London in terms of GCSE results. Education has therefore been central to this account but it is impossible to over-emphasise that one of the biggest changes has been the sense (on the part of some at least) that they can move out into what was formerly white-dominated suburbia and away from the inner city. It is only in the last 15 or so years that many Black and Asian Britons have felt sufficiently confident to venture into what were seen as the bastions of whiteness and working-class mobility in East London – this is perhaps most advanced in Redbridge, least so in Havering (London's whitest borough) and most dramatic in Barking & Dagenham (which had the highest rate of change between 1991 and 2001, albeit from a very low base). This has been made possible not simply by a change in ethos but also, of course, by rising living standards and the death or movement out of such places by the existing and increasingly elderly white populations. At the same time, many of the houses left by both sets of outmovers have been 'bought to let' and now form part of an increased private rental tenure, providing housing for new immigrant groups, students and others displaced by changes in the sub-region's housing and labour markets. This inward and outward movement of the city region's middle classes is, as we argue below, a significant development from the stress on displacement-inducing gentrification that has dominated much of the recent literature on urban change.

## So far so good ...

In many respects, we are reporting here a good news story about upward mobility; but, like most good stories, it has its downside, which is the longstanding poverty of East London which remains, by some margin, the poorest area of London – itself the richest region within the EU. Although this and the ongoing social exclusion of many groups (including the high levels of economic inactivity among the [non-] working class) are not the focus of the book, it would be very misleading to give the impression that either we had airbrushed them out of the story or that they were no longer important. The increasing numbers of people who have become economically marginal remain a vitally important element to any understanding of the contemporary city (Wacquant, 2008), but it is also important that we do not automatically equate their continued marginality with the relative success of some of the social groups that are the focus of this study. Minority ethnic groups remain disproportionately represented at the lower end and bottom of the urban social hierarchy but it would be a major mistake to argue that all minority ethnic groups are socially excluded. The point that we have been making throughout this book is that some at least of East London's established minority groups are clawing their way out of the social exclusion to which they were consigned when they, or their parents or grandparents, migrated to the UK two or three generations back. Many remain and they have been joined by new groups – from Africa, the Balkans, Afghanistan and most recently from the so-called A8 'accession states' to the EU; many are white and, unlike many of the subjects of this study, were brought up in a non-English language culture. Thus the mainstream literature is correct to maintain a continuing link to urban marginality in London and other similar cities (Wills et al, 2010). In East London this remains the case, but some members of these groups are *also* upwardly mobile.

We argue that East London has continued to function as an immigrant reception area much as it did in the 19th century and before. What has changed is the nature of the recent immigrants, initially Indian, Pakistani and African-Caribbean, then Bangladeshi and more recently Black African. However, just like their predecessors, the more successful are gradually pushing out into the suburbs, following the East End Jews of the earlier generations who moved out to the suburbs in the interwar period. At the same time, two new groups, the Eastern Europeans and refugees from the Balkans and the Horn of Africa, are also making their presence felt in East London. The initial areas of immigration were Hackney, Tower Hamlets and Newham, but gentrification, particularly in the first two, is limiting their ability to act in this way, transforming Newham into a classic 'zone in transition', as a migrant reception and sorting area for London, from which over time, as new groups move in, the more successful move outwards to try to improve their housing and living conditions and to escape the stigma of poverty and deprivation often attached to such areas.[1]

Globalisation is a contested concept and we are sympathetic to those sceptics who question the extent to which it has transformed the social and economic relations of contemporary capitalism; at the same time, it is hard to overestimate the effect that the internationalisation of the financial services industry has had on London. In particular, this has driven the recent surge in international migration that, it is estimated, has resulted in a net positive in-migration balance of 150,000 a year into London in recent years (Gordon et al, 2007). Many of these migrants settled in East London, adding to the pressure on the existing population; this has undoubtedly added to the impetus for existing residents to move out. Not only do they see suburbanisation as having positive outcomes for themselves and their households, but they also see the migration process as contributing to a likely further deterioration in the local environment and particularly the educational outcomes for their children. These compare increasingly unfavourably with boroughs like Redbridge.

Migration has always played a role in urban development but it is this renewed focus on international migration that has driven much of the social and economic change in London over recent decades. In 2001 approximately one third of the population of London was born outside the UK and this proportion will have risen even higher by the time of the 2011 Census. This dynamic has, we suggest, provided a 'comfort zone' for many of the (largely British-born) minority ethnic populations of East London, allowing them to make the move out of inner East London for reasons we have already suggested – put very crudely, they have taken comfort from no longer being at the bottom of the pile and so have felt sufficient confidence to move out of what remain some of the zones of first settlement. There have of course also been the push–pull factors of demand for housing in areas like Newham by incoming migrants and gentrifying middle classes, and the fact that the white working and lower middle classes were either dying out or moving out. Not only therefore has suburbanisation joined gentrification in the reshaping of the post-industrial city, but ethnic reshaping has also joined class change in a process in which social change has once more acquired a definite spatialisation – on which we have focused. Suburbanisation is no longer a white-dominated phenomenon but rather has increasingly become appropriated as a means of asserting aspiration by minority ethnic groups.

## Education, education, education ...

Many of our substantive findings have concerned education and schooling: these have ranged from school provision and attainment across East London and the structuring and working of the system of school choice to respondents' perceptions of education and schooling. We have stressed this for three reasons: first, because traditionally secondary education in East London, and in working-class areas in general, was not of high quality and often provided training for work – 'Learning to labour', as Paul Willis (1977) put it in his eponymous book; second, because the changes in the class and ethnic composition of East London have changed educational expectations; and third, because the government's 'choice' agenda and the publication of league tables (and Ofsted inspection reports) has served to focus parental attention on school attainment and quality. This is important because, as we show, there are considerable differences in attainment both between boroughs, but more importantly, between schools. Contrary to the former Labour government's stress on 'failing' schools, we do not view the differences in attainment primarily as a result of deficiencies of management, expectations or teaching, although these undoubtedly play a role, but as a result of differences in the social composition of schools. Other things being equal, a school drawing primarily on a poor area is likely to have lower results than one drawing on an affluent middle-class catchment area.

We found ethnic background and the social character of pupils' residential areas (which we used as an indicator for social background) both played a role in influencing attainment, with the latter being slightly more important. However, we also found that school context was important, in that pupils from less advantageous backgrounds tended to perform better on average in schools with a generally 'socially advantaged' composition. Not surprisingly, parents often take attainment into account when listing their preferences both in terms of seeking out 'good' schools and in trying to avoid less popular schools. We found consistent evidence of a broad hierarchy of school popularity across all boroughs, measured in terms of the applications/places ratio, with a common pattern of two or three very popular schools, and one or two very unpopular ones. The relationship between popularity and attainment was particularly fraught; statistically it was imperfect, with some correlation between the most and least popular schools and good/bad attainment but rather less for those in the middle. More importantly, these measures did not take into account the generally socially advantaged nature of most of the popular schools, nor did they account for the particular circumstances of faith schools.

We have examined the issue of choice at a sub-regional level – seeing East London as a set of 'circuits of schooling' (Ball et al, 1995) that corresponded to how a significant proportion of the respondents across our five research areas saw it. They made often strategic decisions about how to operate within these 'markets' – ranging from the affluent professionals in Victoria Park who decided to prioritise where to live and buy education in the elite private circuit of schooling in inner London to the 'aspirational' members of the minority communities in Newham who invested all in moving out to Redbridge with its high-achieving selective and particularly non-selective schools. Others – particularly, but not exclusively, black respondents – pursued 'the faith option', whereas a small but significant group of white lower professionals sent their children to Newham's rapidly improving secondary schools. Clearly this is a considerable oversimplification of a more complex picture, but these are key elements. We have therefore identified a series of different but overlapping circuits in the East London sub-region; these circuits are structured by class, ethnicity and place and these differences help explain how the various groups behave in relation to the provision of schooling.

In our account of Redbridge, we drew on parental perceptions of school choice to argue that many were attracted to Redbridge precisely because it offered high-quality *non-selective* education alongside high-quality selective education. In the case of most non-white parents, this was seen as part of a generational struggle in which education played a crucial role to improve their children's prospects: most of these parents were aware that schools were also potentially agents of failure, that choices carried risks, and a failure to get into a popular school could undermine the striving of the most ambitious of parents. We identified some strongly articulated 'avoidance narratives' in Redbridge which can be directly related to the existence of an infrastructure of successful non-selective schools in which selective 'circuits of schooling' (whether by fees, faith or ability) are regarded as fallbacks. Similar avoidance narratives were identified in all the other boroughs where we interviewed parents, all of which have a number of unpopular schools.

An important strand to our findings has been that while some respondents eagerly grasped the opportunities offered by the new policy of school choice, many failed in their preferred choices, and have thus become somewhat disillusioned. However, we need to balance this against the overall finding that their perception was of general satisfaction with the schooling their children were receiving and also that they felt, on balance, that schools were improving – a perception which is supported by official data (whatever its flaws). Nevertheless, the 'choice agenda', originally promoted by Tony Blair when Prime Minister, has been somewhat perverse in the manner in which it has created a widespread climate of dissatisfaction and, arguably, has led to a situation in which those who get their children into popular schools feel it is no more than their entitlement while, at the same time, creating resentment among those who either fail in their preferred choices or, more commonly, feel they have been forced to choose a school they would not otherwise choose because the alternatives are even worse – one of the so-called 'sink schools'. In this sense, we suggest that choice is often little more than a rationing mechanism which has some very detrimental side effects – notably, alienated parents who feel that they have been landed with a sub-optimal outcome.

Even if they are reasonably happy with how their child is doing, there is always the nagging doubt that if they had got into their favoured school they would be doing that much better. Inevitably in such circumstances, a sense of personal failure is experienced and schools whose performance measures are often achieved in the context of relatively high levels of social deprivation are justified in feeling themselves demonised in the court of parental popularity. Thus success (in an LEA with a good reputation) far from breeding success is in danger of breeding failure, both in some of its schools and in those who feel they are forced to attend them. Put another way, there was little evidence of 'voice' (Hirschman, 1970) – accommodations were made through individual strategising, gaming and deception but not through collective activity. In the light of this, the arguments for a 'rising tide' in which good provision lifts the less good, would not appear to be working in East London, where choice has created perceptions of failure, increased polarisation and done nothing for improving social justice – despite the fact that, as with elsewhere in England, annual results continue to improve year on year. Nevertheless, despite these feelings of disillusion among our respondents – some more than others – the overall sense was one of guarded satisfaction that things were getting better, that they had been lucky and, more generally in relation to our central theme of 'aspiration', that things were more or less 'on track'. This, we believe, is an important finding, although one fraught with dangers in case they then go 'off track'.

In broad policy terms, our research raises important questions about the feasibility of New Labour's stress on parental choice as a way to drive up school quality and in particular about whether this can be continued in a resource-constrained environment. While in theory it may seem attractive, the demand for places at schools with good reputations and performance far exceeds the number of places available, and many parents and their children are disappointed and are forced to accept places in their local catchment school. To date, this has not caused huge concern among our respondents because, in practice, these young people in such schools are probably achieving better results than in previous years or indeed in similar schools in other boroughs, but the perception is that they may not be doing as well as if they had been in their schools of choice. The ideology of parental choice thus seems rather threadbare in practice. Schools perceived as good are 'positional goods' and access to them is inevitably limited, and a stress on choice, it might be argued, is in danger of creating 'hard to shift' perceptions of failing schools. In short, 'choice' has little to do with driving up quality but is more about managing supply and demand and demonising a small (but increasing) number of schools in relatively deprived catchment areas that are seen as 'unacceptable' or 'failing' in the eyes of many local parents and the former DCSF.

Not surprisingly, the shortage of places at popular schools and the nature of the allocation process with its stress on distance to school as the key allocational procedure has led to a number of parents 'gaming the system', either by moving into or renting flats in the catchment areas of popular schools or calculating which desired schools represent feasible choices and which ones are unfeasible.

## Rethinking urban social change: the limits to gentrification

While gentrification has been, and remains, an important process in transforming the class structure and housing market of some inner-city areas and one about which we have both written about extensively, it is not the 'only game in town' (Watt, 2008) and needs to be examined in the context of a wider set of social and spatial transformations of the city, not least the changes which are taking place within some mature suburban areas as they age and as one population is replaced by another.

Gentrification has been a key concept in understanding a phase in the development of the post-industrial city but there is a danger that an overweening belief in its continued malign influence on urban change is blinding us to the new kinds of movement of emergent as well as well-established groups about the city – such as we have focused on in this book. It is worth noting that we have studiously *not* counterposed the kind of minority ethnic suburbanisation we have identified with more traditional forms of (white) 'urban-seeking' gentrification. Rather, we see the minority ethnic suburbanisation of Redbridge, Walthamstow and now Barking & Dagenham as being a distinct but related process to the traditional upper professional and managerial gentrification of Victoria Park's elegant terraces and the more recent colonisation of Newham's more mundane and mean streets by lower professionals. We hesitate to call this a process of suburban gentrification, as the nature of the groups involved and their reasons for moving are very different. Whereas traditional gentrifiers were seeking the cultural diversity and stimulation of the inner city, along with proximity to central work places and affordable housing, the new suburban residents are, in part, trying to escape from the seeming chaos of the inner city in favour of a more predictable urban social environment. It is therefore more appropriate to see what is happening as simply minority ethnic suburbanisation. However separate the two processes are in terms of actors and motivations, they should be regarded as related aspects of contemporary urban change.

Much of the literature on gentrification has stressed displacement that is seen to be key to the process. We do not deny that most early gentrification in London, New York and elsewhere involved class and tenurial displacement as working-class renters were pushed out by middle-class owners, but there seems evidence to us that much of what is happening in East London today is more often 'replacement', as groups move or die out and are replaced by others who positively value the space they have vacated. While some white groups are being indirectly displaced (or replaced) by minority ethnic inmovers who are changing the ethnic composition of the area, this reflects the overall change that is occurring in the class and ethnic composition of London more generally and East London in particular. For this reason, we prefer to see this as a process of replacement in which different groups are acting out of choice, however constrained they may feel that choice to be. At the same time, there clearly are processes of active indirect or 'exclusionary displacement' occurring – particularly in the Olympic development site in Newham and its fringe areas such as Hackney Wick and Leyton. It would, however, be a mistake, in our view, to generalise this to the kind of change occurring across much of outer East London.

The link between displacement and gentrification has become an act of faith for some scholars (Slater, 2006), but we would suggest that there is a danger that sometimes this can lead to selective vision. Undoubtedly there is direct, or more often what Marcuse (1986) has called exclusionary, displacement in East London, but our research would suggest that the bigger picture is more complex than this and we would draw attention in particular to the growth in private rented tenure in recent years, discussed in Chapter Three. Ironically (given the history of gentrification in London which involved the large-scale displacement of private rented tenants to make way for single-family owner-occupied dwellings), one of the trends in East London, particularly in areas of Newham, has been the transformation of owner-occupied single-family homes into multi-occupied 'buy-to-let' properties. This is, in our view, not gentrification *per se* but rather the conversion of single-family houses into rental multi-occupation for a new and mobile tenancy, many of whom are new migrants or existing residents unable to enter home ownership. In many respects, it can be seen to parallel the shift from ownership to multi-occupation which characterised parts of inner London pre-gentrification in the 1950s and 1960s. We accept that this relatively recent trend is open to debate, but would nevertheless argue that there is a danger in reifying gentrification as a concept in such a way that it blinds us to new trends which have their own, potentially worrying, social consequences. Buy to let may or may not represent a new trend in gentrification but it is perceived by many of our respondents as preventing them from buying a house where they would otherwise expect to have been able to do so, and it is also preventing them, in extreme cases, from sending their children to school in their own catchment area because somebody has rented a flat in a multi-occupied house expressly for that purpose.

The relations therefore between renting, owning and landlordism have become more opaque and complex as have those between replacement and displacement and, for this reason, we have, where possible, avoided the use of the term 'gentrification' precisely because it runs the danger of bringing an overly prescriptive analytical baggage to a description of the kinds of changes we have witnessed among a much wider group of the middle classes than normally associated with gentrification research. As we have argued elsewhere (Butler and Hamnett, 2009), there is a danger of looking at cities through the rear view mirror rather than looking at what is going on out of the windscreen and on the streets and pavements around us.

Thus gentrification theory, while undoubtedly having provided crucial and critical insights into recent urban change, does run the danger of blinding us to some of the more important aspects of contemporary change which are being driven by international as opposed to simply national pressures. Chief among these factors, we would include ethnic as well as class change, outward as well as inward movement, replacement as well as displacement, and buy to let rather than owner-occupation as the major tenurial shift. Additionally, we would argue the need to focus on upward as well as downward social mobility and the central role played by education and the emerging markets in educational choice. Tom Slater (2006) adopts a rather dismissive approach to the integration of education into studies of gentrification, on the grounds that concerns with education and individual forms of social reproduction reflect a middle-class obsession. For our part, we would argue that it is not simply a reflection of middle-class obsessions but rather an indication of important underlying changes in class formation and the manner in which upwardly aspiring groups strategise to achieve change for themselves and their children (Savage et al, 1992; Ball, 2002, 2008). Gentrification is therefore important, but we need to be flexible in terms of the way in which we understand the changed social and economic context, the different actors and the different spatialisations in which these changes are occurring. In particular, it has overlooked the suburbs – one might argue for yet another sub-set of suburban gentrification but this might weaken the concept to make it meaningless. Our approach has been to focus on the twin processes of gentrification and suburbanisation in understanding the contemporary re-making of East London that has been a process of both class and ethnic change. Gentrification research has had relatively little to say about ethnic change and almost nothing to say about suburbanisation. If we have concentrated in this book more on suburbanisation than gentrification, it is in large part because the former has been the dominant process among those already living in East London. They are not exclusive but, in our view, complementary concepts which, taken together, can throw much light on the ways in which cities like London, and its eastern section in particular, are changing.

Within the new constellations of class and ethnicity we have discussed, we suggest that there has been a sense of cautious confidence over the last two decades about the ways in which ethnicity and class background are now not necessarily seen as an inevitable bar to future progress – in contrast to the experience of the recent past. While the suburbanising minority ethnic groups are displaying a new self-confidence about how they navigate the institutions of Britishness – notably by the ways in which they have colonised what might have previously been seen as its suburban heartlands – so too have the other actors in what we term the 'urban contraflow', the white professional middle classes who have chosen to 'live the inner city'. There is nothing particularly new to this rather overt celebration of 'diversity', which was central to accounts offered by the respondents in Victoria Park and Newham about what they found positive about their areas. One of us has previously written about the gentrification of Brixton and Hackney as being 'socially tectonic', in which different social groups slide past each other, maintaining little by way of regular social contact (Butler and Robson, 2001), implying that the middle classes treat the minority ethnic groups and working classes as merely colourful social wallpaper. There are strong elements of this in Victoria Park, where the educational apartheid ensures that there is minimal social contact; however, this does not include all respondents, and in Newham we found evidence of positive social mixing. In contrast to Diane Reay, who is justly sceptical about how middle-class parents sending their children to socially and ethnically mixed schools call this a 'win–win' situation (Reay et al, 2007), we believe that there is some evidence of commitment to improving poorly performing schools, provided there is a minimal critical mass of middle-class children, evidence of school improvement and the opportunities to continue to good sixth form provision. There is therefore in this account of East London's middle classes some evidence for an element of ethnic mixing *within* the middle classes, although there remains plenty of evidence of the kind of tectonics referred to above.

Lest we be misunderstood, inequality remains a huge problem in London, and this is only likely to become more acute with a long-term economic slowdown. We perhaps need to sharpen up some old tools to understand this – those provided by notions of class and capital come to mind rather than the ones of social difference and identity with which social science has equipped itself in recent decades, with the rise of postmodernism and the decline of politics since the rise of Thatcherism and its consolidation under New Labour. However, we also argue there is a need to understand that some groups are able to make gains while others are treading water or even sinking back in the context of an overall restructuring of capitalist social relations. The white working classes made such gains during the long postwar boom (what the French term the '*trentes glorieuses*'), and we ask whether it is fanciful to predict a similar set of social and economic consolidations by the non-white middle classes who make up a significant part of East London's population.

Finally, it is important that we return to three areas identified in the introduction to the book that we have chosen not to focus on explicitly: first, that of gender; second, that of inter-class relations; and third, that of policy. We have not addressed them because our primary aim was to chart the ways in which class and ethnicity have been changing in East London. Our objective has been to analyse the ways in which different groups have been moving in and out of East London and how our respondents have justified this in terms of their aspirations for the future – for them and particularly for their children. With educational assets in such relatively short supply, such moves have been the means for (literally) positioning themselves to maximise their chances of realising those ambitions.

In important respects, gender has been transformed in East London, yet also attitudes to gender have remained remarkably 'unreconstructed'. The matrilocality identified by Young and Willmott in their classic studies of East London (1962) was already giving way to the privatised life in the Essex new towns with a move to the nuclear two-generation family – which forms the other part of their Bethnal Green study. However, while women had responsibility for ensuring that the family survived, their engagement in the formal labour market was minimal. Today, by contrast, we see a transformed East London, with high rates of female economic activity – although these remain significantly lower in some Asian households. What has not changed, however, has been the continuing role of women in their concern for social reproduction; men may speak of their ambitions for their children's future, as we have seen, but invariably women are responsible for implementing them, by gathering intelligence at the school gate about the best schools to go for, attending parents' evenings and even talking to us about it. Thus gender is crucial in terms of understanding how aspiration happens; men may strategise about what they would like their children to do, but it is usually women who make it happen. Thus in this respect not much has changed – if we have joined the long lines of (male) social scientists who have failed to make the implicit explicit, we can only hold up our hands, but in mitigation we could not see a way of doing so without diverting attention from our main story.

The main story has been a book about the middle class in the widest sense. It thus includes those working in the City and on telephone number salaries to those working in 'intermediate' positions as cab drivers, nursery nurses and technicians who – and this was what was distinctive about them compared to the rest of the 'white van man' culture – wanted their children to get into the professional middle classes. We have put to one side the complex debates about the nature and future of the middle class in Britain to concentrate on the ways in which groups have moved around East London and articulated their sense of being middle class – by where they live, where they school their children and whom they associate with and whom they wish to avoid. One thing is clear, however, and that is that they distinguish themselves by the very act of choosing. Choice then is not only a mantra of the politicians but a key activity of every actual or aspirant member of the middle class – it may turn around and bite them, may be meaningless in practice but it is the indicator of who they are and crucially who they are not. Thus we have not discussed the working class or the 'non-working class' but we have faithfully recounted the stories about 'the other' from whom our respondents have chosen to distance themselves, at least rhetorically. Class (not *social* class) thus suffuses the whole book, and again we have had to discipline ourselves to listen to our respondents and ignore the fascinating debates about it. It would have been another project to talk about class interaction (which for the most part does not happen) and we chose not to undertake an old-style community study which looked precisely at these interactions in a local social system.

Finally, we have not chosen to address the issue of policy except in so far as we have, we believe, demonstrated the limits of policy. The promotion of school choice does not itself increase actual choice; choice marginalises otherwise acceptable schools; popular schools and good schools are not necessarily the same; school attainment is largely an outcome of school social composition. None of this is particularly new, although we have used PLASC in a new way to show how these associations work out. What is important to us has been to show that people have high expectations of the schooling system and that, while many are satisfied with the education their children receive and approve of the direction of travel that has been taking place, the structural imbalances are such that, unless huge changes are made, London's education system is not going to meet the expectations of its increasingly middle-class population. Education is both the means for sorting the population to fit the social positions available in society and the means for individuals to transform their life chances – it is not clear to us that the second is going to happen. The new Conservative–Liberal Democrat coalition government's policy appears to be going backwards: ending the school building programme and devaluing what positive aspects there were to its predecessor's academy programme by encouraging every school to become an academy and allowing 'pushy parents' (or, in their absence no doubt, 'consultants') to come up with proposals for 'free schools' that will further drain away the resources needed for a good schooling system for all. We have shown that the middle classes are not able to satisfy their long-term needs; where, then, does this leave other groups who are even more in need of the transforming power of good schools?

## Note

[1] Many of the more affluent migrants at the top of the labour market and often working in the City of London or at Canary Wharf live in Tower Hamlets in the new-build flats that were part of the Docklands Development (see Butler, 2007).

# References

Amin, A. (ed) (1994) *Post-Fordism: A reader*, Oxford: Blackwells.

Ball, S.J. (2002) *Class strategies and the education market: The middle classes and social advantage*, London: Routledge Falmer.

Ball, S. (2008) *The education debate*, Bristol, The Policy Press.

Ball, S.J. and Vincent, C. (1998) '"I heard it on the grapevine": "hot" knowledge and school choice', *British Journal of Sociology of Education*, vol 19, no 3, pp 377–400.

Ball, S., Bowe, R. and Gewirtz, S. (1995) 'Circuits of schooling: a sociological exploration of parental choice of school in social class contexts', *Sociological Review*, vol 43, pp 52–78.

Bernstein, B. (1975) *Class codes and control*, London: Routledge.

Beveridge, W.S. (1942) *Social insurance and allied services*, Cmnd 6404, London: HMSO.

Booth, C. (1889) *Life and labour of the people in London*, London: Macmillan.

Booth, C. (1892) 'Dock and wharf labour 1891–2', Inaugural address as President of the Royal Statistical Society.

Bourdieu, P. and Wacquant, L. (1999) *The weight of the world: Social suffering in contemporary society*, Cambridge: Polity Press.

Branson, N. (1979) *Poplarism 1919–25: George Lansbury and the councillors' revolt*, London: Lawrence and Wishart.

Braverman, H. (1974) *Labor and monopoly capital: The degradation of work in the twentieth century*, London: Monthly Review Press.

Brown, G (2010) 'We can break the glass ceiling', *The Guardian, Comment is Free*, 15 January.

Buck, N., Gordon, I. and Young, K. (1986) *The London employment problem*, Oxford: Clarendon Press.

Buck, N., Gordon, I., Hall, P., Harloe, M. and Kleinman, M. (2002) *Working capital: Life and labour in contemporary London*, London: Routledge.

Burgess, S. and Wilson, D. (2005) 'Ethnic segregation in England's schools', *Transactions of the Institute of British Geographers*, NS30, no 1, pp 20–36.

Burgess, S., Wilson, D. and Lupton, R. (2005) 'Parallel lives? Ethnic segregation in schools and neighbourhoods', *Urban Studies*, vol 42, pp 1027–56.

Butler, T. (1997) *Gentrification and the middle classes*, Aldershot: Ashgate.

Butler, T. (1999) 'The new urban intermediaries? The new middle classes and the remaking of London', *Journal des Anthropologues*, vol 77/78, pp 83–97.

Butler, T. (2007) 'Re-urbanising London Docklands: gentrification, suburbanisation or new urbanism?', *International Journal of Urban and Regional Research*, vol 31, no 4, pp 759–81.

Butler, T. and Hamnett, C. (2007) 'The geography of education', *Urban Studies*, vol 44, no 7, pp 1161–74.

Butler, T. and Hamnett, C. (2009) 'Regenerating a global city', in R. Imrie, L. Lees and M. Raco (eds) *Regenerating London: Governance, sustainability and community in a global city*, London: Routledge, pp 40–57.

Butler, T. and Rix, V. (2000) 'The Royal Docks: continuity and change', in T. Butler (ed) *Eastern promise: Education and social renewal in London's Docklands*, London: Lawrence and Wishart, pp 59–83.

Butler, T. and Robson, G. (2001) 'Social capital, gentrification and neighbourhood change in London: a comparison of three South London neighbourhoods', *Urban Studies*, vol 38, no 12, pp 2145–62.

Butler, T. and Robson, G. (2003) 'Plotting the middle classes: gentrification and circuits of education', *Housing Studies*, vol 18, no 1, pp 5–28.

Butler, T., Hamnett, C. and Ramsden, M. (2006) 'The class geography of black and minority ethnic settlement in London, 1991–2001', Paper presented at The World Congress of Sociology, Research Committee 21, Durban, 23–29 July.

Butler, T., Hamnett, C. and Ramsden, M. (2008) 'Inward and upward? Marking out social class change in London 1981–2001', *Urban Studies*, vol 45, no 1, pp 67–88.

Butler, T., Hamnett, C., Ramsden, M. and Webber, R. (2007) 'The best, the worst and the average: secondary school choice and education performance in East London', *Journal of Education Policy*, vol 22, no 1, pp 7–29.

Callinicos, A. (2010) *Bonfire of illusions: The twin crises of the liberal world*, Cambridge: Polity Press.

Carvel, J. (1984) *Citizen Ken*, London: Chatto & Windus.

Castells, M. (1977) *The urban question*, London: Edward Arnold.

Clark, J., Newman, J. and Westmarland, L. (2008) 'The antagonisms of choice: New Labour and the reform of public services', *Social Policy and Society*, vol 7, no 2, pp 245–54.

Cohen, P. (1996) 'All white on the night? Narratives on nativism on the Isle of Dogs', in T. Butler and M. Rustin (eds) *Rising in the East? The regeneration of East London*, London, Lawrence and Wishart, pp 170–96.

Cohen, P. and Rustin, M. (2007) *London's turning*, Aldershot: Ashgate.

Coppock, J.T. (1964) 'The industries of London', in J.T. Coppock and H. Prince (eds) *Greater London*, London: Faber.

Coppock, J.T. and Prince, H. (1964) *Greater London*, London: Faber.

Crossick, G. (1978) *An artisan elite in Victorian society: Kentish London 1840–1880*, London: Croom Helm.

Cullingworth, J.B. (1970) *Council housing purposes, procedures and priorities*, London: Department of the Environment, HMSO.

Dahrendorf, R. (1959) *Class and class conflict in an industrial society*, London: Routledge and Kegan Paul.

Davidson, M. and Lees, L. (2005) 'New build "gentrification" and London's riverside renaissance', *Environment and Planning A*, vol 37, pp 1165–90.

Davies, N. (2000) *The school report: Why Britain's schools are failing*, London, Vintage.

DCSF (Department for Children, Schools and Families) (2005) *Higher standards, better schools for all: More choice for parents and pupils*, London: The Stationery Office.

Deakin, N. (1974) *New Commonwealth minorities in London: Some issues*, GLC Research Memorandum.

Dench, G., Gavron, K. and Young, M. (2006) *The new East End: Race and conflict*, London: Profile.

Dennis, N., Henriques, F. and Slaughter, C. (1956) *Coal is our life: An analysis of a Yorkshire mining community*, London: Tavistock Publications.

Department for Education and Skills (2003) *Aiming high: Raising the achievement of ethnic minority pupils*, London: DfES.

Deskins, D. (1996) 'Economic restructuring, job opportunities and black social dislocation in Detroit', in J.O. Loughlin and J. Friedrichs (eds) *Social polarisation in post-industrial metropolises*, Berlin and New York: Walter de Gruyter.

Devine, F., Savage, M., Scott, J. and Crompton, R. (eds) (2005) *Rethinking class: Culture, identities and lifestyle*, Basingstoke: Palgrave.

Dunleavy, P. (1981) *The politics of mass housing in Britain, 1945–1975: A study of corporate power and professional influence in the welfare state*, Oxford: Clarendon Press.

Ehrenreich, B. (1989) *Fear of falling: The inner life of the middle class*, New York: Pantheon.

Favell, A. (2008) *Eurostars and eurocities: Free movement and mobility in an integrating Europe*, Oxford: Blackwells.

Fieldhouse, E.A. (1999) 'Ethnic minority unemployment and spatial mismatch: the case of London', *Urban Studies*, vol 36, no 9, pp 1569–96.

Foster, J. (1999). *Docklands: Cultures in conflict, worlds in collision*, London, UCL Press.

Frey, W.H. (1995) 'Immigration and internal migration "flight" from US metropolitan areas: toward a new demographic Balkanisation', *Urban Studies*, vol 32, no 4–5, pp 733–57.

Fried, A. and Elman, R.M. (eds) (1971) *Charles Booth's London: A portrait of the poor at the turn of the century drawn from his* Life and labour of the people in London, Harmondsworth: Penguin.

Garner, R. and Pyke, N. (2002) 'Stop blaming schools, Black head tells parents', *The Independent*, 14 March.

GLA (Greater London Authority) (2004) *The educational experiences and achievements of Black boys in London schools 2000–2003*, London: The Education Commission, London Development Agency.

Goldthorpe, J. and Lockwood, D. (1963) 'Affluence and the British class structure', *Sociological Review*, vol 11, pp 133–63.

Goldthorpe, J.H., Lockwood, D., Bechofer, F. and Platt, J. (1969) *The affluent worker in the class structure*, Cambridge: Cambridge University Press.

Goodwin, M. (1991) 'Replacing a surplus population: the policies of the London Docklands Development Corporation', in J. Allen and C. Hamnett (eds) *Housing and labour markets*, London: Unwin Hyman.

Gordon, I. (1996) 'Family structure, educational achievement and the inner city', *Urban Studies*, vol 33, no 3, pp 407–24.

Gordon, I. and Monastiriotis, V. (2007) 'Education, location, education: a spatial analysis of English secondary school public examination results', *Urban Studies*, vol 44, no 7, pp 1203–28.

Gordon, I., Travers, T. and Whitehead, C. (2007) *The impact of recent immigration on the London economy*, London: City of London Corporation.

Gray, R.Q. (1974) 'The labour aristocracy in the Victorian class structure', in F. Parkin (ed) *The social analysis of class structure*, London: Tavistock Publications, pp 19–38.

Gray, R.Q. (1976) *The labour aristocracy in Victorian Edinburgh*, Oxford: Oxford University Press.

Green, D.R. (1986) 'A map for Mayhew's London: the geography of poverty in the mid-nineteenth century', *The London Journal*, vol 11, pp 115–26.

Green, D.R. (1995) *From artisans to paupers: Economic change and poverty in London 1790–1870*, Aldershot: Scolar.

Green, D.R. (2010) *Pauper capital: London and the Poor Law 1790–1870*, Aldershot: Ashgate.

Hackworth, J. (2007) *The neo liberal city: Governance, ideology and development in American urbanism*, Ithaca, NY, and London: Cornell University Press.

Hall, P. (1962) *The industries of London since 1861*, London: Hutchinson.

Hall, R. and Ogden, P. (1992) 'The social structure of new migrants to London Docklands: recent evidence from Wapping', *The London Journal*, vol 17, no 2, pp 153–69.

Hamnett, C. (1984) 'Housing the two nations: socio-tenurial polarization in England and Wales', *Urban Studies*, vol 43, pp 389–405.

Hamnett, C. (2003) *Unequal city: London in the global arena*, London: Routledge.

Hamnett, C. (2009) 'Spatially displaced demand and the changing geography of house prices in London, 1995–2006', *Housing Studies*, vol 24, no 3, pp 301–20.

Hamnett, C. and Butler, T. (2010) 'The changing ethnic structure of housing tenures in London, 1991–2001', *Urban Studies*, vol 47, no 1, pp 55–74.

Hamnett, C. and Butler, T. (forthcoming) '"Geography matters": the role of catchment area and distance as key determinants of school allocation and educational access in East London'.

Hamnett, C. and Randolph, W. (1983) 'How far will London's population fall? A commentary on the 1981 census', *The London Journal*, vol 8, no 1, pp 96–100.

Hamnett, C. and Randolph, W. (1987) 'Ethnic minorities in the London labour market: a longitudinal analysis, 1971–81', *New Community*, vol 14, pp 333–46.

Hamnett, C., Butler, T. and Ramsden, M. (2007) 'Social background, ethnicity, school composition and educational attainment in East London', *Urban Studies*, vol 44, no 7, pp 1255–80.

Harpin, T. (2005) 'Racism blamed as black pupils struggle', *The Times*, 19 September.

Harris, R., Sleight, P. and Webber, R. (2005) *Geodemographics, GIS and neighbourhood targeting*, London, John Wiley.

Harrison, P. (1985) *Inside the inner city: Life under the cutting edge*, Harmondsworth: Penguin.

Hills, J. et al (2010) *An anatomy of economic inequality in the UK: Report of the National Equality Panel*, London: Government Equalities Office (www.equalities.gov.uk/national_equality_panel/publications.aspx).

Hirsch, F. (1976) *The social limits to growth*, London: Routledge & Kegan Paul.

Hirschman, A. (1970) *Exit, voice and loyalty*, Cambridge, MA: Harvard University Press.

Hobbs, D. (1989) *Doing the business: Entrepreneurship, the working class and detectives in the East End of London*, Oxford: Oxford University Press.

Hoggart, R. (1958) *The uses of literacy*, Harmondsworth: Penguin.

Husbands, C. (1988) 'East End racism, 1900–1980: geographical continuities in vigilantist and extreme right-wing political behaviour', *The London Journal*, vol 8, no 1, pp 3–26.

Imrie, R., Lees, L. and Raco, M. (eds) (2009) *Regenerating London: Governance, sustainability and community in a global city*, London: Routledge.

Jackson, A. (1974) *Semi-detached London*, London: George, Allen and Unwin.

Jackson, B. and Marsden, D. (1962) *Education and the working class: Some general themes raised by a study of 88 working-class children in a northern industrial city*, London: Routledge and Kegan Paul.

Jessop, B., Bonnett, K., Bromley, S. and Ling, T. (1988) *Thatcherism*, Cambridge: Polity Press.

Johnston, R.J., Forrest, J. and Poulsen, M.F. (2002a) 'Are there ethnic enclaves/ghettos in English cities?', *Urban Studies*, vol 39, no 4, pp 591–618.

Johnston, R.J., Forrest, J. and Poulsen, M.F. (2002b) 'The ethnic geography of ethnicities: the American model and residential concentration in London', *Ethnicities*, vol 2, no 2, pp 202–39.

Johnston, R.J., Poulson, M.F. and Forrest, J. (2005a) 'On the measurement and meaning of segregation: a response to Simpson', *Urban Studies*, vol 42, pp 1221–7.

Johnston, R.J., Poulson, M.F. and Forrest, J. (2006c) 'Ethnic residential segregation and assimilation in British towns and cities: a comparison of those claiming single and dual ethnic identities', *Migration Letters*, vol 3, no 1, pp 11–30.

Johnston, R.J., Wilson, D. and Burgess, S. (2004) 'School segregation in multi-ethnic England', *Ethnicities*, vol 4, pp 259–91.

Johnston, R.J., Wilson, D. and Burgess, S. (2005b) 'England's multiethnic educational system? A classification of secondary schools', *Environment and Planning A*, vol 37, pp 45–62.

Johnston, R.J., Burgess, S., Harris, R. and Wilson, D. (2006a) 'School and residential segregation: an analysis of variations across England's local education authorities', *Regional Studies*, vol 40, no 9, pp 973–90.

Johnston, R.J., Burgess, S., Harris, R. and Wilson, D. (2006b) *Sleepwalking to segregation? The changing ethnic composition of English schools, 1997–2003: An entry cohort analysis*, WP 06/155, Bristol: Centre for Market and Public Organisation, University of Bristol.

Judt, T. (2010) *Ill fares the land*, London: Alan Lane.

Kapp, Y. (1976) *Eleanor Marx: The crowded years 1884–1898*, London: Virago.

Kellett, J.R. (1969) *The impact of railways on Victorian cities*, London: Routledge and Kegan Paul.

Kennedy, H., Leung, L. and Poynter, G. (2000) 'Shipping in and shaping up? Profiling company employment policies in London's Docklands and inner east London', in T. Butler (ed) *Eastern promise: Education and social renewal in London's Docklands*, London: Lawrence and Wishart.

Le Grand, J. and Barlett, W. (eds) (1993) *Quasi-markets and social policy*, London: Palgrave Macmillan.

Limb, A. (1999) 'Further education under New Labour: translating the language of aspiration into a springboard for achievement', *Cambridge Journal of Education*, vol 29, no 2, pp 219–28.

Loch, C. (1977) *How to help cases of distress*, Plymouth: Continue Publications Facsimile Editions.

Lockwood, D. (1995) 'Marking out the middle classes', in T. Butler and M. Savage (eds) *Social change and the middle classes*, London: UCL Press, pp 1–12.

Machin, S. and Wilson, J. (2005) 'Public and private schooling initiatives in England', LSE paper PEPG 05-16, prepared for the Mobilising the Private Sector for Public Education Conference, Kennedy School of Government, Harvard University, 5–6 October.

Mackenzie, G. (1974) 'The "Affluent Worker Study": an evaluation and critique', in F. Parkin (ed) *The social analysis of class structure*, London: Tavistock Publications Ltd, pp 237–56.

MacPherson, W. (1999) *The Stephen Lawrence Inquiry*, London, The Stationery Office.

Marcuse, P. (1986) 'Abandonment, gentrification and displacement: the linkages in New York City', in N. Smith and P. Williams (eds) *Gentrification of the city*, London: Unwin Hyman, pp 153–77.

Mason, P. (2009) *Meltdown: The end of the age of greed*, London: Verso.

Mattinson, D. (2010) *Talking to a brick wall: How New Labour stopped listening to the voter and why we need a new politics*, London: Biteback.

Mayhew, H. (1850) *The Morning Chronicle survey of London*, London: Morning Chronicle.

Mearns, A. (1883) 'The bitter cry of outcast London', *Contemporary Review*, vol XLIV.

Milner-Holland Committee (1965) *Report of the Committee on Housing in Greater London*, Cmnd 2605, London: Ministry of Housing and Local Government, HMSO.

Modood, T. (1997) *Ethnic minorities in Britain: Diversity and disadvantage*, London: Policy Studies Institute.

Mollenkopf, J. and Castells, M. (eds) (1991) *Dual city: Restructuring New York*, New York: Russell Sage Foundation.

Olechnowicz, A. (1997) *Working class housing in England between the wars: The Becontree Estate*, Oxford: Clarendon Press.

Park, R., Burgess, E.W. and Mackenzie, R.D. (1925) *The city*, Chicago, IL: University of Chicago Press.

Parker, J. and Dugmore, K. (1978) 'Race and the allocation of GLC council housing – a GLC survey', *New Community*, vol 6, pp 27–41.

Peach, C. (1996) 'Does Britain have ghettoes?', *Transactions of the Institute of British Geographers*, NS21, no 1, pp 216–35.

Peach, C. (1997) 'Pluralist and assimilationist models of ethnic settlement in London, 1991', *Tidjschrift voor Economische en Sociale Geografie*, vol 88, pp 120–34.

Peach, C. (1998) 'South Asian and Caribbean ethnic minority housing choice in Britain', *Urban Studies*, vol 35, no 10, pp 1657–80.

Peach, C. (1999) 'London and New York: contrasts in British and American models of segregation', *International Journal of Population Geography*, vol 5, pp 319–51.

Peach, C. and Shah, S. (1980) 'The contribution of council housing to West Indian desegregation in London, 1961–71', *Urban Studies*, vol 17, pp 333–42.

Phillips, D. (1988) 'Race and housing in London's East End: continuity and change', *New Community*, vol 14, no 3, pp 356–69.

Phillips, T. (2005) 'Is Britain sleepwalking to segregation?', Speech by Chair of the Commission for Racial Equality, 22 September, Manchester.

Platt, L. (2005) 'The intergenerational social mobility of minority ethnic groups', *Sociology*, vol 39, no 3, pp 445–61.

Porter, R. (1994) *London: A social history*, Harmondsworth: Penguin.

Power, S., Edwards, T., Whitty, G. and Wigfall, V. (2003) *Education and the middle class*, Buckingham: Open University Press.

Preteceille, E. (2004) *La division sociale de l'espace francilien: Typologie socioprofessionelle 1999 et transformation de l'espace residentiel 1990–99*, Paris: Observatoire Sociologique du Changement, no 145.

Raco, M. (2009) 'From expectations to aspirations: state modernisation, urban policy, and the existential politics of welfare in the UK', *Political Geography*, vol 28, no 7, pp 436–44.

Reay, D. (2005) 'Beyond consciousness? The psychic landscape of social class', *Sociology*, vol 39, no 5, pp 911–28.

Reay, D., Hollingworth, S., Williams, K., Crozier, G., Jamieson, F., James, D. and Beedell, P. (2007) 'A darker shade of pale? Whiteness, the middle classes and multi-ethnic inner city schooling', *Sociology*, vol 41, no 6, pp 1041–60.

Rex, J. (1961) *Key problems in sociological theory*, London: Routledge and Kegan Paul.

Rex, J. and Moore, R. (1967) *Race, community and conflict: A study of Sparkbrook*, Oxford: Oxford/IRR.

Rhein, C. (1998a) 'Globalisation, social change and minorities in metropolitan Paris: the emergence of new class patterns', *Urban Studies*, vol 35, pp 429–47.

Rhein, C. (1998b) 'The working class, minorities and housing in Paris, the rise of fragmentations', *GeoJournal*, vol 46, no 1, pp 51–62.

Rhodes, J. and Tyler, P. (1998) 'Evaluating the LDDC: regenerating London's Docklands', *Rising East*, vol 2, no 2, pp 32–41.

Rix, V. (1997) 'Industrial decline, economic restructuring and social exclusion in London East, 1980s and 1990s', *Rising East*, vol 1, no 1, pp 118–41.

Rose, D., Pevalin, D.J. and O'Reilly, K. (2005) *The NS-SEC: Origins, development and use*, London: Palgrave Macmillan.

Sarre, P., Phillips, D. and Skellington, R. (1989) *Ethnic minority housing: Explanations and policies*, Aldershot: Avebury.

Savage, M. and Burrows, R. (2007) 'The coming crisis of empirical sociology', *Sociology*, vol 41, no 5, pp 885–99.

Savage, M. and Burrows, R. (2009) 'Some further reflections on the coming crisis of empirical sociology', *Sociology*, vol 43, no 4, pp 762–72.

Savage, M., Bagnall, G. and Longhurst, B. (2005) *Globalisation and belonging*, London: Sage Publications.

Savage, M., Warde, A. and Warde, K. (2003) *Urban sociology, capitalism and modernity* (2nd edn), Basingstoke: Palgrave.

Savage, M., Barlow, J., Dickens, P. and Fielding, A. (1992) *Property, bureaucracy and culture: Middle class formation in contemporary Britain*, London: Routledge.

Schelling, T.C. (1971) 'Dynamic models of segregation', *Journal of Mathematical Sociology*, vol 1, pp 143–86.

Schelling, T.C. (1978) *Micromotives and macrobehaviour*, New York: W.W. Norton & Company.

Sieghart, A.M. (1998) 'The shame of London's schools', *The Times*, 27 November.

Simpson, L. (2004) 'Statistics of racial segregation: measures, evidence and policy', *Urban Studies*, vol 41, no 3, pp 661–81.

Slater, T. (2006) 'The eviction of critical perspectives from gentrification research', *International Journal of Urban and Regional Research*, vol 30, no 4, pp 737–57.

Stedman Jones, G. (1974) *Outcast London*, Harmondsworth: Penguin.

Stillwell, J. (2010) 'Ethnic population concentration and net migration in London', *Environment and Planning A*, vol 42, no 6, pp 1439–56.

Stillwell, J. and Duke-Williams, O. (2005) 'Ethnic population distribution, immigration and internal migration in Britain: what evidence of linkage at the district scale?', Paper prepared for British Society for Population Studies Annual Conference, University of Kent, 12–14 September.

Storkey, M. and Lewis, R. (1996) 'London: a true cosmopolis', in P. Ratcliffe (ed) *Ethnicity in the 1991 Census: Volume Three: Social geography and ethnicity*, London: HMSO.

Swennarton, M. (1981) *Homes fit for heroes: The politics and architecture of early state housing in Britain*, London: Heinemann.

Thompson, P. (1967) *Socialists, Liberals and Labour: The struggle for London 1885–1914*, London: Routledge and Kegan Paul.

Tomlinson, S. (2003) 'New Labour and education', *Children and Society*, vol 17, no 3, pp 195–204.

Townsend, P. (1963) *The family life of old people*, Harmondsworth: Penguin.

Wacquant, L. (2008) *Urban outcasts: A comparative sociology of advanced marginality*, Cambridge: Polity Press.

Wacquant, L. (2009) *Punishing the poor: The neo-liberal government of social insecurity*, London: Duke University Press.

Waldinger, R. (1996) *Still the promised city? African-Americans and new immigrants in post-industrial New York*, Cambridge, MA: Harvard University Press.

Watt, P. (2007) 'From the dirty city to the spoiled suburb', in B. Campkin and R. Cox (eds) *Dirt: New geographies of cleanliness and contamination*, London: I.B. Tauris.

Watt, P. (2008) 'Moving to a better place? Geographies of aspiration and anxiety in the Thames Gateway', in P. Cohen and M. Rustin (eds) *London's turning: The making of Thames Gateway*, Aldershot: Ashgate, pp 149–67.

Watt, P. (2009) 'Living in an oasis: middle-class disaffiliation and selective belonging in an English suburb', *Environment and Planning A*, vol 41, pp 2874–92.

Webber, R. (2004) 'Designing geodemographic classifications to meet contemporary business needs', *Journal of Interactive Marketing* vol 5, no 3.

Webber, R. and Butler, T. (2007) 'Classifying pupils by where they live: how well does this predict variations in their GCSE results', *Urban Studies*, vol 44, no 7, pp 1255–80.

White, P. and Hurdley, L. (2003) 'International migration and the housing market: Japanese corporate movers in London', *Urban Studies*, vol 40, no 4, pp 687–706.

Williams, P. (1986) 'Class constitution through spatial reconstruction? A re-evaluation of gentrification in Australia, Britain and the United States', in N. Smith and P. Williams (eds) *Gentrification of the city*, London: Allen and Unwin, pp 56–77.

Williams, R. (1958) *Culture and society, 1780–1950*, London: Chatto & Windus.

Willis, P. (1977) *Learning to labour: How working class kids get working class jobs*, Aldershot: Gower.

Willmott, P. (1963) *Evolution of a community: A study of Dagenham after forty years*, London: Routledge and Kegan Paul.

Willmott, P. and Young, M. (1961) *Family and class in a London suburb*, London: Routledge and Kegan Paul.

Willmott, P. and Young, M. (1973) 'Social class and geography', in D. Donnison and D. Eversley (eds) *London: Urban patterns, problems and policies*, London: Heinemann, pp 190–214.

Wills, J., Datta, K., Evans, Y., Herbert, J., May, J. and McInwaine, C. (2010) *Global cities at work: New migrant divisions of labour*, London: Pluto Press.

Wilson, W.J. (1996) *When work disappears: The world of the new urban poor*, New York: Knopf.

Wohl, A.S. (1977) *The eternal slum: Housing and social policy in Victorian London*, London: Edward Arnold.

Young, M. and Willmott, P. (1962) *Family and kinship in East London*, Harmondsworth: Penguin.

Zweig, F. (1952) *The British worker*, Harmondsworth: Penguin.

# Index

The following abbreviations have been used: t – table; f – figure. Numbers in *italic* refer to photographic images.